"I grew up in a generation of children required to memorize and recite the Ten Commandments by heart. They set the shape of accepted Christian ethics. Later, I visited many churches with the Ten Commandments inscribed on the walls but lacking the vital context of the opening affirmation of God's redeeming grace: 'I am the LORD your God who brought you up out of the house of bondage'—law without gospel. David Baker's timely book challenges us to reconsider the foundational place of the Decalogue in Christian personal and public ethics. But he is also careful to note the context—both the biblical context of God's people's obedience as a grateful response to saving grace, and the surrounding context of ancient Near Eastern cultures and laws, for helpful comparison and contrast. The result is a richly rewarding textbook, surveying the field of biblical scholarship comprehensively but with a light touch, drawing together many threads in wider biblical theology, and reflecting on the relevance of the Ten Commandments in contemporary church and society."

Christopher J. H. Wright, international ministries director, Langham Partnership

"David Baker is someone who knows the Old Testament, knows the ancient Near East, and knows the scholarly literature, and his study of the Ten Commandments is clear, thorough, wide ranging, and knowledgeable. Further, if you ever want to read anything else, the footnotes and the bibliography are a treasury."

John Goldingay, Fuller Theological Seminary

T0310978

THE
DECALOGUE

Living as the People of God

DAVID L. BAKER

APOLLOS (an imprint of Inter-Varsity Press)
36 Causton Street, London SW1P 4ST, England
Email: ivp@ivpbooks.com
Website: www.ivpbooks.com

First published 2017

British Library Cataloguing-in-Publication Data
A catalogue record for this book is available from the British Library

ISBN: 978–1–78359–550–1
eBook ISBN: 978–1–78359–551–8

Typeset in the United States of America
Printed and bound in Great Britain by Ashford Colour Press Ltd, Gosport, Hampshire

Inter-Varsity Press publishes Christian books that are true to the Bible and that communicate the gospel, develop discipleship and strengthen the church for its mission in the world.

IVP originated within the Inter-Varsity Fellowship, now the Universities and Colleges Christian Fellowship, a student movement connecting Christian Unions in universities and colleges throughout Great Britain, and a member movement of the International Fellowship of Evangelical Students. Website: www.uccf.org.uk. That historic association is maintained, and all senior IVP staff and committee members subscribe to the UCCF Basis of Faith.

For Meg, Abi, and Ivan

Three wonderful children!

CONTENTS

PREFACE

For centuries it was taken for granted in the Western world that the Ten Commandments were relevant for all times and in all places. They were displayed on church walls and windows and formed an essential part of Roman Catholic and Protestant worship. The 1604 Anglican Canons decreed that "the Ten Commandments be set up upon the East-end of every Church and Chapel where the people may best see and read the same" (§82). In Lutheran and Anglican liturgies today, the Ten Commandments or a summary of the law are read in preparation for confession, to convict people of sin so they turn to God for forgiveness. In some Reformed liturgies, they are placed after the confession of sin as guidance for Christian living. Either way, their continuing relevance for Christians is assumed.

But what about national and international ethics? In modern Western societies the relevance of the Ten Commandments is less obvious. Churches in Britain have been largely unsuccessful in opposing the liberalization of Sunday trading laws. In the United States there has been vigorous debate about whether the commandments should be displayed in schools and public places, and on several occasions judges have ruled that stone monuments inscribed with the commandments must be removed. While Christians may regret these outcomes, it is probably unrealistic to expect governments of countries that are becoming increasingly secularized to acknowledge the authority of biblical laws, though many of the principles they express are accepted by civilized peoples throughout the world.

In any case, I am convinced these laws are still important for the people of God, as I aim to show in this book. I tackle the commandments one by one in three contexts:

- First, I place each commandment in the context of ancient Near Eastern law and culture. This context is mentioned only incidentally or not at all in most other books.

- Second, I explain each commandment in the context of the Bible itself (canonical context). This has been done in other commentaries, but it is absolutely essential in my view and could not be omitted responsibly.

- Third, I reflect on each commandment in the context of the world today. Many commentaries limit their scope to the biblical context, leaving readers to draw their own conclusions about the contemporary relevance of the text. There are also a good number of books with valuable insights concerning the relevance of the commandments, but these often lack a firm basis in the study of the text. I aim to bridge the gap by covering both explanation and reflection in one study.

The first part of the book introduces the Ten Commandments, including discussion of their shape and form, origin and purpose. Another matter that could have been included is reception history (how the text has been understood and used over the centuries), but this has been done well elsewhere, and to repeat it here would require a considerably longer book.[1]

My hope is that this book will be useful for teachers and students, preachers and congregations, and all who are interested in understanding the original meaning and contemporary significance of this historic text. To make it accessible for as many readers as possible, I have minimized technical discussions in the body of the text, providing instead footnotes and bibliographies for the benefit of academic readers who wish to study things in more detail.

Finally, I am very grateful to family, friends, and colleagues who have supported and stimulated me during the years I have been writing about the Ten Commandments (or Decalogue, as they are often called by scholars). I began my research on Old Testament law when I was deputy warden at

---

[1] On the reception history of the Ten Commandments, see Slattery 1979; Segal and Levi 1985; Brown 2004: 33-129; Kuntz 2004; Reventlow and Hoffman 2011; Greenman and Larsen 2012; Markl 2013b.

Tyndale House, Cambridge, and preached through the commandments at chapel there. The library resources and scholarly interaction at this unique center for biblical research were immensely important to me. Sabbatical leave granted by Trinity Theological College, Perth, enabled me to make further progress, and the work was completed after my return to Cambridge in 2014. Alan Millard, Abigail Patience, and Diana Hakala read various drafts and made many valuable suggestions. Finally, and most important of all, I mention my wife, Elizabeth. Not only has she read and edited the whole book, but she has also sustained and encouraged me unfailingly over the years. Thank you!

ABBREVIATIONS

NJB	New Jerusalem Bible. London: Darton, Longman & Todd, 1985.
NJPS	New JPS Translation [Tanakh]. Philadelphia: Jewish Publication Society, 1985.
NLT2	New Living Translation. 2nd ed. Carol Stream, IL: Tyndale House, 2004.
NRSV	New Revised Standard Version. New York: National Council of the Churches of Christ, 1989.
REB	Revised English Bible. Oxford: Oxford University Press, 1989.
RHB	*A Reader's Hebrew Bible*. Edited by A. Philip Brown II and Bryan W. Smith. Grand Rapids: Zondervan, 2008.
RSV	Revised Standard Version. New York: National Council of the Churches of Christ, 1952.

Most Bible texts are quoted from the New International Version (2011), but I have substituted my own translation for the Decalogue and a few other laws (marked "DLB") where I feel the NIV does not fully reflect the meaning of the Hebrew. Chapter and verse numbers follow English conventions, assuming that those who know Hebrew will be aware of the differences.

ANCIENT NEAR EASTERN LAWS

AI	*Ana ittišu* tablet 7, including Sumerian Family Laws (ca. 2300–2076 BC; see Driver and Miles 1952: 25-26; 1955: 308-13)
CH	Laws of Hammurabi (ca. 1750 BC; see *COS*: 2.131)
HL	Hittite Laws (ca. 1650–1500 BC; see *COS*: 2.19)
LE	Laws of Eshnunna (ca. 1770 BC; see *COS*: 2.130)
LL	Laws of Lipit-Ishtar (ca. 1930 BC; see *COS*: 2.154)
LU	Laws of Ur-Namma (ca. 2100 BC; see *COS*: 2.153; cf. Civil 2011)
MAL	Middle Assyrian Laws (ca. 1450–1250 BC; see *COS*: 2.132)
SLET	Sumerian Laws Exercise Tablet (ca. 1800 BC; see Roth 1997: 42-45)

REFERENCE WORKS

| ABD | *The Anchor Bible Dictionary*. Edited by David Noel Freedman. 6 vols. New York: Doubleday, 1992. |

ANET *Ancient Near Eastern Texts Relating to the Old Testament.* Edited by J. B. Pritchard. 3rd ed. Princeton, NJ: Princeton University Press, 1969.

APOT 2 *Apocrypha and Pseudepigrapha of the Old Testament in English.* Vol. 2, edited by R. H. Charles et al. Oxford: Clarendon, 1913.

BDB *A Hebrew and English Lexicon of the Old Testament.* Edited by Francis Brown et al. Oxford: Clarendon, 1907. Reprinted with corrections, 1957.

BWL *Babylonian Wisdom Literature.* Edited by W. G. Lambert. Oxford: Clarendon, 1960.

CAD *The Assyrian Dictionary of the Oriental Institute of the University of Chicago.* Edited by Ignace J. Gelb et al. 21 vols. Chicago: Oriental Institute, 1956–.

COS *The Context of Scripture.* Edited by William W. Hallo. 3 vols. Leiden: Brill, 1997–2002.

CTA *Corpus des Tablettes en Cunéiformes Alphabétiques Découvertes à Ras Shamra-Ugarit de 1929 à 1939.* Edited by Andrée Herdner. Mission de Ras Shamra 10. Paris: Imprimerie Nationale, 1963.

DCH *The Dictionary of Classical Hebrew.* Edited by David J. A. Clines. 8 vols. Sheffield: Sheffield Academic, 1993–2011.

DOTPe *Dictionary of the Old Testament: Pentateuch.* Edited by T. Desmond Alexander and David W. Baker. Downers Grove, IL: InterVarsity Press, 2003.

DOTT *Documents from Old Testament Times.* Edited by D. Winton Thomas. Edinburgh: Nelson, 1958.

HALOT *The Hebrew and Aramaic Lexicon of the Old Testament.* Edited by Ludwig Koehler et al. 5 vols. Leiden: Brill, 1994–2000. Edited and translated from German, 1967–1996.

HANEL *A History of Ancient Near Eastern Law.* Edited by Raymond Westbrook. 2 vols. Handbook of Oriental Studies, Section One: The Near and Middle East 72. Leiden: Brill, 2003.

KAI *Kanaanäische und Aramäische Inschriften.* Edited by Herbert Donner and Wolfgang Röllig. 3 vols. Wiesbaden, Germany: Harrassowitz, 1962–1964.

MED	*Macquarie Encyclopedic Dictionary.* 2nd ed. Sydney: Macquarie Dictionary Publishers, 2010.
NIDB	*The New Interpreter's Dictionary of the Bible.* Edited by Katharine Doob Sakenfeld et al. 5 vols. Nashville, TN: Abingdon, 2006–2009.
NIDOTTE	*New International Dictionary of Old Testament Theology and Exegesis.* Edited by Willem A. VanGemeren. 5 vols. Carlisle, England: Paternoster, 1997.
OTP 2	*The Old Testament Pseudepigrapha.* Vol. 2, edited by James H. Charlesworth. New York: Doubleday, 1985.
TDOT	*Theological Dictionary of the Old Testament.* Edited by G. Johannes Botterweck and Helmer Ringgren. 15 vols. Grand Rapids: Eerdmans, 1977–2006. Translated from German, 1970–1995.
ZIBBC	*Zondervan Illustrated Bible Backgrounds Commentary: Old Testament.* Edited by John H. Walton. 5 vols. Grand Rapids: Zondervan, 2009.

JOURNALS AND SERIES

BA	*Biblical Archaeologist*
BAR	*Biblical Archaeology Review*
BASOR	*Bulletin of the American Schools of Oriental Research*
BBR	*Bulletin for Biblical Research*
BJRL	*Bulletin of the John Rylands University Library of Manchester*
BTB	*Biblical Theology Bulletin*
BWANT	Beiträge zur Wissenschaft vom Alten und Neuen Testament
BZ	*Biblische Zeitschrift*
BZAW	Beihefte zur Zeitschrift für die alttestamentliche Wissenschaft
CBQ	*Catholic Biblical Quarterly*
ExpTim	*Expository Times*
FAT	Forschungen zum Alten Testament
FRLANT	Forschungen zur Religion und Literatur des Alten und Neuen Testaments
HBT	*Horizons in Biblical Theology*
HUCA	*Hebrew Union College Annual*

ICC	International Critical Commentary
IEJ	*Israel Exploration Journal*
JAOS	*Journal of the American Oriental Society*
JBL	*Journal of Biblical Literature*
JBQ	*Jewish Bible Quarterly*
JJS	*Journal of Jewish Studies*
JNES	*Journal of Near Eastern Studies*
JNSL	*Journal of Northwest Semitic Languages*
JQR	*Jewish Quarterly Review*
JSNTSup	Journal for the Study of the New Testament Supplement Series
JSOT	*Journal for the Study of the Old Testament*
JSOTSup	Journal for the Study of the Old Testament Supplement Series
JTS	*Journal of Theological Studies*
NICOT	New International Commentary on the Old Testament
OBO	Orbis biblicus et orientalis
OTL	Old Testament Library
RB	*Revue biblique*
SBL	Society of Biblical Literature
SBT	Studies in Biblical Theology
TOTC	Tyndale Old Testament Commentaries
TynBul	*Tyndale Bulletin*
UBS	*UBS Translator's Handbooks*
UF	*Ugarit-Forschungen*
VT	*Vetus Testamentum*
VTSup	Supplements to Vetus Testamentum
WBC	Word Biblical Commentary
WMANT	Wissenschaftliche Monographien zum Alten und Neuen Testament
ZABR	*Zeitschrift für altorientalische und biblische Rechtsgeschichte*
ZAW	*Zeitschrift für die alttestamentliche Wissenschaft*

WHAT IS
THE DECALOGUE?

SHAPE

In spite of their historic significance, few young people in Britain today know what the Ten Commandments are, according to an article in *The Times* a few years ago. A follow-up letter revealed that one adult who claimed to know all ten of the commandments was quite confused about the numbering and thought that "Catholics, Protestants and Jews have different versions of the commandments."[1] So what exactly are the commandments, how does the numbering work, and how do the various traditions relate to each other?[2]

TEN COMMANDMENTS

The term *Ten Commandments* comes from a Hebrew expression that literally means "ten words." It occurs only three times in the Old Testament (Ex 34:28; Deut 4:13; 10:4) and is not attested again until the Greek writings of Philo and Josephus in the first century AD.[3] In the following century it appears in several Christian writings.[4] The English term *Ten Commandments* is rather misleading because the text is much more than a list of commands to obey. Many scholars prefer the term *Decalogue* (from the Greek for "ten

---

[1]Gledhill 2004; Lloyd 2004.
[2]The first four chapters and the final chapter of this book are adapted from three previously published articles of mine (Baker 2004; 2005a; 2005c) by permission of the publishers, all rights reserved.
[3]Philo, *Decalogue*; Josephus, *Antiquities* 3.101.
[4]E.g., Epistle of Barnabas 15:1; Clement of Alexandria, *Paedagogus* 3.12.8; Irenaeus, *Against Heresies* 4.16.3.

words"), and I use that in the remainder of this book. I hope to demonstrate that these ten "words" contain basic principles for the life of God's people in the Old Testament and that these principles are still relevant today.

The Decalogue is recorded twice in the Old Testament, in different contexts and with slightly different wording. The first is Exodus 20:1-21, where God speaks directly to the people of Israel at Mount Sinai after their exodus from Egypt. This is complemented by Deuteronomy 5:1-22, where the Decalogue is repeated as part of Moses' speech to the people before they enter the Promised Land.

Why ten? Does this number have any theological significance? Probably not. It may be a practical number for memorization: one for every finger. Or the number itself may be incidental, simply resulting from the fact that the matters of crucial importance included in the list happen to come to ten.[5]

While all agree that there are ten commandments, there are at least five different ways of numbering them (see table 1). None are exclusive to any one religious tradition, though some are predominantly followed by Protestants, Roman Catholics, or Jews. The differences occur at the beginning and end of the list, and there are three main issues.

First, at the beginning of the list, Exodus 20:2 is different in form from most of the following material, being a statement rather than a command. Some traditions treat it as a historical prologue (A, D), others as the introduction to the first commandment (B, E) or an independent commandment (C). I am inclined to the second possibility, taking it as the introduction to the first commandment. The form of the first commandment is then similar to that of the next four, all of which include an explanation mentioning "the LORD your God." God revealed himself to Israel when he rescued them from slavery in Egypt, and this revelation is the basis of his demand for exclusive worship.[6]

---

[5]Nielsen (1965: 6-10) surveys various possible reasons for the number ten but is unable to come to a clear conclusion. Lang (2003; 2006) argues that in its present form the Decalogue actually has twelve commandments. In his view, there were originally five religious commandments (pentalogue) that were later supplemented with five nonreligious ones to make a decalogue, and this was then expanded further by adding the sabbath commandment and splitting the last commandment in two to make a dodecalogue.

[6]Cf. Judg 6:8-10; Ps 81:9-10; Hos 13:4. While I am inclined to the second possibility, the first and third are also plausible. We know that ancient treaties often began with a historical prologue, which might support the first possibility. Alternatively, the third possibility might be supported by the Hebrew term "ten words," which could accommodate a statement as the first "word." Biddle (2003) discusses the syntax of the commandments, arguing that they are actually all

Table 1. Alternative numbering structures

Content	A[i]	B[ii]	C[iii]	D[iv]	E[v]
"I am the LORD your God" (Ex 20:2)	Prologue		1	Prologue	
No other gods (Ex 20:3)	1	1		1	1
No images (Ex 20:4-6)	2	2	2		
No misusing God's name (Ex 20:7)	3	3	3	2	2
Remembering the sabbath (Ex 20:8-11)	4	4	4	3	3
Honoring parents (Ex 20:12)	5	5	5	4	4
No homicide (Ex 20:13)	6	6	6	5	5
No adultery (Ex 20:14)	7	7	7	6	6
No stealing (Ex 20:15)	8	8	8	7	7
No false witness (Ex 20:16)	9	9	9	8	8
No coveting a neighbor's house (Ex 20:17a)	10	10	10	9	9
No coveting a neighbor's wife (Ex 20:17b)				10	10

[i]Structure A appears to be the oldest, found in Philo (*Decalogue* 50-51), Josephus (*Antiquities* 3.91-92), and Origen (*Homily on Exodus* 8). It is common today in Eastern Orthodox, Anglican, and Reformed churches.

[ii]Structure B is only slightly different from A, and it is uncertain whether Philo and Josephus have A or B in mind since they do not discuss the introductory sentence. This structure is followed in some Jewish traditions (e.g., *Sifre Numbers* 112) and by the NRSV. The Exodus version of the Decalogue in BHS, BHQ, and RHB follows this structure except there is no division between the first and second commandments, so the total number is only nine.

[iii]Structure C is found in the Talmud and Targums as well as the Codex Vaticanus (Exodus) and is commonly used by modern Jews.

[iv]Structure D is found in the Peshitta as well as Clement of Alexandria and Augustine. It is common today in Roman Catholic and Lutheran churches.

[v]Structure E is found in some Masoretic texts and followed in several modern editions of the Hebrew Bible (BFBS; Koren Bible; see also Deuteronomy in BHS, BHQ, and RHB). For further discussion of numbering, see Weinfeld 1991: 86-87, 243-45; Houtman 1996: 3-5; Hakala 2014: 5-13.

Second, the prohibitions of having other gods (Ex 20:3) and making images (Ex 20:4-6) can be understood as two separate commandments (A, B) or just one (C, D, E). It seems to me the two prohibitions cover two distinct issues—gods and images—so they are better understood as separate commandments. On the one hand, it would be possible to worship other gods with or without images. Although images were common in ancient Near Eastern worship, the Nabateans worshiped their gods without them. On the other hand, the prohibition of images was not only concerned with worship of other gods, for it was quite possible to make images of the true

---

statements since there are no imperative verbs. However, this overlooks the fact that the Hebrew "imperative" is only used for positive commands and that negative commands are commonly expressed by the imperfect/jussive preceded by לֹא, as here.

God, as the Israelites did from time to time (e.g., Ex 32:1-5). These points will be discussed further below.

The third issue, which comes at the end of the list, concerns whether the prohibition of coveting is one commandment (A, B, C) or two (D, E). In my view, it is artificial to divide this commandment into two (at least in Exodus) since the repetition of the same verb makes a very close link between the two prohibitions. As will become clear in the detailed discussion below, the second prohibition is an elaboration of the first, not a separate commandment.

To conclude, the first and second ways of numbering the commandments (A, B) fit well with the content. They also have more support from ancient sources, as may be seen in the footnotes to table 1. The only difference between the two is at the beginning of the list, concerning whether the sentence "I am the LORD your God . . ." is a prologue to the Decalogue or part of the first commandment. I prefer the latter, as explained above, though it is not an important point. For almost all the commandments, this numbering coincides with that familiar to Orthodox and Reformed Christians as well as to Jews. Except for the first commandment, Roman Catholics and Lutherans will find the numbering here slightly different from what they are used to (e.g., their second commandment is counted as the third here).

TWO TABLETS

The biblical traditions are unanimous that the Decalogue was written on two stone tablets (Ex 31:18; 34:1, 4, 29; Deut 4:13; 5:22; 9:10-11). These tablets were inscribed on both sides (Ex 32:15) and kept in the ark of the covenant (Ex 25:16, 21; 40:20; Deut 10:1-5; 1 Kings 8:9; 2 Chron 5:10). The use of stone rather than clay may indicate the importance of this document and its intended permanence.[7]

It has generally been assumed the commandments were divided between the tablets, though Kline (1960) has argued the two tablets were identical copies of all ten commandments. This follows from his interpretation of the Decalogue as the text of a treaty between God and Israel, since it was conventional in the ancient Near East to make duplicate copies of a treaty document for the suzerain and vassal respectively.[8] If each tablet contained the

---

[7]Tigay 1996: 48. For further discussion of the material and possible dimensions of the tablets, see Millard 1994.

[8]See also Kline 1963: 13-26; Derby 1993b; cf. Collins 1992; Youngblood 1994. The suzerain was king of the more powerful nation, which would normally initiate a treaty, leaving the vassal king to

whole Decalogue, the ark of the covenant would be an appropriate place to deposit both God's copy and that of the people. However, while making duplicate copies and keeping them in separate places for security makes good sense, to make duplicates and keep them in the same place seems a rather pedantic imitation of the treaty-making procedure. To put God's copy in the ark would be logical because the ark is kept in the most holy place, but to also put the people's copy there would make it inaccessible to them and of little practical use.

So it is likely the ark contained one copy of the commandments engraved on two tablets. This may have been viewed as God's copy, with one or more accessible copies made for reference by the people and their leaders. There is no explicit record of such copies of the Decalogue being made, though Millard (2007) suggests that the "LORD's words and laws" mentioned in Exodus 24:3-4 are the Decalogue, written down by Moses to provide an accessible copy for the people since the original was to be kept in the ark. Later Moses instructs the people to set up stones on Mount Ebal inscribed with "all the words of this law" (Deut 27:2-4). This presumably refers to the laws of Deuteronomy 12–26 and may include the Decalogue too. The instruction is implemented by Joshua (Josh 8:32).

We do not know how the ten commandments were divided between the two tablets. Ancient documents tended to fill the space available in order to economize on writing materials, so the commandments may simply have been spread over the tablets in that way. But it is also possible they were divided into two groups according to content.

In subsequent usage, it has been common to see two groups of commandments in the Decalogue, one of four and the other of six. The first group concerns relationships with God and the second relationships with one's neighbor. This was suggested by Ambrosiaster and Augustine and followed by Calvin.[9] One attraction of this division is that it matches the two great commandments of loving God and loving one's neighbor (Lev 19:18; Deut 6:5; Mt 22:34-40; Mk 12:28-34).

---

decide whether to accept or reject the proposed terms. On whether the Decalogue is to be understood as a treaty document, see "Treaty and Covenant" below.

[9]*Institutes of the Christian Religion* 2.8.12. This has been the traditional division in Roman Catholic and Lutheran churches, though in their numbering the division is actually between the first three and last seven commandments. See also Nielsen 1965: 33-34; Durham 1987: 290.

Others see two groups of five commandments. This division appears to be older and is mentioned in Philo and Josephus.[10] In the first group, each commandment has one or more explanatory clause and always includes the phrase, "the LORD your God."[11] In the second group, the commandments are simple prohibitions and much briefer, though the last is somewhat extended. There is also a distinction in content between these two groups: the first concerns love for God and parents, while the second concerns love for other people. According to Ewald (1876: 160-62), the first group specifies duties owed by those who are inferior and dependent to their superiors, while the second group treats mutual duties between human beings.[12]

A key factor is the interpretation of the fifth commandment. Philo (*Decalogue* 106-7) believes it is placed on the borderline between the two groups because parents stand between the mortal and the immortal. On the one hand, parents are human and might be included in the category of people who are to be loved and protected, as in the following five commandments. On the other hand, they are partners with the Creator in bringing children into the world and are therefore to be honored as the Creator himself is honored.[13]

It follows that honoring parents is part of respect for God, not simply a matter of social relationships. There is more to filial piety than refraining from harming one's parents. Rather it is a fundamental virtue, expressed positively, that follows naturally from honoring God, his Name, and his Day. In Leviticus 19:2-4, honoring parents is closely integrated with honoring God and keeping the sabbath. Of course, this does mean that to harm a parent is a particularly serious crime and often leads to capital punishment (e.g., Ex 21:15, 17), but the emphasis in the Decalogue itself is on the positive aspect. The reward for keeping the fifth commandment is long life "in the land the LORD your God is giving you" (Ex 20:12), complementing the introduction to the first commandment (Ex 20:2; Deut 5:6) and so making a frame (*inclusio*) to round off the first half of the Decalogue.

---

[10]Philo, *Decalogue* 50; Josephus, *Antiquities* 3.101. There are also other suggested divisions that I do not discuss here; on these, see Derby 1993a; Kratz 1994: 215-20; Jackson 1995: 1797-1802; Millard 2000; Motyer 2005: 215-20.

[11]Assuming Ex 20:2 (= Deut 5:6) to be part of the first commandment, as I have argued above.

[12]Weinfeld (1991) suggests that the former group is more distinctively Israelite, whereas the latter contains widely recognized principles (cf. Miller 2009: 168-74). This is partly true, but respecting the name of one's god and honoring one's parents were laws not unique to Israel, and the tenth commandment is by no means a widely recognized principle.

[13]Cf. Blidstein 1975: 1-8; Yisraeli 2009: 403-9.

To sum up, I believe the Decalogue consists of two groups of five commandments, one concerned with loving God and the other with loving one's neighbor. Honoring mother and father forms the conclusion to the first group rather than the introduction to the second. Whether the commandments were actually written on the two tablets in this way cannot be proved (unless one day someone finds the lost ark!).

Table 2. Two groups of commandments

Loving God	Loving Neighbor
1. No other gods	6. No homicide
2. No images	7. No adultery
3. No misusing God's name	8. No stealing
4. Remembering the sabbath	9. No false witness
5. Honoring parents	10. No coveting

IS THE ORDER SIGNIFICANT?

As we have seen, although the numbering of the commandments varies in different traditions, the order is quite stable. The main exception is that the sixth and seventh commandments are transposed in the Septuagint (the ancient Greek translation of the Old Testament), with the prohibition of adultery coming at the beginning of the second group. When Jesus refers to the commandments, adultery follows homicide in Matthew 19:18 and Mark 10:19 but precedes it in Luke 18:20.

It seems the Decalogue is ordered according to the seriousness of the offenses listed. Similar principles may be seen in other ancient Near Eastern laws, with priority given to matters that are considered more important. For example, some laws are ordered on the basis of socioeconomic status, dealing first with matters concerning the temple, then the state, free citizens, serfs, and slaves.[14] Philo (*Decalogue* 121), who follows the Greek order of the commandments by placing adultery before homicide, explains that adultery is at the beginning of the second group because it is the greatest of all offenses against fellow human beings. The same principle applies if we follow the more common order, which locates homicide at the beginning of the second group. There is a descending sequence in each group, beginning with the most serious matter and ending with something slightly

---

[14]Kaufman 1979: 115-18; 1987.

unexpected but nevertheless important: from apostasy to honoring parents, from killing to coveting.

To break a commandment in the first group generally leads to capital punishment (Ex 21:15, 17; 22:20; 31:14-15; Lev 20:9; 24:16; Deut 17:2-7; 19:11-13; 21:18-21). The punishment for making an image is not specified, but it is a very serious offense (Ex 20:5-6; 32:1-35; Deut 27:15) and would probably result in capital punishment too.

In the second group, only the sixth and seventh are capital offenses (Ex 21:12; Lev 20:10; 24:21; Deut 22:22-24). For the eighth and ninth, lesser punishments are decreed (Ex 22:1-4; Deut 19:16-21). The tenth is different in nature, for coveting concerns intention rather than action, and people could hardly be taken to court over it. However, the fact that it is included here is significant because it shows that people could be morally guilty before God without having committed any visible offense at all.[15]

On a slightly different matter, several scholars argue that the order of the Decalogue is the basis for the order of the laws in the central section of Deuteronomy, often called the Deuteronomic Laws (Deut 12–26).[16] This is an attractive idea but not entirely convincing. On the one hand, there are obvious links between Deuteronomy 12–13 and the first two commandments, Deuteronomy 15–16 and the fourth commandment, and Deuteronomy 19–21 and the sixth commandment. On the other hand, it is much more difficult to see a connection between Deuteronomy 14 (clean and unclean foods, tithes) and the third commandment (misuse of the divine name).

Many of the laws in Deuteronomy 12–26 explain and expand principles from the Decalogue, so it is not surprising if their order has been influenced by the order in which those principles appear in the Decalogue. However, it seems the editors of Deuteronomy had other considerations as well, for not all the relevant material is included at the expected place according to this scheme. For example, a group of laws concerning marriage

---

[15]Wright 2004: 291. Smith (1991) suggests a chiastic arrangement for the commandments in the form of an arch, with the prohibition against homicide at the apex, those against idolatry and coveting forming the two bases, and those in between making matching pairs. It may be true that the commandments concerning idolatry and coveting are parallel in meaning (cf. Col 3:5) and that there is an element of chiasm in this, but the rest is rather artificial. To make the structure work, Smith has to count just nine commandments (by making the first into a declaration of exclusive sovereignty after the pattern of ancient treaties), and this goes against the very strong tradition that there are ten.

[16]So Kaufman 1979; Braulik 1991; Olson 1994: 62-125; Biddle 2003; Walton 2012.

and sexuality (Deut 22:13–23:18; cf. seventh commandment) is followed by laws dealing with property (Deut 23:19-25; cf. eighth commandment). This fits the scheme, but the next chapter returns to marriage and divorce (Deut 24:1-5) before taking up property matters again (Deut 24:6, 10-15, 17-22). There is also a good deal of material that has little relevance to any part of the Decalogue (e.g., Deut 14; 17–18; 25–26). So the similarity between the order of laws in the Decalogue and the Deuteronomic Laws should not be overemphasized.

TREATY AND COVENANT

One final point about the shape of the Decalogue concerns whether it is formulated as a treaty document. In a classic article, Mendenhall (1954b) demonstrated that Old Testament covenants are formulated in a similar way to Hittite vassal treaties.[17] The key components of those treaties are now well known:

- preamble identifying the author of the treaty (suzerain)
- prologue recounting the history of relations between the two parties (suzerain and vassal)
- stipulations concerning obligations of the two parties (particularly the vassal)
- provision for a treaty document (deposited in a temple, with periodic public reading)
- list of witnesses (gods)
- curses and blessings on the vassal, threatening divine punishment for disloyalty and promising reward for loyalty

Many of these components are also found in Old Testament texts such as Exodus 19–24, Deuteronomy, and Joshua 24. It seems clear the writers use elements of the ancient treaty structure to express the idea of the covenant, and this is consistent with the fact that the same Hebrew word is used for both treaty and covenant. Nevertheless, the Israelite covenant is unique in forging a relationship between God and his worshipers. Moreover, it includes stipulations about both religious and social behavior, whereas the Hittite treaties tend to focus on military and security issues.

---

[17]See also Beyerlin 1961: 50-64; Baltzer 1964; McCarthy 1978. For examples of the treaties, see *COS*: 2.17-18.

Some treaty components are found in the Decalogue—for example, the historical prologue and stipulations—and this leads Kline (1963) to argue that the Decalogue is itself a treaty document. However, the prologue is very brief and the stipulations are much more wide ranging than the detailed commands of the Hittite treaties. There are no specific curse and blessing clauses, though the former is implied in Exodus 20:5b, 7b, and the latter in Exodus 20:6, 12b. Two key elements of the formulation are completely missing—namely, provision for a treaty document and list of witnesses.

Gerstenberger (1965a: 38) agrees that the ancient Near Eastern treaties used in diplomatic relations between states describe a covenant, a cordial agreement to promote peace and combat common enemies. Naturally stipulations are required for such an agreement, to specify conditions for continuance of the relationship, and the whole is protected by a curse. But Gerstenberger denies that the Ten Commandments are treaty stipulations in this sense. He rejects the view of Mendenhall (1954a: 39) that the covenant is made by God with each Israelite family, arguing instead that the treaty partner is the people of Israel. Further, he considers that the commandments are universal and timeless, reflecting the whole life of society and not bound to particular persons or nations. Thus Gerstenberger concludes that the Decalogue is not a treaty but a collection of moral precepts in the form of commands and prohibitions, as commonly found in the ancient Near East.

In conclusion, Old Testament accounts of the covenant between God and Israel are formulated in a way reminiscent of ancient Near Eastern treaties, but only some elements of the treaty formula are present in the Decalogue itself, while others are conspicuously absent. So the Decalogue expresses the essence of the covenant but is not a treaty document in itself.

FORM

As already mentioned, the Decalogue appears twice in the Old Testament, in two different versions. There are also two slightly different versions not present in the Old Testament. So how do these relate to each other, and can we trace an "original" form?

TWO CANONICAL VERSIONS

The Decalogue is first recorded in the book of Exodus, in the context of an extraordinary event at Mount Sinai two months after the Israelites escape from Egypt (Ex 19; 20:18-21). God appears to Moses and the people in a dense cloud accompanied by thunder and lightning, smoke and fire. They hear a loud trumpet blast, which grows louder and louder, and feel the whole mountain tremble violently. Finally they hear the voice of God (Ex 19:9; 20:1, 22). He identifies himself as their liberator from slavery in Egypt and sets out ten laws for life as the people of God (Ex 20:2-17). The record of this momentous occasion is immediately followed by a collection of laws known as the Book of the Covenant (Ex 20:22–23:33), which develops many of the principles of the Decalogue and gives specific examples of how it should be applied.[1] After this the people confirm their acceptance of a

---

[1] Cf. Sprinkle 1994: 25-27; Tappy 2000; Propp 2006: 305-6; Williamson 2008: 113-14. Kratz (1994) examines the Decalogue in the literary context of Exodus and concludes that it is composed as an introduction to the Book of the Covenant. This confirms the close relationship between the Decalogue and the Book of the Covenant, but the idea that the detailed laws are earlier than the summary goes against the entire biblical tradition of the origin of the Decalogue.

covenant relationship with God in a ceremony on the mountain (Ex 24). Later the importance of the Decalogue is reinforced by the breaking and remaking of the tablets (Ex 32–34).

Forty years later, the Decalogue is repeated at the beginning of Moses' second speech on the plains of Moab (Deut 5–11), which is separate from the main body of laws in Deuteronomy 12–26. This speech explains the meaning of God's covenant with his people, repeatedly reminding the Israelites of their liberation from Egypt, and provides an introduction to the laws. It is recalled that the Decalogue was originally given at Sinai (here referred to as Horeb), though that event is not recounted in detail here (Deut 5:2-5, 22-27). The themes of liberation and covenant are fundamental in both Exodus and Deuteronomy and provide the key to understanding the Decalogue in its biblical contexts.[2]

The content of the two versions is substantially the same, but there are differences in the details of the fourth, fifth, and tenth commandments.[3] Deuteronomy has several extra words and clauses, the theological basis for the sabbath is different in the two versions, and there are a few other small differences. Scholars have drawn various conclusions from these differences. For example, Stamm and Andrew (1967) believe Exodus preserves an older version of the Decalogue, though they consider the written form to be later than that in Deuteronomy because they connect the sabbath command with the Priestly account of creation. Hossfeld (1982) argues for the opposite view, maintaining that the version in Deuteronomy is original and has been reworked and incorporated into the Sinai narrative of Exodus by a postexilic redactor. This hypothesis has been widely refuted.[4] According to Weinfeld (1991), both versions are expansions of an original shorter form, though the account in Exodus is older. He admits there are some apparent Deuteronomic phrases in the Exodus version but argues that this does not prove it to be later, as they could have come from a northern decalogue, which he believes influenced Deuteronomic literature.

---

[2]Wénin 1997: 12-20.

[3]For a synopsis of the texts, see below under the discussion of the commandments in question. A more detailed comparison of the two versions is provided by Charles 1926: xxxiv-xliv; Nielsen 1965: 35-44.

[4]Hossfeld's proposal is followed by Lang (1984) but rejected by many others (e.g., Levin 1985; Graupner 1987; 2000; Weinfeld 1991; Kratz 1994).

In my view, the Exodus version is earlier.[5] It is intrinsically more likely that extra material would have been added than original material omitted. Much of the extra material is characteristically Deuteronomic: for example, the phrases, "as the LORD your God has commanded you," and, "that it may go well with you."[6] The word *field* or *land* is a natural addition to the tenth commandment in view of the imminent prospect of settlement in Canaan (Deut 5:21). As a result of the additions, God's name (YHWH) occurs precisely ten times in the Deuteronomic version of the Decalogue, which may well be deliberate.

TWO ALTERNATIVE VERSIONS

The Nash Papyrus was discovered in Egypt in 1902 and since then has been preserved in the Cambridge University Library. It contains the text of the Decalogue together with the Shema (Deut 6:4-5) and dates from the first or second century BC. Until the discovery of the Dead Sea Scrolls, it was the oldest extant manuscript of any part of the Hebrew Bible. However, although it is a very old manuscript, the form of the text appears to be a combination of that in Exodus and Deuteronomy. Presumably it is later than either and therefore does not provide an independent testimony to the original text. It is close to the Septuagint (Greek translation) of Exodus and may have been taken from the Hebrew text underlying that version.[7]

Yet another version of the Decalogue is found in the Samaritan Pentateuch.[8] It is probably later than that preserved in the Masoretic Text (standard Hebrew text of the Old Testament) and is characterized by harmonization of some of the differences between Exodus and Deuteronomy. The numbering of the commandments is slightly different from the five ways of numbering mentioned above, condensing all the usual content into just nine commandments. This leaves room for a distinctive Samaritan tenth

---

[5]Cf. Cassuto 1951: 250-51; Greenberg 1985: 91-96; Houtman 1996: 10-11; Jungbauer 2002: 9-17; Markl 2007: 209-17; Klingbeil 2010.

[6]Both phrases are used repeatedly in Deuteronomy; see Deut 1:41; 5:32-33; 6:17; 9:12, 16; 12:21 for "as the LORD your God has commanded you" and Deut 5:29, 33; 6:3, 18; 12:25, 28 for "that it may go well with you."

[7]Stamm and Andrew 1967: 13; Greenberg 1985: 94. Charles (1926: vii-xliv), writing not long after the discovery, transcribes and translates the text, and compares the three versions in detail, arguing that the Nash Papyrus agrees with LXX (Septuagint) in preference to all other authorities, and that it is closer to Deuteronomy but also makes use of Exodus. For a popular but up-to-date account of the papyrus, see Sweeney 2010.

[8]See Bowman 1977: 16-27; Greenberg 1985: 91-94.

commandment: a decree to build an altar and place stones inscribed with the law on Mount Gerizim.[9]

Both alternative versions of the Decalogue are ancient and of great interest, but they are probably later than those in the canon and give no reason to amend the traditional texts with which we are familiar.

CAN WE TRACE AN "ORIGINAL" FORM?

There have been many attempts to reconstruct the "original" form of the Decalogue. Ewald (1876: 159, 163) argues that if the additions and explanations found in Exodus and Deuteronomy are removed, we are left with two series of five laws that "exhibit perfectly that sharp clear brevity which every law ought to possess." It is "undoubtedly" these that were written on the two tablets, as follows:

I.

1. Thou shalt have no other God before me.

2. Thou shalt not make to thyself any graven image.

3. Thou shalt not idly utter the name of Jahveh thy God.

4. Thou shalt remember the Sabbath day, to keep it holy.

5. Thou shalt honor thy father and thy mother.

II.

1. Thou shalt not murder.

2. Thou shalt not commit adultery.

3. Thou shalt not steal.

4. Thou shalt not bear false witness against thy neighbor.

5. Thou shalt not covet thy neighbor's house.

Likewise Charles (1926: xliv-liv) believes that originally the ten commandments each consisted of one terse clause. He suggests the last one was even shorter than in Ewald's proposal—simply, "Thou shalt not covet." Sellin goes further in his reconstruction, arguing that the two positive commands were originally phrased negatively as prohibitions of work on the sabbath

---

[9] Cf. Deut 27:1-8. Several abbreviated forms of the Samaritan Decalogue have been found on inscriptions (Bowman 1977: 9-16).

and the cursing of parents.[10] Other scholars have made similar attempts and produced a variety of hypothetical "original" decalogues.[11] Weinfeld actually suggests three different reconstructions in two articles and a commentary.[12] On the other hand, Kratz rejects the reconstruction of a primitive Decalogue. He argues that the form in Exodus was composed for its literary context and that it included from the beginning most of those elements often considered to be expansions, though he admits the theological basis for the sabbath command may be secondary.[13]

There seem to be two issues: Was there an earlier ("original") form of the Decalogue, and—if so—can it be reconstructed? That there has been some development in the form of the Decalogue is clear from the different versions in Exodus and Deuteronomy. The most significant difference is in the theological basis for the sabbath command, and it could be that each tradition is adding an explanation to an earlier shorter form. Beyond this we move into the realm of speculation. On the one hand, the Decalogue in Exodus is presented as the direct words of God, and it may be questioned whether mere humans would dare to edit these. On the other hand, Cassuto (1951) argues that the author of Deuteronomy did not feel it inappropriate to do this very thing,[14] so there may also have been a process of editing that led to the form we now read in Exodus.

The striking difference in length and style between the first five commandments and the second five suggests that the former have been expanded, in which case there would once have been a shorter, simpler

---

[10]Sellin 1924: 83-84, followed by Alt 1934: 118-19; von Rad 1957: 191.

[11]Cf. Stamm and Andrew 1967: 18-22, 58; Nielsen 1965: 78-118; Cazelles 1969; Lemaire 1981; Harrelson 1997: 33-34. Rabast (1949: 35-38) argues that the Decalogue was originally worded metrically and was in fact a dodecalogue.

[12]Weinfeld 1985a: 12-14; 1985b: 6-8; 1991: 247-48. There are no cross-references between the three, so it is unclear which suggestion he considers most likely.

[13]Kratz 1994; cf. Graupner 2001. From a rather different perspective, Kline (1996) argues that the idea of "later expansive revisions" is incompatible with the understanding of the Decalogue as a treaty, for "treaties were not subject to revisionary tampering." Phillips (1983a), in contrast, argues that the examples of Deuteronomic and Priestly reinterpretation of the Decalogue show that the text was not sacrosanct but could be reworked to take account of new circumstances, just like other Hebrew law. Schunck (1984) believes that the ninth and tenth commandments were added in the eighth century BC as a response to the socioeconomic injustice at that time.

[14]He writes, "According to the customary literary usage followed both in the Bible and in the other literatures of the ancient East, when someone's utterance is cited it is related that someone else referred to it, the statement is not repeated in the *ipsissima verba*, but certain changes and variations are introduced," so "when Moses reminds the people of God's words, he does not repeat them exactly" (250-51). See also Markl 2013a: 22-24.

form. However, this cannot be proved, nor can we say exactly what that form was. In any case, there is no reason to assume the earliest form must have consisted of uniform, short sentences, all in the negative. Nor should we rule out the possibility that some of the explanations are original, included from the beginning because they seemed necessary to make the point clear. Ancient Near Eastern law codes are not always short and simple in form; they include explanations and expansions when required. Moreover, "no one in the climate of opinion in which the Jewish lawgiver lived could have commanded a people to serve only one God, to do so without images, and to afford a slave an equal opportunity with his master for a day's rest, without a threat or promise, or both, and a good reason to boot."[15]

So it is possible there was an earlier form of the Decalogue, simpler and shorter than the forms in the Bible. But it cannot be proved with certainty, nor is there is any way of establishing its exact wording. In any case, it is the texts of Exodus and Deuteronomy that have become canonical for Judaism and Christianity, and it is in this form that the Decalogue has had an unparalleled influence in world history.

OTHER SIMILAR TEXTS

Several other texts in the Old Testament show similarities to the Decalogue, and parallels can be found to almost all the individual commandments.[16] In the Pentateuch, Exodus 34:11-26 has sometimes been called a "ritual decalogue," and it focuses on observances related to worship, overlapping to some extent with the Decalogue (concerning, e.g., worship of one God, idolatry, and sabbath).[17] Leviticus 19 appears to be a reworking and expansion of the Decalogue related to specific cases, with eight of the ten commandments quoted or alluded to in Leviticus 19:4 (first and second commandment), 19:12 (third), 19:3b, 30 (fourth), 19:3a (fifth), 19:16 (sixth),

---

[15]Goldman 1956: 65-66; cf. Cassuto 1951: 237.

[16]Cf. Charles 1926: lix-lxiv; Wenham 1979: 264; Weinfeld 1985a: 4-9, 18-26; Weiss 1985; Harrelson 1997: 21-33; Rodd 2001: 82-85.

[17]Goethe (1773, according to Nielsen 1965: 13-15) and Wellhausen (1889: 85-96, 327-33) believed the "ritual decalogue" to be older than the "ethical decalogue" of Ex 20 and Deut 5, but these terms are misleading generalizations, and the dating is based on an evolutionary idea of Israel's history that has long been discredited (Gressmann 1913: 473-79; Alt 1934: 117n95; Durham 1987; Harrelson 1997: 28). Also, the division of commandments into ten in Ex 34 is uncertain; it could equally be considered a dodecalogue.

19:11, 13 (eighth), and 19:15-16 (ninth).[18] Deuteronomy 27:15-26 contains twelve curses that overlap in content with the Decalogue but differ in form and character.

The prophet Ezekiel has several lists of basic moral and religious obligations in his exposition of individual responsibility (Ezek 18:5-9, 10-17, 18), some of which are also found in the Decalogue (regarding, e.g., idolatry, adultery, and theft). Another list includes honoring parents, sabbath observance, homicide, and adultery (Ezek 22:6-12). Hosea and Jeremiah also make two brief lists of crimes, almost all of which are in the Decalogue (Hos 4:2; Jer 7:9). Two of the psalms set out ethical requirements for those who worship God (Ps 15; 24:3-4).[19]

These similarities are not surprising. The Decalogue is foundational for the life of Israel as a nation and has had an influence on the writing of other laws, prophecy, and liturgy. However, none of the texts mentioned is as comprehensive in scope as the Decalogue.

There are also similarities with a few ancient Near Eastern texts. The Sumerian Instructions of Shuruppak contain warnings about stealing, killing, and adultery.[20] The "Negative Confession" in the Egyptian Book of the Dead has clauses with similar content to the third, sixth, seventh, eighth, ninth, and tenth commandments, though the form is quite different from the Decalogue.[21] However, the similarities do not prove literary dependence on these ancient Near Eastern texts. The prohibition of homicide, adultery, theft, and the like is common in many cultures, and the parallels simply show that the Decalogue originated in a world that recognized a distinction between right and wrong in such basic areas of human life.

To sum up, while there are other texts in the Old Testament and ancient Near Eastern literature that summarize desirable conduct and list specific sins to be avoided, there is nothing quite like the Decalogue.

---

[18]The seventh commandment is mentioned in Lev 20, and there may be an allusion to the tenth in the command to love one's neighbor in Lev 19:18. On the relationship between the Decalogue and Lev 19, see Wenham 1979: 264; Weinfeld 1991: 250-53; Hartley 1992: 309-11; Milgrom 2000: 1600-1602.

[19]Cf. Ps 50:14-20; Is 33:14-16. Mowinckel (1927: 141-56; 1962: 177-80) describes these as "entry liturgies" for the covenant renewal festival that paved the way for the formation of the Decalogue, but Weinfeld (1985a: 25) rejects the comparison because they mention only "refined moral demands" and omit gross sins such as homicide, theft, and adultery.

[20]Lines 28-31, 33-34, 39-40 (*COS*: 1.176).

[21]Chapter 125 (*ANET*: 34-36; cf. *COS*: 2.12). Burney (1908: 350-52) also mentions an ancient Babylonian ritual formula that parallels the sixth, seventh, and eighth commandments.

ORIGIN

As we have seen, the Decalogue is unique. There is no other ancient text comparable to it in the Bible or elsewhere. Its uniqueness, however, is not limited to matters of shape and form, but also extends to its origin and purpose.

MOSES AND THE DECALOGUE

According to Exodus and Deuteronomy as well as later tradition, Moses had a major role in imparting the Decalogue to Israel. Until the nineteenth century this was widely accepted by both Jews and Christians, but in more recent times it has been questioned. There have been three major stages in the discussion: pre–World War II, mid-twentieth century, and post-1970.

First, historical-critical scholarship at the end of the nineteenth century and during the first third of the twentieth century tended to reject the traditional view that the Decalogue originated in the time of Moses. This was argued by Wellhausen and followed by many who accepted his radical reconstruction of the history of Israel.[1] Several scholars suggested the Decalogue originated in the teaching of the eighth-century prophets,[2] though Wellhausen himself dated it later still and connected it with the Priestly tradition.

However, although most critical scholars accepted Wellhausen's reconstruction in general, not all agreed with his late dating of the Decalogue.[3]

---

[1]Wellhausen 1883: 392-93; 1889: 333; cf. Budde 1899: 31-33.
[2]E.g., Kuenen 1885: 244-45; Addis 1899.
[3]E.g., Gressmann 1913: 471-79.

Ewald (1876: 19-20) asserted, "There is no well-founded doubt that the Ten Commandments are derived from Moses, in their general import, their present order, and even in their peculiar language." Burney (1908: 350-52) referred to similarities with the Egyptian Book of the Dead as evidence that Moses was the promulgator of the Decalogue. And Charles (1926: xliv-lix) argued that in its earliest and tersest form it came from Moses and was presupposed by the Book of the Covenant.

During the mid-twentieth century there was a reversal of the trend to date the Decalogue late, and the majority of scholars argued for Mosaic origin.[4] For example, Rowley believed there was an even older "ritual decalogue," one going back to pre-Mosaic religion, that is preserved in Exodus 34. He suggested Moses was responsible—before God—for the issue of an ethical decalogue more in keeping with the new character of Yahwism as he mediated it to Israel. Mendenhall, contra Wellhausen, believed the tribal federation to be a conscious continuation of an earlier tradition going back to the time of Moses. They were bound by a covenant, the text of which was the Decalogue. Stamm and Andrew (1967: 39) surveyed various possibilities but preferred to ascribe the Decalogue to "that pre-eminent personality Moses, rather than to a later unknown author." Even Nielsen (1965: 139), who doubted the Decalogue derived from Moses, conceded that the "genuinely Mosaic tradition really did have an essential contribution to make to the *content* of the decalogue" (emphasis original).

On a slightly different tack, Beyerlin (1961: 145-46) argued that a primitive form of the Decalogue originated in the Mosaic period, but during the stay at Kadesh rather than at Sinai. Likewise Kapelrud (1964) concluded that the covenant and Decalogue originated at Kadesh, earlier than many other scholars supposed. While this may still seem relatively reassuring to those who hold on to the hope that the Decalogue is genuinely ancient, several questions remain unanswered. How was it in fact formed? Did Moses write it, and if not, who was the anonymous author of this extraordinary document? And why does the narrative claim it originated at Sinai if in fact it came from Kadesh?

Since 1970 the situation has changed once more, and widely differing views are now found among scholars on the dating of the Decalogue. For

---

[4]E.g., Buber 1946: 119-40; Cassuto 1951: 235-36; Rowley 1951; Mendenhall 1954a; Goldman 1956: 36-68.

example, according to Harrelson, "the Ten Commandments as a series are from Moses . . . a remarkable discovery of this founder of Israelite religion, and they underlie and sum up the very heart and center of Israel's religion."[5] Durham believes it impossible to establish a precise date for the origin of the Decalogue but is confident of "an earlier rather than a later dating."[6] Kratz dates the Decalogue much later—between the time of Hosea and the composition of Deuteronomy 5—while Graupner considers it a pre-Deuteronomic attempt to generalize and expand older laws.[7] Hossfeld believes the Decalogue to have been compiled in the same period as Deuteronomy (and only later inserted into Exodus) on the basis of Exodus 34:12-26, Hosea 4:2, and Jeremiah 7:9.[8] Different again, Houtman (1996: 9) thinks the Decalogue in its present form is from "the last period of the existence of ancient Israel as a nation," composed as a succinct statement of the basic rules underlying the covenant between God and his people.

Clearly there is no consensus. On the one hand, many scholars believe the Decalogue to be early, indeed one of the earliest parts of the Old Testament; on the other hand, there are various attempts to date the Decalogue much later. It is impossible here to evaluate all these views in detail.

One key issue is whether Moses was a historical figure at all. Some critical scholars today doubt this, and it must be admitted there is no way of proving Moses' historicity beyond question since the only evidence available is from the Old Testament traditions themselves. Nevertheless, this evidence is very strong and should not be dismissed unless there is stronger evidence to the contrary. Many other scholars still regard the traditions about Exodus and Sinai to have a basis in history.[9] This is expressed well by Bright (1981: 127) in his classic history of Israel:

> Moses . . . was, as the Bible portrays him, the great founder of Israel's faith. Attempts to reduce him are extremely unconvincing. The events of exodus and Sinai require a great personality behind them. And a faith as unique as Israel's demands a founder as surely as does Christianity—or Islam, for that matter. To deny that role to Moses would force us to posit another person of the same name!

---

[5]Harrelson 1997: 35; cf. de Vaux 1971: 449.
[6]Durham 1987: 282; cf. Phillips 1984b; Greenberg 1985: esp. 110-11.
[7]Kratz 1994; Graupner 2001.
[8]Hossfeld 1982: 281-82, followed by Otto 1992.
[9]See de Vaux 1971: 327-472; Albright 1976; Coats 1988: 11-17; Beegle 1992; Davies 2004.

Assuming Moses did exist, it seems to me entirely probable that he was the one who imparted the Decalogue to the people he led—at least in its "original" form.[10] Otherwise, if Moses did not give the Decalogue to Israel, who was the unknown figure—presumably even greater than Moses—who was able and authorized to do this, and why is he or she not identified?

ISRAEL AND THE DECALOGUE

We have relatively little evidence concerning the subsequent use of the Decalogue in the life of the nation. Mowinckel (1927) proposed that ancient Israel held a New Year covenant renewal ceremony at which a summary of the law, including prototypes of the Decalogue, was proclaimed. He then argued that the present form of the Decalogue emerged in prophetic circles, probably among the disciples of Isaiah. Though not necessarily following this view of the origins of the Decalogue, many scholars have accepted the idea that it had a role in Israel's worship.[11]

Another influential view has been that of Gerstenberger (1965a; 1965b), who locates the life setting of the Decalogue among the extended family and the wise rather than the priests and prophets. He believes the commandments reflect everyday life. At the most basic level it is the father addressing the son, speaking from experience and with the sacred authority granted to elders within a clan. These rules for social conduct are in due course incorporated into the law, according to Gerstenberger, and become a prerequisite for acceptable worship, as in the entrance liturgies of the sanctuaries. Later, a representative sample of the commandments becomes the center of worship. These insights point to a much wider role for the Decalogue in society than simply in formal worship and could indicate an earlier origin than Gerstenberger assumes. According to the Bible, early Israel is an extended family, and Moses may be seen as a father figure, even though Abraham is the founding father of the nation. Indeed, God himself is sometimes portrayed as the Father of his people (Ex 4:22; Deut 14:1; Hos 11:1), though this is relatively rare.

In my view, it is an oversimplification to associate Old Testament law exclusively with any one group, whether priests (Wellhausen), prophets

---

[10]For more on the Decalogue's form, see the preceding chapter above.
[11]E.g., Stamm and Andrew 1967: 28-30; Childs 1974; Greenberg 1985: 114-16; Collins 1992.

(Mowinckel), or wisdom teachers (Gerstenberger). On the contrary, the Decalogue belongs to the whole nation—the people and their leaders.[12]

A good starting point for understanding the role of the Decalogue in Israel's life is given by Weinfeld (1991: 262-64). He proposes three major stages in the nation's use of the Decalogue:

- "At the dawn of Israelite history the Decalogue was promulgated in its original short form as the foundation scroll of the Israelite community, written on two stone tablets . . . placed in the Ark of the Covenant."

- The Decalogue was read in the sanctuaries at annual ceremonies to renew the covenant, probably at Pentecost (the festival traditionally connected with the giving of the law).

- In Second Temple times it was read daily together with the Shema.

In the light of the evidence available, this proposal seems reasonable. Bearing in mind the discussion above, I suggest two further points to supplement Weinfeld's outline:

- The Decalogue, or at least the principles it expresses, is assumed by the prophets and has a formative influence on the message they proclaim.

- The Decalogue provides guidelines for social conduct within the extended family, and these guidelines are implicit in the wisdom literature.

One matter worth mentioning briefly at this point is motives and sanctions. Laws are toothless without sanctions and ethics ineffectual unless people are motivated to follow them. So why should Israel obey the Decalogue? How is it to be enforced? The Decalogue itself does not stipulate penalties for infringement, and it is left to more detailed laws to do this. For example, all the requirements of the Decalogue are repeated and elaborated in the other law collections (except the prohibition of coveting, which by its very nature cannot be proved and punished). Many of these laws specify

---

[12]Cf. Durham 1987: 279-80. Freedman (2000) interprets the narrative from Exodus to 2 Kings in relation to the Decalogue, arguing that it contains a hidden pattern of commandment violations. In order to make it work, Freedman has to follow the unusual order of the sixth to eighth commandments found in Jeremiah (theft, homicide, adultery), claiming that Baruch was the Deuteronomic historian and so following this order. It is an ingenious theory with interesting insights along the way, but Rodd (2001: 82) demolishes it in a paragraph.

punishment, and the severity varies depending on the nature of the offense and circumstances in which it has been committed.

However, this leads to another point. Apart from the threat of punishment, which is common in ancient Near Eastern law, Old Testament law is distinctive in its inclusion of theological and ethical explanations. The simplest is the opening words of the Decalogue: "I am the LORD your God" (Ex 20:2). Similar words are used throughout the collection of laws in the second part of Leviticus, known as the Holiness Code (Lev 18–26). Some explanations are based in salvation history, especially calls to remember Israel's liberation from bondage in Egypt, as in the Deuteronomic expansion of the fourth commandment (Deut 5:15; cf. Ex 22:21; 23:15; Lev 23:43). A theological basis is given for the prohibition of shedding human blood: "for in the image of God has God made mankind" (Gen 9:6). There are also ethical appeals, such as the prohibition of taking a millstone as security for debt, "because that would be taking a person's livelihood as security" (Deut 24:6; cf. Ex 23:8; Deut 25:3). On these explanations, von Rad (1957: 198) comments, "Jahweh wants obedience, admittedly; but he also wants men who assent inwardly as well. . . . Thus Deuteronomy, which makes a more earnest endeavor than any other code to explain the commandments . . . has the right to say 'very near to thee is the word, in thy mouth and in thine heart' (Deut 30:14)."

WORDS OF GOD

As we have seen above, scholars have debated for more than a century whether Moses wrote the Decalogue and have weighed the merits of various alternative theories. However, what has rarely been done is to consider the actual claims of the biblical text. Clines (1995) points out that the Bible claims God spoke the words of the Decalogue (Ex 20:1; Deut 5:22), but commentators do not take this claim seriously.[13] Instead, they say someone else spoke them, without acknowledging that this implies God did not do so (e.g.,

---

[13] An exception to this generalization is Nicholson (1977: 426), who recognizes that "the Decalogue, in contrast to other legislation in the Sinai narrative in Exodus, is presented as having been spoken directly by God to Israel rather than mediated through Moses" (cf. Phillips 1984a; 1984b). Nicholson believes the present position of the Decalogue is motivated by theological concerns, not merely editorial convenience. Deut 4 and 5 "attach both theological and apologetic significance to the direct transmission of the Decalogue to Israel at Horeb." Likewise, Ex 20:22 refers to God speaking from heaven to Israel to give the Decalogue, unlike Ex 19 where God speaks to Moses. Another exception is Miller (2004b). However, neither Nicholson nor Miller discuss the *actual* origin of the Decalogue and whether or not the biblical presentation is credible.

Hyatt). Or they change the subject and make the issue whether or not they were spoken by Moses (e.g., Charles). Or they imply the text never intended to mean that God actually spoke the words (e.g., Barr). Or they pretend God did actually speak the words, even though it is clear they do not believe it (e.g., Patrick). Clines himself prefers to take what the biblical text says seriously and therefore rejects its claim because he does not believe it to be true, arguing that it was formulated by people whose particular interests were served by its contents.

I also take the biblical text seriously and am intrigued by its extraordinary claims, so I will begin by clarifying exactly what claims are made before considering whether or not they are credible. Both Exodus and Deuteronomy repeatedly identify the Decalogue as words of God, spoken by him directly to the people (Ex 20:1, 22b; Deut 4:10, 12, 33, 36; 5:4, 22-27; 9:10b)[14] and written by him on tablets of stone (Ex 24:12; 31:18; 32:16; Deut 4:13; 5:22; 9:10; 10:1-4).[15] In contrast, Moses is the mediator for the Book of the Covenant (Ex 20:22a; 21:1; 34:32), the Holiness Code (Lev 18:1; 19:1; etc.), and the Deuteronomic Laws (Deut 4:14; 6:1; 31:9, 24-26). He takes on this role in response to the request of the people themselves after their terrifying experience of hearing God speak (Ex 20:18-21; Deut 5:23-27). So there is undoubtedly something remarkable about the Decalogue from the perspective of the biblical narrative.

Apart from the narrative context, which claims divine origin for the Decalogue, the question arises whether the Decalogue itself is formulated as words of God. As it stands, the prologue and the first two commandments are expressed as divine speech using the first-person singular, while the following commandments refer to God in the third-person. Nielsen (1965: 128-30) suggests that the Decalogue was originally a collection of laws with references to God in the third person and that at a later stage in the tradition

---

[14]Cf. Deut 18:16. Deut 5:5 appears to say that Moses mediated the Decalogue, and this is interpreted by some as a relic of an older tradition which has been displaced by the direct, divine delivery of the commandments to the people and by others as a later harmonizing gloss, while a third view is that Deut 5:4-5 reflects two different but equally old traditions. Cf. Childs 1974: 351-60.

[15]It is not clear in Ex 34 whether the new copy of the Decalogue is written by God (Ex 34:1) or Moses (Ex 34:28). Cole (1973: 227) claims the narrator sees no conflict between the two, for they are alternative ways of describing the same events, and deduces that we should not interpret the phrases literally. Childs (1974) points out that Deut 10:1-4 refers to God writing the tablets and suggests that God should be understood as the subject of the verb in Ex 34:28 as well as in Ex 34:1. This is possible, though it is not the most natural reading in the context.

the third-person forms were changed to the first—appearing now as if it were a divine utterance, at least in the first part. However, while it is conceivable such a change could happen, it appears the use of the first person for direct speech in ancient Oriental languages is less consistent than in modern Western ones.[16] For example, God's self-revelation in Exodus 34:6-7 uses the third-person form, and the great king in the Hittite vassal treaties speaks of himself using both the first and the third person.[17] So the mixture of first- and third-person forms in the commandments does not conflict with the assertion of the narrative that all these words are spoken by God. Whether they are supposed to have been spoken directly or through a mediator cannot be determined from the text of the Decalogue itself.

In any case, is clear that the "ten words"—in a specific sense that does not apply to most other words in the Bible—are presented as the direct words of God. Undoubtedly such a presentation creates a problem for many readers today, especially in the Western world. What are we to make of it? On the one hand, Kline (1996) has no difficulty in taking the biblical account at face value. On the other, as already mentioned, Clines (1995) concludes that it is simply not true. As he has shown, there are various attempts to cloud the issue, to find a way of saying that these words come from God without him having to actually speak them. I will not attempt a philosophical argument about whether it is possible or likely that God spoke audibly from heaven and was heard by the people of Israel at Mount Sinai. However, from an exegetical perspective, it may be noted that comparable claims are made concerning three other momentous experiences in the history of God's people: Jesus' baptism (Mt 3:17; Mk 1:11; Lk 3:22) and transfiguration (Mt 17:5; Mk 9:7; Lk 9:35), and Paul's conversion (Acts 9:4-7[18]).[19] Looking outside the Bible, rabbinic literature often refers to the *bat qol* (lit. "daughter of the

---

[16]Even modern languages are not always consistent; e.g., authors sometimes refer to themselves in the third person ("one") or first-person plural ("we").

[17]See *COS*: 2:17-18.

[18]Here it is stated that Paul's traveling companions heard the voice but did not see the speaker, while according to Paul's later retelling of the event his companions saw the light but did not hear the voice (Acts 22:9). It is arguable that inconsistencies like this are not surprising in trying to remember such an extraordinary and overwhelming event, and the differences between the two accounts tend to confirm its essential historicity, whereas identical testimony would more likely be invented.

[19]Visions in both the Old and New Testaments include voices from heaven (e.g., Is 6:3-8; Ezek 1:25, 28; Acts 10:13-15; Rev 4:1; 10:4, 8; 11:12; 14:13). But this is rather different from Exodus 20 and Deuteronomy 5, where an audible voice from heaven is recorded in a historical context.

voice"; i.e., an echo), which seems to be a way of referring to divine speech without stating blatantly that God spoke audibly.[20] In modern times, there are many claims to similar phenomena, especially among people who have been converted to Christianity in a situation where reading the Bible or hearing the gospel is virtually impossible. Whatever we think about this, there seems to me no good reason for rejecting a priori the possibility that the biblical narratives are referring to real historical events. The authors and editors appear to have understood them as such.

The claim of the narrative that the words were not only spoken by God but also written by him on the tablets has no parallel elsewhere in the Bible, except perhaps the writing on the wall in Daniel 5 (described as being written by a human hand, apparently detached, that had been sent by God; Dan 5:5, 24). Most commentators do not even discuss the historicity of this point, and it seems to be assumed that it was in fact Moses or someone else who actually inscribed the tablets.[21] It is impossible to prove what really happened since there were no witnesses to the event apart from Moses himself. However, as in the case of God speaking from heaven, I see no reason to rule out the possibility that the text is recording a real event, perhaps using figurative language. That certainly seems to be what the writer(s) intended the readers to understand. And we should not assume ancient people were naive and unable to distinguish fact from fiction. It is well known that the Babylonians and Egyptians were capable of sophisticated mathematics and engineering, history and literature.

Modern Western disbelief in miracles is based on the assumption that God—if he exists—always acts predictably and according to the laws of nature. In contrast, most theology in the ancient world, as in much of the Eastern world today, allows for the possibility of occasional divine intervention in the routine life of this world. It seems Clines (1995) assumes the former view, and consistent with this he concludes that the Decalogue was not spoken by God. I tend toward the latter view, taking seriously the claim of the biblical text that the "ten words" are words of God in a unique sense, while leaving open the question of exactly how they were originally communicated.

It certainly is an extraordinary claim: the words of this text are the words of God! I am reminded of a story told about Rabbi Zusya of Hanipol:

---

[20]See Strack and Billerbeck 1922: 125-34.
[21]There is ambiguity on this point in Ex 34, as mentioned above (see footnote 15).

> At the very start, when the maggid recited the verse from the Scriptures which he was going to expound, and began with the words "And God said" or "and God spoke," Rabbi Zusya was overcome with *ecstasy*, and screamed and gesticulated so wildly that he disturbed the peace of the round table and had to be taken out. And then he stood in the hall or in the woodshed, beat his hands against the walls and cried aloud, "And God *said!*"[22]

The Decalogue is unique in being ascribed to God. Unlike the Book of the Covenant, Holiness Code, and Deuteronomic Laws—for which the role of Moses as mediator is stressed—the Decalogue is presented as the direct words of God. However we understand this, I believe there is good reason to accept the biblical tradition that the Decalogue originated in the time of Moses and played a key part in the formation of Israel as a nation, indeed as the people of God.

---

[22]Miskotte 1963: 12.

PURPOSE

There is one further matter to clarify before moving into a study of the commandments themselves. What is the purpose of the Decalogue? To be more specific, who is it written for, and what is it designed to do for them?

LAWS FOR GOD'S PEOPLE

Who is the author of the Decalogue addressing? There are three main answers to this question.

First, it has been suggested that the Decalogue is intended for *all people everywhere*. Westermann (1978: 21) describes the first commandment as an example of a command that applies "to everyone and for all time," unlike more specific commands such as Genesis 12:1. Similarly Cohen (1994) considers the Decalogue to present self-evident values to those sensitive to natural justice, a natural rule for human beings created as reflections of God.

A quite different answer is given by Phillips (1970), who argues that initially only free adult males were subject to Israelite criminal law, whereas in Deuteronomy women are considered equal members of the covenant community and are thus liable for breaching the law. Slaves and resident aliens also did not possess legal status, at least in earlier times. Because of this, Phillips believes the Decalogue is addressed to *free adult male Israelites*. Crüsemann (1983) takes this argument further, claiming the Decalogue applies only to adult men who are responsible for administering justice and active in worship, especially farmers who own land and citizens who own slaves. He believes its main principle is to secure freedom for independent farmers and claims that this is why only certain laws are included, whereas other central features of Old Testament law and ethics are absent, such as taboo rules (e.g., clean/unclean, blood), cultic matters (e.g., sacrifices, festivals), economic and state matters, and rules for care of the weak in society. In a similar way, Clines (1995: 32-37)—while admitting that the authors of the Decalogue may have *intended* to address the whole community—argues that the text actually expresses the class interests of middle-aged, urban, property-owning males in Israelite society. Although other groups are mentioned incidentally (women, resident aliens, slaves), they are not addressed directly, nor are their interests and responsibilities the primary concern of the commandments.[1]

A third answer to the question about the audience of the Decalogue is that it is addressed to *all Israel*, the people of God.[2] Having said that, some scholars differ as to whether it is for Israel as a people or as individuals. Zimmerli (1975: 138) concludes his study of the Decalogue by stating that it is "addressed first and foremost to Israel as a nation . . . not . . . the individual." Weinfeld (1991: 249) disagrees, arguing that it applies to every individual in Israelite society, unlike other laws that depend on certain personal or social conditions. The Decalogue is formulated in the second-person singular, "as if directed personally to each and every member of the community," to avoid the possibility of individuals evading responsibility, which might happen if the command was addressed to a group.[3]

I will consider these views in turn. First, it is true that the principles enshrined in the Decalogue are relevant to all human beings in every culture and age, and many of them are also found in the laws and ethics of other nations. However, the context of the Decalogue makes it clear that these particular principles are imparted at a particular time to a particular people: the people of God, Israel. Also, some of the laws are quite distinctive to Israel—for instance, exclusive worship of one God, without images, and sabbath observance.

---

[1]Cf. Block (2011: 30-33), who argues that, strictly speaking, the Decalogue is addressed to "individual male heads of households," but not for their own interests. Rather it is intended to restrain their tendency to abuse others, especially members of their own households and also neighbors.
[2]E.g., von Rad 1957: 195.
[3]As pointed out by Philo and Nahmanides; cf. Albeck 1985: 287-88.

The second view, which states that the Decalogue is addressed primarily to property-owning male Israelites, is also problematic. For example, Crüsemann's (1983) claim that central features of Old Testament law are absent from the Decalogue can be counteracted by pointing out that the first two features he mentions (taboo rules and cultic matters) are *not* in fact central in the context of the whole Old Testament, as proclaimed repeatedly by the prophets. Moreover, the latter two (economic matters and care for the weak) *are* referred to in the fourth, eighth, and tenth commandments. The one religious observance included in the Decalogue is the sabbath, which could be observed by everyone without expense, travel, or special equipment. In contrast, the pilgrimage festivals are not included, and these may well have been observed predominantly by property-owning male Israelites who had the resources and leisure to spend several weeks away from home journeying to the central sanctuary. Childs (1974) points to the simplicity with which the Decalogue is formulated, indicating that it is not addressed to a specific segment of the population but rather to the whole community. Likewise, McConville (2002a: 122) shows that—at least in its Deuteronomic form—the Decalogue "does not support a social structure in which a particular class has special rights or responsibilities," for this would be against the spirit of Deuteronomy that treats all members of God's people as equals (e.g., Deut 15:12-18; 17:14-18).

I believe the third view to be correct—the Decalogue is addressed to the whole people of God. This is surely implied in the biblical context of the Decalogue, where the words are spoken to "[all] the people" (Ex 20:18), "all Israel" (Deut 5:1), the "whole assembly" at Sinai (Deut 5:22). Elsewhere, women and children are specifically included among those who hear and are expected to obey the laws (Deut 29:10-13; 31:12-13; Josh 8:34-35; Neh 8:2; cf. Ezra 10:1; Jer 44:15, 20). Likewise, the Decalogue is for the people of God, both as individuals and as a community. The two are not mutually exclusive, for the actions of individuals affect the community and vice versa. The worship of one God, without images, and the observance of the sabbath would be matters of community policy, but the effectiveness of the policy would depend on the cooperation of individuals. Honoring God's name and one's parents—together with refraining from killing, adultery, stealing, and false testimony—would be primarily matters of individual behavior. Nevertheless, the community would be responsible for ensuring conformity, because the effects of misbehavior would affect the people as a whole. The use of the singular *thou* is consistent with this, since it is used in the Old Testament to address individuals and also the people as a corporate entity.

THE CONSTITUTION OF ISRAEL

Another question concerns the nature of the Decalogue. What role is it intended to play in the life of Israel, as a people and as individuals? There are four main views.

Gressmann (1913: 477) is typical of scholars in the early part of the last century when he describes the Decalogue as the *Hebrew catechism* at the time of Moses. It was widely understood at that time to be a summary of the key points of Israelite religion, itemized so they could be counted on the fingers and easily memorized.[4] According to this view, it is intended primarily for teaching within the community of the people of God.

Phillips (1970; 1983a) believes the Decalogue constitutes *ancient Israel's criminal law*, enforced by means of capital punishment. He starts with the premise that the Old Testament concept of covenant is based on the Hittite treaty form, understanding God as suzerain and Israel as vassal. It follows that any breach in the stipulations amounts to apostasy and leads to divine action. A broken commandment could lead to punishment for both the individual offender and the whole community and might even result in a repudiation of Israel's covenant relationship with God. As a result, if an individual breaks a commandment, it is treated as an offense against the community—in other words, a crime. Following Greenberg (1960), Phillips argues that crimes in biblical law—unlike other ancient Near Eastern law—concern injury to God or a person, never property. Further, the penalty is always death, whereas this is not the case for offenses against property.

A third view is that the Decalogue itself is not primarily law but basic *moral and ethical principles* that deal with issues central to Israel's national life throughout her history.[5] This fits with the research of Mendenhall (1954a), who notes a distinction in ancient Near Eastern law between what he terms "policy" and "technique." The former is the sense of justice in a community, determined and enforced by the deity and accepted by the community as binding and functional as the source for law. The latter stipulates how community policy is translated into specific actions. So also in the Bible,

---

[4]E.g., Gunkel, according to Buber 1946: 130.
[5]Cf. Bailey 1963; Childs 1974; Biddle 2003.

the Decalogue is understood as a statement of the essentials of Old Testament ethics (i.e., policy), while detailed laws in the Book of the Covenant, Holiness Code, and Deuteronomic Laws explain how these principles are to be put into practice (i.e., technique). Unlike law collections such as Exodus 34 and Leviticus 19, the Decalogue is brief but complete: "he added nothing more" (Deut 5:22). The commandments reflect the essential nature of God and his relationship to his people, so the Decalogue may be described as "the essence of the Sinaitic covenant," "the quintessence of Old Testament law," the authoritative summary of God's will as expressed in the laws of Israel.[6] Philo and Muhammad are examples of those who have understood the Decalogue in this way.[7]

A fourth way of looking at the Decalogue is as the *constitution of Israel*.[8] That it is a central part of the process by which the nation is formed is suggested by the introduction to the first commandment: "I am the LORD your God, who brought you out of Egypt" (Ex 20:2). It provides theological and ethical guidelines for the people freed from Egyptian slavery, laying a foundation for the life of the liberated community that continues to be the standard for the people as they live together and order their lives for the common good.[9]

So is the Decalogue the Hebrew catechism, criminal law, ethical essentials, or the Israelite constitution?

It is true that those learning the Jewish and Christian faiths have often been expected to learn the Decalogue. But that does not make it a catechism. The Decalogue is not instruction for a person who has to demonstrate their readiness for membership into a religious community. Catechisms are usually formulated as statements of doctrine (third person) and confessions of faith (first person). But "the soul of the Decalogue" is in the word *Thou* (second person), as Buber (1946: 130) points out. Nothing is stated or confessed; instead, commands are given.

There is also some truth in the idea that the Decalogue is ancient Israel's criminal law, for the first seven offenses are crimes against God and society,

---

[6]Kline 1996; Wenham 1978: 27; Graupner 2001.

[7]Greenberg 1985: 117; Houtman 1996: 7-8. For a survey of Jewish literature in which the Decalogue is viewed as a summary of the law, see Hakala 2014: 45-65.

[8]E.g., Volz 1932: 25; Buber 1946: 135-36; Houtman 1996: 7; Miller 2009: 6-7; cf. Huffmon 1995: 363-65. For a thorough study of the Decalogue understood as the constitution of God's people, see Markl 2007.

[9]McConville 2002a: 121; cf. Miller 1989; 2002; 2004b; 2004c.

and the penalty for these seven is generally death. However, there is a serious problem with this view: the last three commandments (traditionally understood) are not criminal law! Phillips (1970: 130-52) is aware of this and has a solution. He makes them fit by interpreting the eighth commandment as prohibition of kidnapping (i.e., stealing a person, as in Ex 21:16), limiting the ninth to false witness that leads to the death penalty (e.g., 1 Kings 21), and arguing that the tenth is concerned with protecting the status of community elders. However, these interpretations are quite unconvincing; at most Phillips shows that the first seven commandments are criminal law.

Closer to the mark is the view of the Decalogue as the essentials of Old Testament ethics. There are all sorts of laws in the Pentateuch, and the Decalogue provides an "executive summary" of the essential points for maintaining Israel's relationship with God. While all the laws express the divine will, these are the most important ethical principles, believed to be directly revealed by God and not to be diverged from in any circumstances.

However, in my opinion, the most helpful view is the last: the Decalogue is the Israelite constitution. It begins by stating the basis of Israel's special relationship with God and continues by listing her primary obligations in maintaining that relationship. These obligations include responsibilities toward both God and other people. While we should not draw too close a parallel with modern constitutions, in its biblical context the Decalogue is foundational for the national life of Israel. Its similarity in form to ancient Near Eastern treaties may also point in this direction.

Like the Magna Carta of Britain or the Pancasila ("five principles") of Indonesia, the Decalogue determines foundations for perpetuity. Younger nations often appreciate such foundations more than those who have long been free, and Old Testament Israel is no exception (Ps 19:7-10; 119). Far from being a dry legal document or a burden to bear, the Decalogue is a charter of freedom to be embraced and celebrated.

The Decalogue sets out ground rules for the people of God, covering both their relationships with God and others. The first five commandments concern religious and family matters that are of great importance for Israel and relate to its distinctiveness as a nation. Interestingly, these obligations do not include circumcision, considered so important by Jews in later days.[10]

---

[10]Circumcision is the sign of the Abrahamic covenant (Gen 17:10-27) and is referred to in several early narratives (Gen 21:4; 34:13-24; Ex 4:25-26; Josh 5:1-9). However, it is mentioned only briefly

The next four commandments express ethical principles that were widely accepted in the ancient world. The last commandment concerns thoughts and is presumably not intended to be enforced in a human court, though that does not make it any less important than the first nine. Clearly the Decalogue is not intended to satisfy the needs of law courts. "If this is a law code, it isn't written for people to look over their shoulders in case the magistrate sees them, but it is written to make people look up, in case God sees them, or look inside themselves because God is even interested in their thoughts."[11]

To put it another way, the Decalogue expresses the response that God expects from the people he has brought into being. It outlines a vision for the life of Israel after its liberation from Egypt. As such it is instrumental in forming the nation, and the principles it enshrines continue to provide an ethical basis for the people of God in both the Old and New Testaments.

---

in the laws (Ex 12:44-48; Lev 12:3) and nowhere else in the Old Testament except in a figurative sense (esp. concerning "circumcision of the heart"; e.g., Lev 26:41; Deut 10:16; 30:6) and negatively in reference to non-Israelites who are described as "uncircumcised" (esp. the Philistines; e.g., Judg 14:3; Is 52:1).

[11]David Instone-Brewer, personal communication.

LOVING GOD

1 FIRST OF ALL

In the first commandment God introduces himself and establishes his identity as the one God who makes all other "gods" pale in significance. He tells us who he is and how important it is to recognize him. All the other commandments follow on from this first core statement. This clear stance on the unity of God is quite distinct compared with Israel's neighbors.

ONE GOD

Ancient Near East. Ancient Near Eastern societies were almost all polytheistic. In such societies, people believed in many gods—male and female, old and young, powerful and relatively weak. Generally they were thought to be just and wise, though they were also fallible and sometimes incompetent. Their activities were similar to those of human beings: eating and drinking, work and rest, sex and war. Polytheism was inherently tolerant, since each god was believed to have their own role, and people often worshiped several gods. Fourteenth-century Egypt during the reign of Akhenaten was a rare exception, when worship of the sun god Re or Aten was promoted to the exclusion of all others.[1]

It is commonly stated that Israel's monotheism was a revolutionary breakthrough, the culmination of intellectual and religious development over many centuries.[2] According to von Rad (1957: 208), the insistence on the worship of one God to the exclusion of all others is "unique in the

---

[1]For a helpful summary of polytheism in the ancient Near Eastern world, see Walton 2006: 87-112. On Akhenaten, see Redford 1992; 1997; Millard 1993; Allen 2006; Higginbotham 2006.
[2]E.g., Gnuse 1997: 129.

history of religion." However, there may be vestiges of a much more ancient monotheism, for, according to their myths, most ancient Near
Eastern gods were born or created, and their origins can be traced back to
one primordial deity.[3]

While there are few parallels to the Israelite belief in one God, the
demand for exclusive loyalty in the first commandment may be compared
with ancient Near Eastern treaties where the suzerain who initiates a
treaty demands fidelity from his vassal to the exclusion of all others. This
demand is often given a historical basis with reference to the suzerain's
benevolence toward his vassal—for example, in Hittite treaties with
Amorite kingdoms.[4]

There are also ancient Near Eastern parallels to the self-presentation
formula with which the first commandment begins. For example, several
Sumerian and Babylonian law collections begin or end with words like this:

> I am Hammurabi, the shepherd, selected by the god Enlil, he who heaps high
> abundance and plenty, who perfects every possible thing for the city
> Nippur . . .[5]

Many West Semitic royal inscriptions have comparable introductions—for
example, the well-known Moabite Stone reads,

> I am Mesha, the son of Kemosh[-yatti], the king of Moab, the Dibonite . . .[6]

In each case the formula serves to introduce the author and assert his authority to make the law or decree in question. Comparable formulae are
used to introduce gods in oracles addressed to Esarhaddon, the
seventh-century king of Assyria:

> I am the great divine lady, I am the goddess Ishtar of Arbela, who will destroy
> your enemies from before your feet.[7]

First commandment. In a similar way, the Decalogue begins with a
self-presentation formula, which introduces the God who speaks these ten
"words" to the people of Israel at Mount Sinai:

---

[3]Walton 2006: 93-94.
[4]*COS*: 2.17.
[5]CH prologue; cf. CH epilogue; LU prologue; LL prologue.
[6]*COS*: 2.23. See also several Phoenician (*COS*: 2.30-32) and Old Aramaic (*COS*: 2.35-36; 2.38)
  inscriptions.
[7]*ANET*: 449-50.

> **²I am the LORD your God,⁸ who brought you out from the land of Egypt, where you were slaves.⁹ ³You shall not have other gods¹⁰ besides me.¹¹** (Exodus 20:2-3/Deuteronomy 5:6-7)

The first sentence is considered a prologue in some traditions, while the second sentence forms the first commandment. Others regard the first sentence as the first commandment and the second sentence as part of the second commandment. Still others take the two sentences together as the first commandment, and that seems to me most satisfactory. The first sentence provides the context and motivation for the actual commandment in the second sentence.

First, God introduces himself by name (Ex 20:2a; Deut 5:6a), as on previous occasions when he reveals himself to Moses in the Sinai desert (Ex 3:13-15) and in Egypt (Ex 6:2-8). Where God's name occurs in the Old Testament, most Christian and Jewish translations replace it with "the LORD," using small capitals to distinguish it from other uses of the word "Lord."¹² I follow this convention here. This practice dates at least as far back as the Septuagint, where the Hebrew name is translated into Greek as "Lord" (*kyrios*). The New Testament follows the precedent of the Septuagint in using the title "Lord" instead of the divine name. Since there is no need to distinguish this from the actual name, which never appears, it is printed without small capitals in English Bibles (e.g., Mt 1:20, 22; 3:3; 4:7, 10; Jn 12:13; Rom 10:13; Heb 8:8-9; 1 Pet 3:12).

In Hebrew Bibles, God's name is written with four consonants (YHWH), usually supplemented with the vowels of the word "Lord" (*adonay*) to indicate how it is intended to be read. The name Jehovah is common in older

---

⁸So most translations and commentaries, though the NET has "I, the LORD, am your God" (cf. NJPS). Zimmerli (1953) argues at length for the correctness of the traditional translation.

⁹Lit. "from the house of slaves," a common biblical term for Egypt (cf. Ex 13:3, 14; Deut 6:12; 7:8; 8:14; 13:6, 11). Tigay (1996) suggests it may be a term for slave barracks.

¹⁰Lit. "there shall not be for you other gods," an idiom reminiscent of the clause "I will be your God," in the covenant formula, which is literally, "I will be for you God" (Ex 6:7; Lev 26:12; cf. Deut 26:17).

¹¹So the NJPS (Ex); Craigie 1976; Schmidt 1995: 79; Houtman 1996; Lundbom 2013; cf. LXX (Ex); Targums. Alternatively "beside me" (NJPS Deut); "before me" (NIV; NRSV; ESV; NET; Childs 1974; cf. LXX Deut); "in my presence" (Durham 1987; Weinfeld 1991; McConville 2002a; Dozeman 2009); "to rival me" (NJB); lit. "before/beside/upon/over my face." The GNT rephrases the entire sentence as "worship no god but me."

¹²A notable modern exception is the JB, followed by the NJB, which prints the name of God as "Yahweh." Another substitute often used by Jews for the name of God is *Hashem* (Hebrew for "the Name," as in Lev 24:11 and Deut 28:58).

English literature and is still perpetuated by the Jehovah's Witnesses today. However, this name is a misunderstanding, originating with Christian students of Hebrew in the Middle Ages who tried to pronounce the Hebrew form as it stands (*YaHoWaH*), not realizing it was intended to be pronounced *adonay*. The Koren Bible prints the divine name without vowels to eliminate the possibility of mispronunciation in this way. As a result, the original pronunciation of the four-letter Name (Tetragrammaton) has been forgotten, though it is conjectured that it was "Yahweh."

God's name ("the LORD") is supplemented by a statement of who he is: "your God." The original Hebrew uses the second-person singular, addressing each person individually as well as the people as a whole. This holy God is not remote in heaven, inaccessible to human beings; he makes himself known to Israel as "*your* God." In this way he not only tells them who he is but who they are. They are the people of God! This is consistent with the classic formulation of the covenant relationship in one of the earlier revelations of God's name in Exodus: "I will take you as my own people, and I will be your God" (Ex 6:7).

Next, God reminds the people he is their liberator, the one "who brought you out" (Ex 20:2b; Deut 5:6b). On both previous occasions God reveals his name to Moses and tells him about the plan to liberate his people from slavery in Egypt and take them to the Promised Land (Ex 3:7-12, 16-22; 6:5-6, 8). That liberation is now past history rather than future hope and becomes the basis for a new stage in the relationship between God and his people. Later on, the prophet Hosea recalls the historical link between God's revelation of his name and liberation of his people, alluding to the first commandment:

> I am the LORD your God
> > from the land of Egypt;
> you know no God but me,
> > and besides me there is no saviour. (Hos 13:4 RSV; cf. Hos 12:9)

The first two lines are identical to the first part of the first commandment (except for the omission of "who brought you out"), as can be seen in the literal translation of the RSV. The following lines allude to the second part of the commandment. Several other texts paraphrase the first commandment in a similar way, in every case linking it with the exodus from Egypt

(e.g., Deut 6:12-15; 13:4-5; Judg 6:8-10; 2 Kings 17:35-39; Ps 81:9-10). Incidentally, these paraphrases strengthen the view taken here that both the
self-presentation of the God of the exodus and the prohibition of other gods
are part of the first commandment.

Finally, after this historical and theological introduction, the commandment itself is simple and uncompromising: "You shall not have other
gods besides me" (Ex 20:3; Deut 5:7 DLB). The phrase translated "besides
me" has been much discussed. Weinfeld (1991: 276-77) considers six possible meanings, concluding that "in my presence" is the most accurate.
Miller (2009: 19-20) lists four meanings, arguing that all are present in the
command: "before me," "beside me," "besides me," and "over against me."
In my view, there are two main points. Understood literally, the phrase
means that images of other gods are not to be placed in the temple or anywhere else God is present ("before me," "in my presence," "beside me").
However, it is surely not limited to the prohibition of pagan images, which
are in any case ruled out by the second commandment. More broadly, it
means that the people of Israel are not to worship any other god in addition
to—or instead of—the LORD ("besides me," "except me," "to rival me"). In
practice it seems the problem was not so much turning to other gods instead of the LORD (apostasy) as it was worshiping other gods in addition
to the LORD (i.e., syncretism; e.g., 1 Kings 11:4-6; 2 Kings 17:33; Jer 7:9-10;
Zeph 1:4-6).

Is this monotheism? In the Old Testament world of competing gods and
goddesses, it was crucial to determine one's loyalties. The issue is not
framed theoretically in the first commandment. It is not primarily a
question about the existence of God: Is the LORD one god among many, or
the greatest of all gods, or the only God there is? Rather, it is very practical,
calling Israel to decide who they will worship as God (cf. Ex 15:11; 34:14).
Their ancestors had been polytheistic (Josh 24:2; cf. Gen 35:2), and the
historical and prophetic books repeatedly mention Israelites worshiping
other gods. Such worship is consistently condemned by the biblical writers
as a turning away from the worship of the one God that was practiced by
Abraham and taught by Moses.

The first commandment presupposes polytheism and in that context requires Israel to reject all other gods and worship only One. This is not really

a statement of monotheism in the modern sense of the word (the belief that there is only one God).[13] If we want to use a technical term, the closest would be monolatry, which denotes exclusive worship of one God without denying other gods may also exist.[14]

Toward the end of Moses' first sermon in Deuteronomy, he reminds the people of the extraordinary events they have experienced during the preceding years and explains that they were shown these things so they would know that "the LORD is God; besides him there is no other" (Deut 4:35; cf. Deut 4:39). However, it seems Moses does not actually deny the existence of other gods (Deut 4:7, 34). Rather, he calls Israel to worship the LORD instead of them because he is the one who has demonstrated his power and love for his people (Deut 4:20, 32-34, 36-38; cf. 32:36-39). Likewise, the Shema (Deut 6:4-5) is a call to exclusive and whole-hearted worship of the LORD, refusing to follow any other gods (Deut 6:14). This is crucially important to the continuance of the covenant community, so deviance has to be punished by death (Deut 13; cf. Ex 22:19).

Joshua addresses the people after they enter the Promised Land with a plea to commit themselves to the LORD who brought them there, and at the same time he rejects all other gods (Josh 24:14-24). David prays, "How great you are, Sovereign LORD! There is no one like you, and there is no God but you" (2 Sam 7:22), remembering that other nations and their gods have been driven out before Israel (2 Sam 7:23). Solomon agrees, articulating a more universal perspective in his prayer "that all the peoples of the earth may know that the LORD is God and that there is no other" (1 Kings 8:60). Nowhere is the issue of commitment seen more clearly than in Elijah's dramatic

---

[13]There is general agreement that monotheism is one of Israel's most distinctive contributions to civilization. Nevertheless, there has been an extended scholarly debate about when Israel herself began to be monotheistic. Albright (1946: 257-72) traces the beginning of monotheism in Israel to Moses. Similarly, Kaufmann (1961: 122-49, 212-44) considers that Moses more or less eradicated polytheism and that thereafter Israelites were predominantly monotheistic. But many other scholars believe the religion of pre-exilic Israel and Judah to have been largely polytheistic and argue for a gradual evolution from polytheism to monotheism. Some emphasize the role of the monarchy in this development (e.g., Hezekiah and Josiah), whereas most see the exile as the formative period. However, Tigay (1986) adduces archaeological evidence to argue that from the time of Moses most Israelites were de facto monotheistic. On the rise of monotheism, with a spectrum of different conclusions, see Eichrodt 1933: 220-27, 363-64; Albright 1946; Lang 1983; Tigay 1986; Petersen 1988; Millard 1993; Gnuse 1997; de Moor 1997; Smith 2001; 2002; Assmann 2008; Heiser 2008; MacDonald 2012; MacDonald and Brown 2014.

[14]An alternative term sometimes used is *henotheism*, which denotes a form of polytheism that recognizes the existence of many gods but only worships one of them.

confrontation with the prophets of Baal on Mount Carmel, when he challenges the people: "If the LORD is God, follow him; but if Baal is God, follow him" (1 Kings 18:21).

From Moses to Elijah, the writers of Deuteronomy and the Deuteronomic history highlight the challenge to choose between God and the gods. But in the prophets, especially the second part of Isaiah, we move from a choice between the One and the many to an unequivocal assertion that there is really only one God:

> Before me no god was formed,
>> nor will there be one after me. (Is 43:10)
> I am the first and I am the last;
>> apart from me there is no God. (Is 44:6)
> You are my witnesses. Is there any God besides me?
>> No, there is no other Rock; I know not one. (Is 44:8)
> I am the LORD, and there is no other;
>> apart from me there is no God. (Is 45:5; cf. Is 45:6, 18, 21)
> I am God, and there is no other;
>> I am God, and there is none like me. (Is 46:9)

It follows that other so-called gods are simply lifeless images (Is 40:18-20; 41:7; 44:9-20; 46:1-7). This is the closest Old Testament equivalent to monotheism. In terms of the ancient Near Eastern understanding of deity, however, it is not so much a claim that other gods do not exist but that they are powerless and insignificant. In other words, they are not really gods at all. Whether they are something else is a hypothetical question that is neither asked nor answered, because in ancient Near Eastern terms existence is bound up with function, and something without a function is effectively nonexistent.[15]

In any case, there is no doubt Israel's view of the divine world was significantly different from that of her neighbors. The gods of the ancient Near East belong to a pantheon, and they frequently interact with each other. It is common for gods to have consorts. Sometimes decisions affecting gods and

---

[15] Walton 2006: 88-91. Miskotte (1963: 225) argues that the assertion, "I am the LORD, and there is no other" (Is 45:5), is not a metaphysical statement but "a theological negation: besides me there is nothing that has being and value, nothing that can help and give hope." The prophets "teach us, not so much that there are no other gods, but rather that we must constantly choose the Lord in the midst of the gods" (226).

human beings are made in a divine assembly, while at other times there is
conflict so that more powerful or wise gods achieve their goals. In contrast,
the God of Israel is not part of a pantheon, nor does he have a consort. He
is One, taking full responsibility for his plans and actions and communi-
cating with his people by means of priests and prophets. He does not share
his power with other gods, nor is he the most powerful of all gods—he alone
is God.[16]

REFLECTION

Law and gospel. The relationship between the Testaments is sometimes expressed as a contrast between law and gospel: Old Testament religion is
thought to be based on law, in contrast to the New Testament gospel of love.
But that is not the teaching of the Bible. It is true that Paul contrasts law and
faith (e.g., Gal 3), stressing that there is no point in relying on obedience to
the law as a way of salvation because it is only through faith in Christ that
we can be saved. That does not mean there is anything wrong with the law,
however, so long as it is used according to its original intention: as guidelines
for life in the covenant community. It was never intended to bring salvation.
Obedience to law is the *consequence* of covenant, not its condition. People
do not achieve a relationship with God by means of good behavior, faithful
piety, or sustained effort. On the contrary, God saves people by his grace,
bringing them into relationship with himself, and they are expected to respond in gratitude by obeying his law (e.g., Rom 1:5; 8:3-4; 13:8-10). So
gospel and law are complementary, not antithetical.[17]

One of the key texts relating to this issue is the Decalogue. It is particularly clear in the introduction to the first commandment: "I am the Lord
your God, who brought you out from the land of Egypt, where you were
slaves" (Ex 20:2 and Deut 5:6 DLB; cf. Deut 5:15; 6:20-25). Significantly, God
gives the Decalogue to the people he has *already* freed from slavery in Egypt.
He does not require obedience as a condition for achieving that freedom. In

---

[16]This is not quite the same thing as saying that he alone is divine. The Old Testament occasionally
mentions other divine or heavenly beings who are part of the divine assembly or council and
subordinate to God (e.g., Job 1–2; 1 Kings 22:19-22; Ps 82; 89:6-7; Is 6:1-8; Jer 23:18; Zech 3:1-5).
For further discussion, see commentaries on these texts.

[17]The subject of Paul and the law is much too complex to discuss thoroughly here. I mention just
a few works for further reading: Sanders 1983; Badenas 1985; Westerholm 1988; Dunn 1996;
Rosner 2013; Green 2014.

the Old Testament, just as in the New, obeying the law is intended to be a response to God's love, not a way to persuade God to love. A Jewish parable illustrates this point:

> A stranger came into a city and said to the inhabitants, "I will be your king." The people answered, "What have you ever done for us, that you should be our king?" So he proceeded to do many things for the benefit of the city and the people. He built a defense wall, he brought in water to the city and he defended them against their enemies. Then he said to them again, "I will be your king." And the people immediately agreed. In the same way, God delivered the Israelites from Egyptian slavery, and He parted the Red Sea; He gave them manna from heaven, the water and the quail; and He fought for them against Amalek. Then He said to them, "I will be your king" and the people immediately agreed.[18]

So the Decalogue begins by reminding the people of God's love for them, which was demonstrated in their liberation from Egypt. Then it sets out laws for them as the people of God to put into practice in the future. These "ten words" are commonly called "commandments" in English, suggesting they are rules to be obeyed or obligations to be fulfilled. That is partly true, but they are much more than that. In the context of biblical theology, it is more accurate to see them as guidelines for responding gratefully to the grace of God, who loves and saves his people before they do anything at all.

The first response of the Israelites to their liberation is to sing the praises of God, as we see in Exodus 15. Later on, God gives his people the law, beginning with the Decalogue, a gift that also stirs them to praise and thanksgiving (Ps 19:7-11; 119). Miller (2009: 17) comments, "If we ever find these commands too 'binding,' it may be because we do not really know what it means to be slaves who have been liberated from terrible slavery into a new service." The people of Israel are freed from slavery to be God's servants (Lev 25:42), and the service of God is "perfect freedom," as expressed inimitably in the Book of Common Prayer.[19]

Faith and worship. The first commandment is crucial for both faith and worship. On the one hand, Martin Luther emphasizes faith,

---

[18]Albeck 1985: 265-66.
[19]"Collect for Peace," Morning Prayer 1. For further discussion of law and gospel, with bibliographical references, see Baker 2010: 73-75. On the law as gift, see Stevens 2004.

understanding the commandment as a call to believe in God alone. He paraphrases it like this:

> "See to it that you let Me alone be your God, and never seek another," i.e.: Whatever you lack of good things, expect it of Me, and look to Me for it, and whenever you suffer misfortune and distress, creep and cling to Me. I, yes, I, will give you enough and help you out of every need; only let not your heart cleave to or rest in any other.

Faith—confidence in God's grace—is the one and only way to fulfill the commandment. So the commandment is to be kept not merely with outward works but with inward trust, as living children of God.[20]

On the other hand, John Calvin emphasizes worship. He focuses on the preeminence of God, who alone deserves to be worshiped and to have complete authority over his people. His people must not have other gods, because that would be to transfer to another what belongs to God alone: adoration, trust, invocation, and thanksgiving.[21]

Faith in one God, who alone is worthy of worship, is at the heart of the first commandment. However, the commandment is not primarily an affirmation of monotheism. It is a call to make choices and set priorities, to put the one God before all other rivals for one's loyalty and devotion whether spiritual or material, true or false. Faith is not just a matter of reciting a creed, signing a doctrinal statement, or affirming belief in one God (cf. Jas 2:19). Nor is worship limited to singing hymns, reading liturgies, preaching sermons, and celebrating sacraments. These may be requirements for participation in a faith community and doubtless serve to foster faith and deepen devotion. But the first commandment goes deeper than any of them, challenging hearers to decide what is really most important in their lives.

The covenant relationship between God and his people demands total and exclusive commitment by each of the partners. God's commitment to his people is never in doubt in the Bible, whereas they often are not fully committed to him. So the first commandment may be seen as a call to the people of God to renew their commitment to the One who has saved them from slavery and who has promised his protection and blessing for the

---

[20]Luther 1520: 17-23; 1529: 5-10.
[21]Calvin 1536–1559: 379-83. On Luther's and Calvin's interpretations of the first commandment, see further Oden 2005; Price 2008; Coetzee 2014.

future. Its ongoing message for Jews is clear. Christians too, as members of the renewed people of God and spiritual descendants of Abraham, may recognize that the commandment is addressed to them as the will of the One who is their God (Rom 4; 11:17-24) and has saved them from spiritual slavery (Rom 7:14, 24-25; Gal 4:3-8; 5:1; Heb 2:14-15).[22]

---

[22]For helpful surveys of Old Testament teaching on God, see Scullion 1992; Fretheim 2007. For in-depth theological reflection, see Brueggemann 1997a; Goldingay 2003. There is also a short but thought-provoking article titled "God or Nothingness" by Hart 2005.

$\mathscr{2}$ WORSHIP

The first commandment warns the people of God not to worship other gods; the second is concerned with *how* to worship the true God. The detailed attention given to the second commandment (like the fourth and tenth) suggests this is one with which Israel had particular problems. An obvious reason is that the Old Testament prohibition of images is quite different from usual practice elsewhere in the ancient Near East.

IMAGES

Ancient Near East. It was very common in the ancient Near East to depict gods and goddesses by means of statues and carvings. The images were varied, including representations of human beings, animals, plants, and astral bodies. Such images were probably not intended to look like the gods but rather symbolize one or more of their characteristics.[1]

Images were central to most ancient Near Eastern worship, but opinions vary as to whether pagans worshiped the images themselves or treated them as symbols of divine presence. According to Weinfeld (1991: 288) there was no distinction between the gods and their images in the ancient Near East, and pagans could not conceive of a god without an image. However, Bernhardt (1956) has shown that even primitive people did not identify an image with the god it represented, but thought of it as the place where the divine spirit dwelt.[2] For example, an Egyptian creation account tells us that

---

[1]Curtis 1990: 41-42; 1992.

[2]Bernhardt 1956 was not available to me, so I have used the summaries in Clines 1968: 81-83 and Childs 1974: 408.

after Ptah made everything "the gods entered their bodies—of every kind of wood, every kind of mineral, every kind of fruit . . ."[3] All the same, even though the gods were not identified with their statues in theory, it may well be that idolaters would overlook the distinction in practice and view the images as fetishes, having inherent magical powers.[4]

Elaborate rituals were used to transform an image so it was imbued with the divine presence and became the "pure epiphany of its god."[5] The material image was understood to be animated by the divine essence, not simply representing the god but manifesting its presence. Thus the image was believed to be alive and able to eat the food, drink the water, listen to the music, and smell the incense brought by worshipers. However, the image and the god were not the same: the god was the reality embodied in the image.[6]

As a result, images functioned as mediators between people and their gods. On the one hand, the gods were thought to reveal themselves through their images. On the other hand, statues were placed in temples to mediate the prayers of worshipers to the god. One statue has an inscription mentioning that it is "near the ear of my lady [the goddess] that she might speak my prayer to her."[7]

Unsurprisingly, there are no ancient Near Eastern laws comparable to the second commandment, at least among those that have survived to the present day. Nevertheless the idea of worship without images is not completely unknown. For example, Pharaoh Akhenaten destroyed images in his efforts to exalt the worship of the sun god, and the Nabateans used standing stones rather than images to represent their gods.[8]

Second commandment. In contrast to other religions where images were commonly used in worship, the commandment categorically prohibits this practice for the people of God:

---

[3]Conclusion to the "Memphite Theology" (COS: 1.15).

[4]Tigay 1996: 53; Propp 2006: 168.

[5]Berlejung 1997: 72; cf. Walker and Dick 1999.

[6]For further discussion, see Morenz 1960: 150-58; Jacobsen 1987; Curtis 1990: 42-44; Lorton 1999; Walls 2005: 1-67; Walton 2006: 114-18.

[7]von Rad 1957: 214; Curtis 1990: 35, 39-40.

[8]On Akhenaten, see Redford 1997. On the Nabateans, see Patrich 1990. For further examples from the West Semitic area, see Mettinger 1995. However, Lewis (1998: 50) emphasizes that "the repudiation of divine images is very rare in the ancient Near East apart from Israel."

> [4]You shall not make for yourself an image[9] or any likeness[10] of anything that is in the heavens above, or that is on the earth below, or that is in the waters under the earth. [5]You shall not bow down to them or serve them; for I the LORD your God am a jealous[11] God, visiting the iniquity of parents on children[12] and on the third and fourth generation of those who hate me; [6]but showing steadfast love[13] to thousands of generations[14] of those who love me and keep my commandments. (Exodus 20:4-6/Deuteronomy 5:8-10)

In some traditions this double prohibition is regarded as part of the pre-ceding commandment about other gods, while others take it as a commandment on its own. The latter seems to me preferable because there are two separate issues: whether Israelites may have other gods and how God is to be worshiped.

The essence of the commandment is stately succinctly in the first few words as the prohibition of images (Ex 20:4a/Deut 5:8a). The Hebrew word refers to a carved image, generally made of wood or stone and chiseled into shape.[15] Later it comes to include metal figures as well (Is 40:19; 44:10; Jer 10:14). The next clause emphasizes that there are no exceptions to the

---

[9]So NIV 2011; RSV; NJB; REB; Childs 1974; Houtman 1996; McConville 2002a; Dozeman 2009; cf. GNT; Targums; Vulgate. NRSV and NIV 1984 have "idol" (so also Lundbom 2013; cf. LXX). In practice, images would often be made for use as idols, but "idol" is not the essential meaning of the Hebrew word.

[10]So ESV; NJB; NJPS; NET. Alternatively "in the form" (NRSV; NIV).

[11]So most English translations and commentaries, though NJPS has "impassioned" (followed by Weinfeld 1991; Schmidt 1995: 79). In some contexts the same Hebrew word is translated "zeal-ous" (Num 25:11, 13; 2 Sam 21:2; 1 Kings 19:10, 14; cf. Is 9:7). According to Tigay (1996: 65), the term combines the meanings "jealous" and "zealous"; it "reflects the emotional tie between God and Israel that was described metaphorically by the prophets as a marital bond."

[12]This is a literal translation, as in ESV; RSV; KJV; cf. NJPS. The expression is difficult to translate into modern English. Suggestions include "punishing children for the iniquity of parents" (NRSV; cf. NIV); "I punish the parents' fault in the children" (NJB); "responding to the transgres-sion of fathers by dealing with children" (NET); "I lay the sins of the parents upon their children; the entire family is affected" (NLT2). For a novel interpretation of the word "visit" (פקד) in the second commandment, see Ararat 1995: 51-53.

[13]So NRSV; ESV; see also "faithful love" (NJB); "covenant faithfulness" (NET). Less satisfactory translations are "love" (NIV; cf. GNT); "kindness" (NJPS); "mercy" (KJV).

[14]So GNT; cf. Targums; Peshitta. Alternatively, "the thousandth generation" (NRSV; NJPS; Childs 1974; Weinfeld 1991; Dozeman 2009) or "a thousand generations" (NIV; NET; NLT2). The word "generation" is not in the Hebrew but is probably implied in view of the contrast with the three or four generations of Ex 20:5/Deut 5:9 and is explicit in the Targums. See also the references to "a thousand generations" in Deut 7:9; 1 Chron 16:15; Ps 105:8. However, several translations take the meaning as simply "thousands" (RSV; ESV; NJB; REB; cf. LXX and Vulgate).

[15]The Hebrew noun is פֶּסֶל, from the verb פסל ("cut," "carve," "hew"), which is often used in connection with stone (e.g., Ex 34:1, 4).

rule: likenesses of anything in any form are unacceptable (Ex 20:4b/Deut 5:8b). Not only images of other gods are forbidden, for that is already excluded by the first commandment, but also images of the true God or anything else.[16]

The question arises whether the problem is the act of making an image in itself or the use of such images in worship (i.e., idolatry). To put it another way, would it be acceptable to make an image for purely artistic or educational purposes? Many Muslims and some Jews understand the second commandment to prohibit all images used for any purpose. But elsewhere in the Old Testament, the cherubim are given a place in the tabernacle, as are designs using flowers and fruit (Ex 25:18-22, 31-36; 28:33-34). Moses is commanded by God to make a bronze snake (Num 21:8-9). Solomon makes extensive use of imagery in his temple furnishings, including pomegranates, lilies, gourds, bulls, lions, cherubim, and palm trees (1 Kings 7:13-37). Returning to the Decalogue, the second prohibition in this commandment ("You shall not bow down to them or worship them," Ex 20:5a/Deut 5:9a DLB) is clearly concerned with images for worship, so it may be concluded that the commandment is not designed to rule out painting pictures or making models. Similar prohibitions of image making are found throughout the biblical law collections, in every case concerned with idolatry (Ex 20:23; 34:17; Lev 19:4; 26:1; Deut 4:15-19; 27:15).

As in the first commandment, there is theological motivation for obedience (Ex 20:5b/Deut 5:9b). The people are warned that the LORD is a "jealous" God. A better translation might be "zealous," since jealous has rather negative connotations in English, though I am not sure how much that really relieves our discomfort with the term. In any case, it is not so much a question of intolerance as exclusiveness. Israel's covenant relationship with God demands loyalty, like a marriage relationship, as expounded graphically by the prophets (Is 54; Jer 3; Ezek 16; Hos 1–3). In such a relationship, disloyalty provokes jealousy (Deut 32:16; Song 8:6; Ezek 16:38; Zech 1:14; 8:2-3). God will be angry and hurt if his covenant partner is unfaithful—not just temporarily, but up to a lifetime (three to four generations;

---

[16]Cole 1973; Durham 1987; Miller 2009; cf. von Rad 1957: 215-16; contra Houtman 1996. Dozeman (2009), following Obbink (1929), argues that the divine reaction of jealousy only makes sense if images of other gods are intended, and thus sees the second commandment as a concrete continuation of the first.

cf. Gen 50:22-23; Job 42:16). This warning may relate to the first two commandments, both of which are concerned with worship of the one God.[17]
Elsewhere, God's jealousy is mentioned in connection with worshiping other
gods (Ex 34:14; Deut 6:13-15; 32:16-17; Josh 24:19-20) as well as with making
images (Deut 4:23-25; 32:21; Ps 78:58; Ezek 8:3, 5, 10).

These are harsh words, intended to provide the people with strong motivation for obedience to God's commandments. However, even a lifetime is
relatively short compared with the extent of God's love—thousands of generations (Ex 20:6/Deut 5:10). It is striking that this final verse focuses on
mutual love between the covenant partners. Several other texts assure the
people that God loves them while at the same time warning them that he
will punish their sin. Perhaps most important is the proclamation to Moses
at Sinai after the golden calf incident (Ex 34:6-7), often quoted later in the
Old Testament (e.g., Num 14:18). Deuteronomy 4 combines a reminder
about God's jealousy (Deut 4:24) with a reassurance that he is merciful
(Deut 4:31). The almost infinite scope of divine love is emphasized again in
Deuteronomy 7:9 without mention of wrath continuing to subsequent generations. On the contrary, Deuteronomy 7:10 simply warns of swift punishment for those who reject God.

There has been much discussion about the justice (or injustice) of punishing people for the sins of their parents and grandparents. Four points may
be made here.[18] First, the warning is given in a tribal society where family
solidarity is fundamental, and the Old Testament gives many examples of
whole families being blessed or punished as a result of actions by the head
of the family (e.g., Noah, Achan). Next, three or four generations of descendants are the most anyone could expect to see, so the punishment may be
intended as a deterrent to the ancestors, who will see their children and
grandchildren suffer as a result of their sin, rather than implying transfer of
guilt to the descendants themselves. Third, the concluding phrases of
Exodus 20:5-6 ("those who hate me" and "those who love me") suggest the

---

[17]The immediate reference of the word "them" in Ex 20:5/Deut 5:9 is to the "image or any likeness"
prohibited in Ex 20:4/Deut 5:8, a complex expression which is plural in meaning though singular in form (cf. Schmidt 1995: 80). It is possible that it also refers back to "other gods" in Ex 20:3/
Deut 5:7, in which case it connects Ex 20:5-6/Deut 5:9-10 with the first two commandments
(Tigay 1996).

[18]This paragraph is based on the helpful exegesis of these verses and the excursus on
cross-generational retribution by Tigay (1996: 66-67, 436-37).

punishment only applies if the descendants perpetuate their ancestors' rejection of God. Fourth, the everyday principles of justice in Israelite society apply to individuals rather than groups: "Parents are not to be put to death for their children, nor children put to death for their parents; each will die for their own sin" (Deut 24:16). Ezekiel 18 applies the same principle to God's justice in dealing with the whole nation (cf. Jer 31:29-30).

Idolatry in Israel. How far Israelite practice was consistent with the principle of the second commandment is uncertain. The biblical historians give the impression Israel was prone to idolatry, the golden calves made by Aaron (Ex 32) and Jeroboam (1 Kings 12:25-33) being notorious examples. These images were probably intended to represent the LORD or his throne rather than other gods, but in any case they are roundly condemned by Moses and the author of Kings. The bronze snake made by Moses was originally a visual aid, but in later history it was treated as an idol and eventually destroyed by Hezekiah (2 Kings 18:4). On the whole, it seems likely worship in the tabernacle and temple was conducted without images, and divergences from this principle were more common in local sanctuaries like the "high places" (e.g., Lev 26:30; 1 Kings 3:2; 11:7; 14:23).[19] Apparently some individuals had their own shrines too; for example, Micah appointed a personal priest to look after his silver image, ephod, and household gods (Judg 17).

Archaeological evidence to support the existence of idolatry in Israel has been adduced in the discovery of almost a thousand small terracotta figures in Judah dated from the late monarchy period. Most take the form of a woman with large breasts, and they may represent the Canaanite goddess Asherah.[20] Israelites were tempted to worship her, as we know from frequent references in the Old Testament (e.g., 1 Kings 14:15, 23; 15:13; 2 Kings 17:10; 21:7). Many of the figures appear to have been deliberately damaged, perhaps in the reforms of Hezekiah and Josiah. Asherah is often mentioned in the Bible together with the god Baal (e.g., Judg 3:7; 6:25-32; 1 Kings 16:31-33; 18:19), and portrayals of him have been found in ancient Israelite sites.[21] Baal is well known from ancient Near Eastern texts (especially as the storm god

---

[19]Cf. von Rad 1957: 215-16.

[20]While many scholars believe these figures represent the goddess Asherah (e.g., Kletter 1996; cf. Hadley 2000; Johnston 2003), others consider them to be charms or votive figures in human form, perhaps connected with motherhood (Moorey 2003: 47-68; Tigay 1986: 91-92; Millard 2014: 123-24).

[21]Dever 1987: 226; Keel and Uehlinger 1992: 195-98.

of Ugarit) and seems to have been the greatest threat to Israelite loyalty to the LORD—from the plains of Moab (Num 25:3, 5) till Josiah's reforms near the end of the monarchy (2 Kings 21:4-5).

However, Tigay (1986) has argued on the basis of evidence from Hebrew inscriptions that the majority of Israelites were Yahwistic and a relatively small number worshiped other gods. Moreover, Mettinger (1997) believes images were not generally used in everyday Israelite religion at the beginning and that the prohibitions of idolatry in the law and prophets reflect a later period. Two-dimensional images of humans and animals have been discovered that date to the biblical period (for example, on ninth-century ivories from Samaria and assorted seals from the eighth and seventh century), but these do not appear to be objects of worship. Israelite depictions of God are extremely rare.[22]

In later periods it was common for Jewish synagogues to be decorated with both human and animal figures. But archaeological finds from the Hasmonean and Herodian periods (ca. 140 BC–AD 100) include hardly any human or animal images in contrast to preceding and succeeding periods. This may suggest the second commandment was interpreted more strictly at that time, prohibiting all kinds of images, whereas in other periods it was only taken to prohibit idols (i.e., images for worship).[23]

REFLECTION

Images as idols. As explained above, the second commandment is not against the visual arts in themselves but against their misuse for creating objects of worship, specifically making images to be used as idols. The first part of Psalm 115 may be seen as a reflection on the commandment (cf. Ps 135:15-18). The question of the nations in Psalm 115:2 ("Where is their God?") would be an understandable reaction if they should visit the temple in Jerusalem and look in vain for an image of the local god. Perhaps with this in mind, the psalmist contrasts the religion of a living God (Ps 115:3) with

---

[22]Hendel 1997: 212-19; Tigay 1986: 91; Uehlinger 1997: 152; Hendel 1988: 367; Lewis 1998: 42-43. A fourth-century Jewish coin depicts a male figure seated on a winged chariot. Some early scholars read the inscription as YHW and identified the figure with YHWH, comparing it with the vision of God in Ezekiel 1. It is now clear that the inscription should be read YHD (= Judah), and the figure more probably represents Zeus (Meshorer 1982: 21-29).

[23]Konikoff 1973; Hurowitz 1994. For a helpful survey of idolatry in Israel, see Curtis 1992. On the second commandment in LXX, Philo, and Josephus, see Tatum 1986. On rabbinic laws concerning idolatry, see Urbach 1959.

religions that worship lifeless objects (Ps 115:5-7). It is emphasized that these idols are "made by human hands" (Ps 115:4), whereas God is the "Maker of heaven and earth" (Ps 115:15).

These points are developed further by the prophets in a devastating critique of idol worship. The folly of worshiping one's own creation is repeatedly pointed out (e.g., Is 2:8; 44:9-20), and the impotence of dumb idols is contrasted with the power of the true God, the Creator of heaven and earth (Jer 10:3-16). Countless derogatory terms are used to denote the idols; for example:

- *gillul* ("idol"; e.g., Jer 50:2; Ezek 6:4-13; 22:3-4) is probably a play on the word for dung (*gél*), implying that idols are disgusting.

- *elil* ("idol"; e.g., Is 2:8, 18, 20; 10:10-11; Hab 2:18) literally means "worthless thing."

- *shiqquts* ("detestable thing"; e.g., Ezek 5:11; 7:20; 20:7-8) derives from a Hebrew root associated with unclean animals.

- *to'éva* ("abomination"; e.g., Is 44:19; Jer 16:18; Ezek 5:9, 11) refers to something that is utterly unacceptable for the people of God.

- *shéqér* ("deception," "falsehood") and *hével* ("futility," "vanity") suggest that workmen who make these worthless things are deceiving those who worship them (e.g., Jer 10:14-15).

The issue of images and idols in the Christian church came to a head in the iconoclastic controversy of the eighth- to ninth-century Byzantine Empire. It began with an edict of Emperor Leo III in 726 that equated images with idols and ordered their destruction, and it raged for more than a century. Baranov (2007: 541) discusses the commandment in relation to this controversy, which he considers "perhaps the most important period in Church history, when an Old Testament text became the focal point of a theological debate." He shows that both sides of the debate accepted the authority of the second commandment but interpreted it in radically different ways. This mostly affected the Eastern church, but during the sixteenth century the issue surfaced again in the West, when the Reformers opposed the veneration of images and many of them were subsequently destroyed.[24] In the

---

[24]There are several detailed studies of Reformation attitudes to images: e.g., Phillips 1973; Eire 1986; Michalski 1993.

twenty-first century there are still significant differences of opinion between Eastern Orthodox, Roman Catholic, and Protestant Christians concerning the role of images and the visual arts, but on the whole there is mutual acceptance, and iconoclasm is no longer a major issue.[25]

Idol worship may not be a problem in the modern Western world in literal terms. But there is still a challenge for those who live there to question presuppositions and commitments and be open to the possibility of self-delusion, as Barton (1999) suggests. Theologians need to be careful that theology does not become a form of idolatry.[26] Even if we don't make physical images of God, it is possible to treat human ideas of divine reality as though they were absolute. Idolatry is making one's own gods, so in an indirect way idolaters are worshiping themselves and their creations. To put it another way, idolatry is bringing God down to earth and making him into the image of mankind. It is convenient because God is confined within limits that we feel safe with; it is comfortable because God is domesticated, leaving us the feeling that we can control our lives.[27]

At an everyday level, there are glossy magazines packed with images of people and things. There are images of celebrities that inform inquisitive readers about the latest romance or marriage or divorce or baby. There are images of cars that suggest people gain prestige and power by what they drive, all in the attempt to impress others. There are images of clothes that tempt those who are already well dressed to indulge in something new to wear, promising they can become more attractive to others. These are just a few examples of how people and things are idolized in secular societies, treating them almost like gods. There is even a TV series called *Idols* that has been immensely popular throughout the world in various shapes and forms. Of course, no one thinks the singers on these shows are really gods, but the title implies they are hoping to become idols and be adored by the masses.

---

[25]See Boldrick et al. (2013) for a wide-ranging study of iconoclasm from prehistory to the Taliban. On the latter, the following note regarding the Taliban destruction of the Bamiyan Buddhas in 2001 is telling: "Western popular coverage of Taliban statements and actions was almost uniformly condemnatory . . . with few journalists or analysts attempting to make sense of what the Taliban were doing. Statements by Mullah Umar saying the statues would be destroyed because they 'have been used as idols . . . Only Allah, Most High, deserves to be worshipped, not anyone or anything else,' and his infamous comment 'We do not understand why everyone is so worried . . . All we are breaking are stones' were quoted in the Western media primarily as examples of the Taliban's incomprehensible irrationality" (Elias 2013: 150).

[26]Miller 2009: 57-58.

[27]Cf. Stott 1990: 287, 291.

Listening to God. The reason for prohibiting images, even images of the true God, is not given in the commandment itself, but the matter is explained at length in Deuteronomy 4.[28] The Hebrew words translated "image" or "idol" (Deut 4:16, 23, 25) and "form" or "likeness" (Deut 4:12, 15, 16, 23, 25) are the same as in the second commandment. This passage emphasizes that God revealed himself by a voice, not a form, so the people need to beware of making carved images (Deut 4:10-12, 15-18, 23, 25). Other nations believed images made it possible for humans to relate to the gods. But images are an inappropriate response to a God who has made himself known by his word. We are to listen to God, not look at him. It is true that God appears in human form several times in Genesis (Gen 3:8-24; 18; 32:24-30) and occasionally later in the Old Testament (e.g., Ex 24:9-10; 1 Kings 22:19; Is 6:1; Ezek 1:26), but the writers are reticent in what they say, and we learn virtually nothing of what God looks like.[29] There is certainly no suggestion that such experiences are or should be normal in this world.

Some interpreters suggest the second commandment reflects the spirituality of Israelite worship in contrast to primitive religion, others that God chooses to reveal himself dynamically in history rather than statically in an image. There may be some truth in these ideas, but perhaps more importantly the issue turns on God's witness to himself as distinct from any human witness. To substitute an image for God's revelation is inevitably false witness. God cannot be imprisoned in the forms of this world but is free and sovereign. No practice or place of worship can guarantee his presence. No institution or movement has control over him. He is the One who Is ("I AM") and Speaks ("thus says the LORD"), and no image carved by human hands can be adequate to represent him.[30]

Idolatry is the fundamental sin in the Old Testament, according to Reno (2006). Likewise in Romans 1:21-25, godless human beings fail to glorify God and instead worship images they have made themselves. Reno examines the Augustinian tradition, which highlights pride as the primal sin of humanity, concluding that Augustine's view of "sin grounded in self-love" is consistent with biblical teaching about idolatry:

---

[28]For a detailed study of Deuteronomy 4 and the second commandment, see Holter 2003.
[29]For a detailed study of some of these appearances, see Satyavani 2014.
[30]Cf. von Rad 1957: 217-19; Childs 1974; Lochman 1979; Durham 1987; Miller 2009: 51-52.

The spiritual project of the Enlightenment is to bring humanity . . . back to its true home—our inner dignity, our rational capacity for self-directed life, and our unique individualities. Thus the motto of modernity: Our heart is restless until it finds its rest in itself. (178)

However, we are designed to find rest in God, not ourselves. Such illusions of divinity move from pride to idolatry: "Pride's project of finding rest in the self will always find concrete expression as the worship of idols" (180).

Seeing God. So does God ever become visible? Yes! We read in Genesis that God has made his own images: human beings (Gen 1:26-27; 5:3; 9:6).[31] Moreover, according to the New Testament, Jesus Christ is the image of God (2 Cor 4:4, 6; Col 1:15). As Lochman (1979) puts it, God is seen in his self-giving, love, judgment, and grace—but specifically in the life, death, and resurrection of Jesus. So we can see what God is like through Jesus, the Word who became flesh. Through human beings too, if they are faithful to God's purpose in creating them, people around may catch a glimpse of the divine.

Since we are images of God, it follows that we should focus on representing God well in our own lives rather than making other images to represent him. Perhaps this is part of what it means to worship God in spirit and truth (Jn 4:23-24). In any case, it will be good preparation for the day when there will be no need of a temple (Rev 21:22), let alone images, for the people of God will worship before his throne in the heavenly city (Rev 22:3-4). Then the prophecy of Matthew 5:8 will be fulfilled: "Blessed are the pure in heart, for they will *see* God" (emphasis mine).[32]

---

[31]The Hebrew word translated "image" in Genesis (צֶלֶם) is different from that in the second commandment, but its meaning is essentially the same (Miller 2009: 58-59). It is used for images in a neutral sense (1 Sam 6:5, 11) as well as images used as idols (Num 33:52; 2 Kings 11:18; Ezek 7:20; 16:17; Amos 5:26). For a valuable study of the relationship between the image of God and idolatry in biblical theology, see Lints 2015 (esp. chap. 5).

[32]It is impossible to cover all the issues raised by the second commandment here. On idolatry in the New Testament, see Marcus 2006. For a wide-ranging Jewish study of idolatry, see Halbertal and Margalit 1992. For a biblical theology of idolatry from a Christian perspective, see Beale 2008. Goudzwaard (1981) shows how modern ideologies (regarding, e.g., revolution, one's nation, material prosperity, guaranteed security) tend toward idolatry. Duff (2006) reflects on contemporary American politics in the light of the second commandment. See also Barton 2007.

3 REVERENCE

As we have seen, the Decalogue begins with the one God who created the world, made a covenant with Abraham, freed his descendants from slavery, and revealed himself at Mount Sinai. The first two commandments call for a response to this God in faith and worship, rejecting every competing claim to divinity and focusing our attention on listening to God rather than trying to see him. Next, the third commandment is concerned with reverence for God, specifically proper use of his holy name.

GOD'S NAME

Ancient Near East. The introduction to the Babylonian Epic of Creation elevates the importance of names to such an extent that someone or something not yet named can hardly be considered to exist. At the end, the divine assembly bestows fifty names on Marduk, thereby giving him the roles and authority required to act as king of the gods.[1]

The significance of a god's name is also evident in Egyptian writings, In the Legend of Isis and the Name of Re, a wise woman called Isis sets out to discover the secret name of the "noble god" Re.[2] He is very reluctant to reveal it because knowledge of the name could give others power over him. The story illustrates the ancient Near Eastern belief that a name does not simply identify a person but also defines who one *is*.

---

[1]Enuma Elish tablets 1 and 7 (*COS*: 1.111; cf. Walton 2006: 90).
[2]*COS*: 1.22. On the names of gods in Egyptian religion, see Morenz 1960: 21-24.

In the Book of the Dead, the deceased arrives at the judgment hall and approaches Osiris (the god of the dead) with the words, "I know you and I know your name and the names of the forty-two gods who are with you." He makes a declaration of purity, listing thirty-six sins not committed, including blasphemy. Then he carefully addresses each god by name, declaring his innocence of sundry wrongdoings, including reviling a god. Finally there is a closing recitation in which the deceased again denies having cursed a god.[3]

Another Egyptian text that demonstrates the seriousness of frivolous or false use of divine names is the prayer stele of Neferabu, a workman in the necropolis of Thebes. He confesses,

> I am a man who has sworn wickedly by Ptah, the Lord of truth, and he has made me see darkness by day.

and advises,

> Beware of Ptah, the Lord of truth. He leaves no man's action unnoticed. Keep from mentioning the name of Ptah falsely. See, the one who mentions his name falsely comes to ruin.[4]

Religious texts from Mesopotamia also show a concern to avoid misusing divine names. For example, one text reads,

> My god, I did not know how severe your punishment is.
>   I frivolously took a solemn oath in your name.
>   Like one . . . who . . . casually swore a solemn oath by his god.[5]

Similarly, in the Hittite Prayer of Kantuzilis, the supplicant claims not to have sworn an oath in the name of his god and then broken it.[6] Oaths in the name of a god were widespread in the ancient Near East and would often be imposed by a court in a case with inconclusive evidence. An accused person who denied the charge could be required to swear an oath in a temple or before an image, calling on the god to curse them if they were in fact guilty.

---

[3]Chapter 125 §§A8, B38, 42, and the first paragraph of words to be spoken by X in *ANET*: 34-35; cf. *COS*: 2.12: p. 60, column 1; p. 62, column 1.

[4]Verso lines 2-6 in Beyerlin 1975: 36. For further examples, see Wilson 1948, esp. nos. 32-35, 42-46, 50-62; Huffmon 1995: 369-70.

[5]Dingir.šà.dib.ba Incantations, section 1, lines 23-24 (Lambert 1974: 275; cf. 279, line 87; 289, line 12); Poem of the Righteous Sufferer, tablet 2, line 22 (*COS*: 1.153, p. 488, column 2). For further examples, see Huffmon 1995: 368-69.

[6]Line 12 (*ANET*: 400; Beyerlin 1975: 168).

Fear of divine retribution could make this quite effective in ascertaining the truth, and sometimes the parties involved would choose to compromise or lose the case rather than risk the consequences of taking an oath.[7]

The examples quoted so far are not legal texts. The only laws known from Israel's neighbors that cover misuse of divine names come from Assyria. In the Middle Assyrian Laws, blasphemy is mentioned together with stealing from a temple in separate laws covering both women (§§A1-2) and men (§§N1-2). There are also two relevant clauses in the Middle Assyrian Palace Decrees where capital punishment is decreed for a woman in the palace who uses a god's name blasphemously in a quarrel (§10) or for other improper purposes (§11).[8] Another relevant legal document is a treaty found at Ebla that has several clauses on blasphemy. It is considered a very serious offense, often punished by death.[9]

Third commandment. The next sentence of the Decalogue is counted as the second commandment in Roman Catholic and Lutheran tradition and the third in most others:

> You shall not misuse[10] the name of the LORD your God; for the LORD will not leave unpunished anyone who misuses his name. (Exodus 20:7/ Deuteronomy 5:11)

First-person pronouns are used for God in the preceding commandments ("I," "me"), but the style changes to the third person for the next three ("the LORD," "he"). Some of the rabbis conclude from this that the Israelites hear God speak only the first two commandments, but this is contrary to the claim of the text that all ten are received without human mediation.[11] It is probably simply a stylistic variation. A similar variation is found in the Book of the Covenant, while the Holiness Code tends to use the first person and the Deuteronomic Laws the third-person form.

---

[7]Oaths are often mentioned in the laws: e.g., LU §29; SLET §8; LE §§22, 37; CH §§20, 23, 131, 249, 266; MAL §§A47, C1; HL §75. For further discussion, see Jasnow 2003: 313-15; Lafont and Westbrook 2003: 194-96; Oelsner et al. 2003: 924-25; Slanski 2003: 495; Veenhof 2003: 445-46; Westbrook 2003a: 33-34; 2003b: 374-75.

[8]Roth 1997: 201-2; cf. Greengus 2011: 260-61.

[9]Catagnoni 2003: 236-37.

[10]So NIV; NJB; NLT2; cf. "make wrongful use of" (NRSV); traditionally "take . . . in vain" (KJV; RSV; ESV; NET); lit. "lift to emptiness." NJPS has "swear falsely by," which is part of the meaning but unnecessarily limits the scope of the commandment.

[11]Goldman 1956: 22-24.

More significant is the fact that the second person is used for the audience ("you"), as in all ten commandments. This is unusual in Old Testament law and unique in the ancient Near East.[12] Evidently the Decalogue is a personal address to the people, not a textbook for lawyers. The divine Lawgiver speaks directly to those from whom he expects obedience. "The law given by God has a fundamentally personal and interrelational character" and "obedience to law is thus seen to be a response within a relationship, not a response to the law as law" (Fretheim 2003: 192).

The language of the third commandment is quite general, which is perhaps deliberate because it permits a range of application, covering all kinds of misuse of God's name. The warning of punishment for those who break it may suggest this commandment was taken less seriously than others at some point in the history of Israel and needed reinforcing.

One matter addressed by the third commandment is taking a false oath in the name of God.[13] The Old Testament gives examples of statements made under oath in a court of law (Ex 22:9, 11; Num 5:19-22; Hos 10:4; Mal 3:5) and oaths used to strengthen ordinary statements (Judg 21:1, 5; 1 Sam 29:6; 1 Kings 17:12; cf. Mt 26:72, 74). Either way, to swear in the name of God is to appeal to him as a witness, to guarantee the truth of what is being said. But if someone is not telling the truth, they are calling on God to confirm that their lie is true, which is outrageous! Perhaps they do not really believe in a God of judgment at all. As Philo points out, "It is a most impious thing to invoke God to be witness to a lie" (*Decalogue* 86).

Another important use of God's name was in making vows. Biblical examples include Jacob (Gen 28:20-22), Jephthah (Judg 11:30-31), Boaz (Ruth 3:13), Hannah (1 Sam 1:11), Jonathan (1 Sam 20:12-13), and Herod (Mt 14:6-10). In each case, the vow is kept, even though for Jephthah it results in the sacrifice of his daughter and for Herod the execution of a prophet. Clearly, to make a vow in the name of God and not keep it would be misuse of the name (cf. Ps. 15:4; Eccles 5:4-5; Sir 18:22-23), though it is

---

[12]Cf. McConville 2002b: 20-25.

[13]Cf. Lev 19:12; Ps 24:4; Jer 7:9; Hos 4:2; Zech 5:3-4. So Targum Jonathan; Peshitta; Josephus, *Antiquities* 3.91. NJPS translates the commandment, "You shall not swear falsely by the name . . .", and Tigay (1996) takes it as a prohibition of false oaths. Huffmon (1995: 366-67) compares the Hebrew terminology here (תִּשָּׂא אֶת־שֵׁם, lit. "lift the name") with an expression used elsewhere in the Old Testament for swearing oaths (אֶשָּׂא . . . יָדִי, lit. "lift my hand"; e.g., Deut 32:40; cf. Ezek 20:6, 15). He also surveys the various expressions used for making oaths in the name of God, the most common being חַי־יְהוָה ("as the LORD lives"; e.g., Judg 8:19; 1 Sam 14:39, 45).

doubtful readers are expected to approve the actions of Jephthah and Herod.

The commandment is also applicable to profane use of the sacred name (cf. Ex 22:28). A biblical example is the account of a half-Israelite who "blasphemed the Name with a curse" during a fight (Lev 24:10-12). The incident is reported to Moses, who takes the matter to God. Capital punishment by stoning is decreed (Lev 24:13-16) and implemented (Lev 24:23). The same fate awaits Naboth after being falsely accused of blasphemy (1 Kings 21:13). However, the commandment does not cover profanity in general, such as the use of Anglo-Saxon four-letter words instead of their politer equivalents derived from Latin. As Biddle (2003: 109) points out, the use of appropriate language in particular contexts is a cultural issue, not a religious one, and the Bible itself does not eschew strong language where required (e.g., Amos 4:1-2; Phil 3:8).

Yet another way the commandment can be understood is as a prohibition of using God's name for magical purposes. Mowinckel (1921–1924: 54-60) argues on the basis of the Hebrew term used here that the commandment is concerned with harm caused by magical use of the name, and this may well be part of the meaning. Elsewhere in the ancient Near East it was common to use a god's name in incantation formulae in the attempt to harness divine power for human ends. "The reason for this prohibition was that to use the name of a god in magic . . . was a way of having power over that god, of using him for your own purpose."[14]

Avoiding the name. God's name has an important role in Israel's faith from early days (Gen 4:1, 26; Ex 3:15; 6:3;[15] 34:5-6), and Moses teaches the

---

[14]Andrew 1963b: 305. So also Eichrodt 1957: 30; von Rad 1964; Phillips 1970: 54; cf. Klopfenstein 1964: 315-20; Childs 1974; Durham 1987; Arand 1998. Still more ways of misusing God's name would be to give it to an idol (Staples 1939) or to prophesy falsely (Miller 2009: 105-8).

[15]At first sight there appears to be a contradiction between Gen 4 (dating the first use of the name YHWH to the lifetime of Adam and Eve) and Ex 3 and 6 (suggesting that the name was first revealed to Moses). The matter has been extensively debated by commentators with varied conclusions (see Childs 1974: 112-15). In my view, the best explanation is that Gen 4:26 refers to the beginning of public worship, following the beginning of cattle breeding, music, and metalworking mentioned in Gen 4:20-22 (so Westermann 1974; Wenham 1987). The phrase "call on the name of the LORD" (Gen 4:26) is used elsewhere in Genesis to denote worship (Gen 12:8; 13:4; 21:33; 26:25). If this explanation is correct, the emphasis is on the activity rather than the use of a particular name. In Ex 3:13-15 there is more emphasis on the name YHWH and its meaning, but even here a key point is that the God who reveals himself to Moses is the same God who was known by Israel's ancestors. Gen 17:1 and Ex 6:3 agree that God appeared to Abraham as El Shaddai ("God Almighty"), and both texts explicitly identify that God with YHWH.

people to take their oaths "in his name" (Deut 6:13; 10:20; cf. Jer 4:2; 12:16). At the same time, misuse is a continuing danger (e.g., Lev 20:3; 24:16; Ps 139:20; Is 48:1; Jer 5:2; Hos 4:15). Several ancient Israelite letters discovered by archaeologists begin by greeting the recipient in the name of God: "May Yhwh give you good news at this very time."[16] Others include blessings using the name of Yhwh.[17] There are also examples of Israelite oaths that take the same form as in the Bible: "As Yhwh [your God] lives . . ." This is an appeal to God for confirmation of good intent, in the belief that he will punish the speaker if they fail to keep their word.[18]

The name of God reveals who he is, which is why it is so important for Moses to know it (Ex 3:13). Moses' enquiry does not receive an entirely straightforward answer, to be sure, but both the expression "I AM WHO I AM" (Ex 3:14) and the four-letter name Yhwh (Ex 3:15; translated "the Lord," probably related to the Hebrew verb "to be") hint at the eternity and reality of the One who thereby reveals himself to his people. God does not withhold his name from Moses, but he remains sovereign. He is not to be manipulated or controlled by his worshipers.

In due course it became common to avoid pronouncing the four-letter Name at all, perhaps to sidestep the risk of profaning it in any way. Ben Sira advises his readers not to get into the habit of naming the Holy One (Sir 23:9-10). Philo argues that anyone who utters the name "unseasonably" should suffer capital punishment, commenting that people do not even call their own parents by name out of respect for them.[19] A member of the Qumran community who enunciated the most holy name for any reason was liable to be expelled (1QS 6:27–7:2). The Mishnah forbids use of God's name except in specified circumstances (*Sotah* 7:6; *Sanhedrin* 7:5; 10:1).

Ancient Jewish and Christian tradition has refused to say the sacred name, generally replacing it with "the Lord" or "the Lord" following the precedent of the Old and New Testaments in Greek as well as the Hebrew

---

[16]Lachish Letter 2, lines 1-2; cf. Letters 3, 4, 5, 6, 8, and 9 (*COS*: 3.42; *ANET*: 322). God's name is printed here as Yhwh rather than Lord since the practice of replacing the former with the latter is unlikely to have been known at that time in history.

[17]Arad Ostraca nos. 16, 18, 21 (*COS*: 3.43); cf. Deut 21:5; Ruth 2:4; Ps 129:8; 1 Chron 23:13.

[18]Lachish Letters 3 and 6 (*COS*: 3.42); cf. 1 Kings 17:12; Jer 4:2; Hos 4:15.

[19]Philo, *On the Life of Moses* 2: 206-8. As may be seen from §§193-204, Philo does not base his argument on the third commandment but on Lev 24:16, translated in LXX as "anyone who names the name of the Lord is to be put to death" (MT has "anyone who *blasphemes* the name of the LORD . . .").

Bible. Nevertheless, some scholars today renounce this tradition and refer to God by what is assumed to have been the original pronunciation of his name (Yahweh). This may be done out of a desire for authenticity, but often the effect is to downgrade the Ineffable to the Pronounceable.

REFLECTION

Name calling. There is a well-known saying in Shakespeare's *Romeo and Juliet*:

> What's in a name? that which we call a rose
> By any other name would smell as sweet.

So the saying goes, though whether people *really* think that is another matter. Many modern women change their surnames when they get married, while others deliberately choose not to do so. Some people change their names because they do not like them or for other reasons. An example from ancient Egypt is Pharaoh Amenhotep IV, who changed his name to Akhenaten to promote exclusive worship of the god Aten. In Old Testament Israel, a name is something sacred, summing up in a word the character of the named person and having an almost mystical relationship with them. Significant events in the Bible are sometimes marked by a change of name: Abram becomes Abraham, Jacob becomes Israel, and Simon becomes Peter.

To know someone's name can be a step toward gaining power over them or from them; this is true to some extent in Western cultures and much more so in the East. I remember Harold Loukes, a well-known figure in religious education during the 1970s, emphasizing in one of his Oxford lectures that the first thing teachers must do is memorize the names of the children they are teaching, a method certainly helpful for effective classroom management.

In Asian cultures, however, the name has deeper significance. Among the Batak people of Sumatra, where I once lived and worked, personal names are used mainly for children and tend to be avoided when addressing adults. A parent is called by the name of their firstborn child ("father of . . . ," "mother of . . ."), and when the next generation grows up, grandparents are called by the name of their first grandchild ("grandfather of . . . ," etc.). This is linked to magic and traditional religion as well as the fear that spirits may gain power over a person if they know his or her name. It is also connected with the great respect shown for elders in society, so most people are addressed in accordance with their titles and positions, and only the young are normally called directly by name.

Looking at it from this perspective, the third commandment may be a warning against attempts to manipulate God or obtain power by using his name. That is not to say that God really can be manipulated, but it is possible for religion and piety to become absorbed with enrolling God on *our* side rather than offering ourselves for the service of *his* Kingdom. God's name is not to be a tool for achieving human ends, nor does knowledge of his name confer power over him. In contrast, the Bible exhorts readers to submit their wills to that of God (2 Chron 30:8; Job 22:21; Ps 81:11; Prov 3:6; Heb 12:7; Jas 4:7).

Blasphemy. In 2006, there was controversy after cartoons published in Denmark ridiculing Muhammad were reprinted in several other European countries. Charlie Hebdo's Paris offices were burned in 2011 after the magazine's front cover made fun of the prophet. The "Innocence of Muslims," a video broadcasted on YouTube, provoked widespread protests in 2012. In many parts of the Muslim world, these were seen as tantamount to blasphemy because to denigrate God's prophet is taken as an insult to God himself. It seems to me that there are several things we could learn from this.

First, there is a belief among some people in politically correct Western societies that free speech is an ultimate good, something to be defended at all costs. Undoubtedly, it is a privilege to be able to speak one's mind without fear of reprisal, but this freedom needs to be balanced by other good principles, such as love for other people and respect for their beliefs. Free speech is good; love for one's neighbor is better still.

Second, these incidents show how deeply we misunderstand each other—in this supposedly "globalized" society—and particularly how superficial the understanding of Islam is in the Western world. Stereotypes such as Islamic oppression of women and support for violence only scratch the surface. We might just as well conclude that Christianity is a religion of sex (from films made in the United States, a predominantly Christian country) and violence (from the situation in Northern Ireland, where for many years two ostensibly "Christian" groups were at war with each other). Many Westerners failed to understand just how deeply these cartoons and videos affected people in the Islamic world, where Muhammad is revered as the greatest of the prophets. No one there would dream of speaking a word against him. And in this case there was a double offense: making an image (any depiction of the prophet is avoided, even for good purposes) and pouring scorn on the prophet (blasphemy).

By contrast, in nominally Christian countries like Britain and Australia, God's name is often used in profane speech with little awareness of his presence. But to lace ordinary conversation with words such as *God* or *Jesus*, whether in anger or frivolity, is surely to misuse them and break the third commandment—apart from the fact that the speaker apparently does not realize the significance of what they are saying. One result of such a misuse of words was the child who heard the Christmas story and asked, "Why did they name the baby after a swear word?"

Apart from profane speech, God's name may be used lightly in other ways: for example, by attributing personal desires and plans to him. Could it be that the platitudes of the pious are more of a problem than the curses of the atheists? "What is dangerous is not intellectual atheism, which is un-popular, but mild religion, which is very popular indeed. . . . The real enemy is not irreligion but *vague religiosity*" (Trueblood 1961: 32, 38).

Another form of blasphemy is treating God as though he does not exist. According to Psalm 14:1, "The fool says in his heart, 'There is no God.'" But Radner (2005: 87, 93) suggests that the modern problem is not so much that many people declare themselves to be atheists but that "on some basic level, we are *all* atheists," emptying God's name of its power and living as though God was not there. The clearest reference to the third commandment in the New Testament is concerned not with atheists but with the chosen people, who broke God's law and caused his name to be blasphemed among the nations (Rom 2:23-24).

Reverence. A helpful definition of reverence is "the feeling or attitude of deep respect tinged with awe" (*MED*). I suspect this is at the heart of the third commandment. It is not simply a matter of avoiding specific words or expressions, but how we think, speak, and act in relation to the Almighty. When we talk about God, do we show "deep respect tinged with awe"? If we show respect to other human beings, why do we not show even more respect to the One who alone is Holy, Creator of heaven and earth, Ruler of the universe, and Judge of all? On New Year's Eve 1823, the German philosopher Goethe reflected,

People treat [God's name] as if that incomprehensible and most high Being, who is even beyond the reach of thought, were only their equal. . . . This expression becomes to them, especially to the clergy, who have it daily in their mouths, a mere phrase, a barren name. If they were impressed by His greatness they would be dumb, and through veneration unwilling to name Him.[20]

Three biblical texts may illuminate this point. First, Moses learns something about reverence for God at the burning bush, where he is told, "Do not come any closer. . . . Take off your sandals, for the place where you are standing is holy ground" (Ex 3:5). Second, in Jesus' model prayer for his disciples, the first request after the opening address is for God's name to be revered on earth as it is in heaven ("hallowed be your name," Mt 6:9). Third, in John's vision of heaven, "deep respect tinged with awe" might encapsulate the experience of those who come into the very presence of God:

Then I heard every creature in heaven and on earth and under the earth and on the sea, and all that is in them, saying:

"To him who sits on the throne and to the Lamb
   be praise and honor and glory and power,
   for ever and ever!" (Rev 5:13)

The mention of the Lamb brings us to a final point. As we have seen, God's name (YHWH) is never used directly in the New Testament, the word "Lord" always serving as a substitute. However, a new and very significant name appears in the New Testament. God the Father and the Holy Spirit are always mentioned in terms of their roles without names, but the Son of God is given a personal name when he is born (Mt 1:21, 25; Lk 1:31; 2:21). In the gospels he is simply called "Jesus," though after the resurrection this name is usually supplemented with the title "Lord" or "Christ," or both. The "name of Jesus" is often mentioned in Acts, especially in connection with baptism (Acts 2:38; 8:12, 16; 10:48; 19:5), healing (Acts 3:6, 16; 4:10, 30; 16:18; 19:13), and preaching (Acts 4:18; 5:40; 9:27). Paul prays that the name of Jesus may be honored by his followers in the present age (2 Thess 1:12) and is confident that one day it will be the focus of worship by everyone "in heaven and on earth and under the earth . . . to the glory of God the

---

[20]Eckermann and Goethe 1823–1832: 29.

Father" (Phil 2:10-11). On this basis, therefore, the third commandment may be understood to include misuse of Jesus' name, as well as other divine names and titles in Scripture, thus upholding reverence for God the Father, Son, and Holy Spirit.[21]

---

[21]For a helpful discussion of the name of Jesus in connection with the third commandment, see Miller 2009: 111-14.

4 REST

The next commandment is the longest in the Decalogue, perhaps because it is so distinctive. So far as we know, no other nation in the ancient world celebrated the sabbath, and thus the commandment requires explanation and justification to persuade Israel to keep it. And that is not easy! In the eighth century BC, we read of traders who are anxious for the sabbath to end so they can get back to their business (Amos 8:5). By the time of Nehemiah (the fifth century BC), people in Judah are treading winepresses and holding markets on the sabbath (Neh 13:15-22). No doubt they would have liked today's 24/7 shopping culture![1]

SABBATH

Ancient Near East. None of the ancient Near Eastern laws make provision for holidays. There is an incidental reference to a holiday[2] in a clause on marriage in the Middle Assyrian Laws (MAL §A42), but no further details are given. From third-millennium Lagash there is a liturgy for the New Year festival that reads, "During seven days no grain was [ground], the maidservant made herself equal to her mistress, the manservant walked side by side with his master."[3] However, by the first millennium Babylonian slaves had to work all year, and there is no evidence of them being given regular free time.[4]

---

[1]This chapter reuses some previously published material in a revised form (Baker 2009: 287-96) by permission of the publisher, all rights reserved.

[2]So *COS* and *ANET*; lit. "empty day" (*CAD* 14: 176); contra Driver and Miles 1935: 411, 482, who translate *ra-a-ki* as "anointing."

[3]Andreasen 1974a: 281-82.

[4]Dandama[y]ev 1984: 248.

The Egyptian calendar had three ten-day "decades" each month, which is probably the nearest ancient parallel to the Israelite pattern of seven-day weeks. A craftsmen's village has been discovered at Deir el-Medina on the west bank of the Nile River, where laborers were expected to work for nine days followed by one day's rest. In practice, this seems to have been inadequate, for the men were often absent from work for a two- or three-day "weekend."[5]

It is possible the Hebrew word for "sabbath" (*shabbat*) is related to the Akkadian word *šapattu*, which denotes the fifteenth day of the month (i.e., the day of the full moon).[6] There is no connection in meaning, however, since the sabbath consistently refers to a weekly day of rest that is quite independent of the lunar cycle.[7] Nor is there any evidence that *šapattu* was a day of rest at all.[8] The number *seven* occurs in various Ugaritic texts and may have had a special significance in ancient Canaan (as it did in Israel), but there is no evidence of a connection with holidays or religious celebrations.[9]

Fourth commandment. The essence of the fourth commandment (or the third commandment in the Roman Catholic/Lutheran tradition) is the same in both versions of the Decalogue. However, there are significant differences in the wording. As discussed above (see pp. 14-15), the version in Deuteronomy is probably a revision of that in Exodus, though it is also possible that both versions are expansions of a shorter "original" form. To make it easier to compare the two versions, the texts are printed in parallel columns with the differences in italics.

Exodus 20:8-11 DLB	Deuteronomy 5:12-15 DLB
[8]*Remember* the sabbath day, to set it apart as holy.[10]	[12]*Keep* the sabbath day, to set it apart as holy; *as the LORD your God has commanded you.*

---

[5]So Davies 1999: xix. But others understand the evidence from Deir el-Medina to indicate an eight-day work week with rest on the ninth and tenth days (Oakes and Gahlin 2002: 121).

[6]*CAD* 17.1: 449-50; *HALOT*: 1410; cf. *COS*: 1.130, line 206; Stamm and Andrew 1967: 90-92.

[7]The noun שַׁבָּת ("sabbath") derives from the root שבת ("rest," "stop"). On these terms, see North 1955; Andreasen 1972: 94-121; Robinson 1980; Haag 1993; Bosman 1997.

[8]Phillips 1970: 65; Robinson 1988: 160.

[9]See Baker 2009: 225-26.

[10]So NET; cf. "keep it holy" (ESV; RSV; cf. NRSV; NIV; NJB; NJPS). The same verb is used in Ex 20:11 and Gen 2:3, where the former meaning is clearly appropriate. Several translations in those verses have "made it holy." I have chosen this translation so that the Hebrew verb can be translated in the same way in all three verses.

⁹Six days you shall labor,¹¹ and do all your work. ¹⁰But the seventh day is a sabbath to the LORD your God; you shall not do any work, you or your son or your daughter, your male or female slave,

or your livestock, or your resident alien who is in your town.¹²

¹¹*For in six days the Lord made heaven and earth, the sea, and all that is in them, and he rested on the seventh day;*

that is why the LORD *blessed*

the sabbath day *and set it apart as holy.*

¹³Six days you shall labor, and do all your work. ¹⁴But the seventh day is a sabbath to the LORD your God; you shall not do any work, you or your son or your daughter, *or* your male or female slave, *or your ox or your donkey* or *any of* your livestock, or your resident alien who is in your town, *so that your male or female slave may rest like you.*

¹⁵*You shall remember that you were a slave in the land of Egypt, and the Lord your God brought you out from there, with a strong hand and an outstretched arm;*

that is why the LORD *your God has commanded you to keep*¹³ the sabbath day.

The sabbath is to be set apart from all other days as a holy day (Ex 20:8/ Deut 5:12). It is dedicated to God and so has a religious function. The sabbath is first of all a holy day and only then acts as a holiday. From this perspective, stopping work ensures that no one is distracted from divine worship by other activities. Note the two different subjects for the verb "set apart as holy": God (who first made the sabbath holy, Ex 20:11) and human beings (who are to keep it holy, Ex 20:8; Deut 5:12).

The first word is different in the two versions of the commandment.¹⁴ Exodus begins with the command to "remember" (Ex 20:8), a word that

---

¹¹Cf. Ex 20:2 and Ex 20:5, where the same Hebrew root means "slave" and "serve" (i.e., worship) respectively.

¹²Lit. "within your gates." The term "gate" is used as a part referring to the whole (metonym), just as the English word *crown* may be used for *king*.

¹³Lit. "make." Eder 2006 prefers the literal translation, arguing that the use of this particular word is significant for the meaning of the commandment.

¹⁴The Hebrew has זָכוֹר ("remember") in Exodus and שָׁמוֹר ("keep," "observe") in Deuteronomy.

refers not merely to mental activity but to observance of an obligation (cf. Ex 13:3). It is also used of God keeping his covenant (Ex 2:24; 6:5; 32:13). The Deuteronomic version prefers the term *keep* (Deut 5:12), which has a wide meaning but is frequently used for observing covenant obligations (e.g., Deut 4:2, 6, 40; 5:1, 10, 29; 6:2, 17; 7:11; 13:4; 16:1). The word *remember* may have been avoided here because it is used with a different meaning in Deuteronomy 5:15. Deuteronomy also inserts its characteristic refrain, "as the LORD your God has commanded you" (Deut 5:12; cf. Deut 4:5; 5:15, 16, 32, 33; 6:17, 25; 13:5; 20:17; 26:13, 14; 28:45).

The sabbath creates a regular pattern of six days' work followed by a day of rest (Ex 20:9-10/Deut 5:13-14). It has a social function as a holiday, providing rest and refreshment for tired workers. Positively, the seventh day is "a sabbath to the LORD your God" (cf. Ex 16:25; 31:15; 35:2; Lev 23:3, 38); negatively, it is a day when all work is forbidden. It is made very clear that the sabbath is not an option but a fundamental rule for every one of God's people. Looked at in this way, work is stopped so that all may take a break from their labors and be renewed for the coming week. This is particularly important for the poor, who are employed as hired workers or forced to work because of their status as slaves, contra the wealthy, who are free to choose when they work and how much time they spend on leisure activities. Because of this, the sabbath has been described as "perhaps . . . the greatest social revolution in the history of mankind" (Eder 2006: 108).

According to the older version in Exodus 20:10, seven groups are specifically told to observe the sabbath: household head ("you"), son, daughter, male slave, female slave, livestock, and resident alien. This is probably intended as a merism to indicate "everyone": old and young, male and female, slave and free, natives and resident foreigners, humans and animals. The reference to livestock is expanded in Deuteronomy 5:14 so that altogether a total of nine groups is mentioned: six human and three animal. Deuteronomy also adds a clause to emphasize the sabbath as a day of rest for slaves. This is probably intended to avoid any possibility that free Israelites might think they alone are entitled to the benefits of belonging to the people of God, though it should be noted that Exodus does emphasize this point in a separate law (Ex 23:12). The expression "like you" is significant because it grants equal sabbath rights to all human beings.

The Exodus commandment ends with a statement of its theological basis: the imitation of God (Ex 20:11; cf. Ex 31:17). As God rested after the sixth day of creation and blessed the seventh day, so human beings should treat the seventh day as holy (cf. Gen 2:2-3). The sabbath is "built into the very structure of the universe."[15] However, it is distinct from all other festivals and seasons, which occur in relation to the sun (yearly) and moon (monthly), because it creates an independent rhythm of its own (weekly).

Deuteronomy also gives a theological basis for the commandment, but it is quite different (Deut 5:15). The stated reason is commemoration of the exodus from Egypt, though the connection of this with sabbath observance is not immediately clear. The same reason is given elsewhere for freeing slaves in the seventh year (Deut 15:15) and caring for widows, orphans, and resident aliens (Deut 24:18, 22). In view of the specific mention of slaves and resident aliens in the sabbath law (Deut 5:14), it seems the intention is to remind Israel of their previous hardship as slaves in a foreign land and to encourage them to care for those in their own land who suffer similar hardships, in particular by allowing them regular time for rest and worship.[16] The same reason is given for celebrating the Festival of Weeks (Deut 16:12), which also specifically includes these vulnerable people. Again, the Deuteronomic version inserts its characteristic refrain: "[the LORD] your God has commanded you" (cf. Deut 5:12).

On the one hand, Exodus explains why the sabbath is a holy day on the basis of the story of creation. On the other, Deuteronomy is concerned with why the sabbath should be kept, grounding it instead on the story of salvation. The former directs attention to the God of the covenant, the latter to the people of the covenant. These different theological bases for the sabbath are complementary, not contradictory.

A serious celebration. Several texts specify the death penalty (the punishment for most of the Ten Commandments) for breaking the sabbath rule, showing how seriously this commandment is taken in the Old Testament (Ex 31:14; 35:2; Num 15:32-36). However, we should note that it is one of only two commandments formulated positively, which may suggest

---

[15]Childs 1974: 416; cf. Sarna 1991.
[16]Cf. Driver 1902; Sarna 1991; Derby 1994; Tigay 1996; Eder 1997; Christensen 2001; Biddle 2003; Kahn 2004; contra Childs (1974: 417), who argues that the concern of the Deuteronomist is theological, not humanitarian: Israel is commanded to observe the sabbath in order to remember her own deliverance from slavery.

an emphasis on celebration rather than abstinence, joy rather than duty (cf. Is 56:2; 58:13-14).

The sabbath law is repeated in the Book of the Covenant:

> Six days you shall do your work, but on the seventh day you shall stop; so that your ox and your donkey may rest, and your home-born slave and the resident alien may catch their breath. (Ex 23:12, DLB[17])

Several other passages in Exodus also deal with the sabbath. It is recounted how the provision of manna on the sixth day of the week is twice the normal amount to allow for rest on the seventh day (Ex 16:5, 22-30). A detailed law on the sabbath is recorded together with instructions for building the tabernacle, perhaps to emphasize that even creating a place for worship of God is not important enough to override the principle of regular rest and refreshment (Ex 31:12-17). In this passage, the sabbath is described as a sign of the covenant, a theme taken up later by the prophet Ezekiel (Ezek 20:12, 20; cf. Is 56:2, 4, 6; Jer 17:19-27), who decries the profaning of sabbath as rebellion against God (Ezek 20:13, 16, 21, 24; 22:8, 26; cf. Neh 13:17-18). Another brief law emphasizes that the sabbath rule still applies during the busy time of harvest (Ex 34:21).

Exactly what is meant by the prohibited "work" is not specified in the commandment, but elsewhere it is understood to include gathering and preparing food (Ex 16:22-30; though cf. Ex 12:16), plowing and harvesting (Ex 34:21), gathering wood and lighting fires (Ex 35:3; Num 15:32-36), buying and selling (Neh 10:31; 13:15-18; Amos 8:5), wine making (Neh 13:15), and transporting goods (Neh 13:15; Jer 17:21, 24, 27).[18]

Several fifth-century Aramaic documents refer to the sabbath and other Jewish holidays. For example, one of the Elephantine letters refers to the delivery of vegetables, apparently taking place on the sabbath. It is likely the boatman would have been Egyptian, so it does not prove Jews themselves were breaking the sabbath at this time, though it would still go against the principle of allowing employees to rest.[19] We can learn a great deal about the

---

[17]For notes on this translation, see Baker 2009: 291.

[18]On the Old Testament sabbath, see also Jenni 1956; de Vaux 1961: 475-83; Andreasen 1972; 1974b; Tsevat 1972; Hallo 1977; Lohfink 1977: 203-21; Siker 1981; Dressler 1982; Beuken 1985; Robinson 1988; Hasel 1992; Cole 2000; Shead 2002; Barker 2003; Geller 2005; Gosse 2005; Frey 2006; Timmer 2009; Grund 2011.

[19]COS: 3.87G. Differently, Lindenberger (2003: 50) translates the word בשבה as "on account of the sabbath" and understands the letter to be instructing the recipient to arrive in good time to take

understanding and practice of the sabbath in ancient Judaism from documents such as 1–2 Maccabees, Jubilees, the Dead Sea Scrolls, and the New Testament and authors such as Philo and Josephus.[20]

REFLECTION

A special day. Times and seasons in the ancient Near East were reckoned on the basis of solar and lunar phases, as were many in Israel (Gen 1:14). But the sabbath is different, being quite independent of the natural order. It is based simply on the command of God and is therefore denoted "sabbath to the LORD" (Ex 20:10; Deut 5:14; cf. Ex 16:23, 25; Lev 23:3; 25:2, 4). All the major law collections in the Bible deal with the sabbath, and it stands at the head of the calendar of festivals in Leviticus 23.

Alongside its primary purpose of facilitating worship, the weekly sabbath is intended for the well-being of all God's people. There is a clear contrast in this matter between Israel and neighboring nations. Although people elsewhere would presumably have stopped work for the purpose of religious observance, no extant law collection outside the Old Testament actually legislates holidays. Without such legislation, it is likely that slaves and other poor people continued to work while the wealthy enjoyed their celebrations.

Sabbath observance is assumed in the New Testament. It was Jesus' custom to go to the synagogue on the sabbath (Lk 4:16, 31; cf. Mk 1:21; 6:2), and his disciples rested "in obedience to the commandment" (Lk 23:56; cf. Mt 24:20). Jesus is never recorded as having broken the sabbath, though he was more flexible than some contemporary Jewish leaders on what activities were permitted on the holy day. As a result, he provoked conflict with them by healing (Mk 3:1-6; Lk 13:10-17; 14:1-6; Jn 5:5-18; 9:1-16) and allowing his disciples to pluck grain (Mk 2:23-28), though an exorcism performed on a sabbath caused only amazement (Mk 1:21-28). He justified this flexibility with various arguments: while some were based on Scripture (Mt 12:5, 7; Mk 2:25-26; Jn 7:21-24) and common sense (Lk 13:15-16; 14:5), others were more controversial (Mt 12:6; Jn 5:17). In every case, Jesus treated the sabbath as a blessing rather than a burden—a law for life, not for death—and never

---

the delivery before the sabbath begins. The sabbath day is also mentioned in several other Aramaic texts (Hasel 1992: 853; Lindenberger 2003: 44, 54).

[20]See Rowland 1982; McKay 1994; Doering 1999; Weiss 2003: 10-85. For a wide-ranging symposium on the sabbath in both ancient and modern Judaism, see Gordis 1982.

hinted that it was superseded. Some opponents were apparently convinced by his approach or were at least left speechless (Lk 13:17; 14:6), whereas others were hardened in their opposition (Mt 12:14; Jn 5:18).

Perhaps Jesus' most important argument was his well-known saying (or pair of sayings):

> The Sabbath was made for man, not man for the Sabbath. So the Son of Man
> is Lord even of the Sabbath. (Mk 2:27-28)

Again it is implied that the sabbath has continuing validity for Christians so long as it is observed as intended by God (Mk 2:27) and in submission to Jesus as Lord (Mk 2:28). There is an early rabbinic parallel to the first sentence: "The Sabbath is given to you, but you are not given to the Sabbath."[21] This suggests that Jesus' statement fell within the spectrum of views held by Jews at the time. Mark does not record the Pharisees' response in this instance, but they were inclined toward a rigid interpretation of the law and were probably unconvinced. They would surely have objected to the second sentence (Mk 2:28) if understood as a messianic claim, though some interpreters view this as an editorial comment by Mark rather than a statement of Jesus, in which case the Pharisees would not have heard it.[22]

Paul followed Jesus' practice of using the sabbath to teach in synagogues (Acts 13:14, 42, 44; 17:2; 18:4; cf. Acts 16:13) and several times claims to have kept the Jewish law faithfully, no doubt including sabbath observance (Acts 25:8; 26:5; 28:17; cf. Acts 21:20-24; 1 Cor 9:20). His letters do not contain specific teaching about the sabbath. Twice he refers to differences of opinion among Jewish and Gentile Christians about observance of special days, including the sabbath, but apparently does not take a strong line himself (Rom 14:5-6; Col 2:16).

For the past two millennia the seven-day week has been followed throughout much of the world, often with one day set apart for rest. The origin of this pattern has been debated extensively with no definite conclusion. Most ancient calendars are related to the phases of the sun and moon, consisting of days, months, and years; but there is no astronomical

---

[21]*Mekhilta Shabbata* I:27-28 (see Lauterbach 1935: 198).
[22]On Jesus and the sabbath, see further Jeremias 1971: 208-9; Bacchiocchi 1977: 17-73; Beckwith and Stott 1978: 21-26; Carson 1982a; Sanders 1990: 19-23; Weiss 2003: 86-110; Ringe 2005; Miller 2009: 158-62; Burer 2012. Contrary to the view presented here, a few scholars consider Jesus to have suspended the sabbath (e.g., Rordorf 1962: 54-79; Goppelt 1975: 92-95).

basis for the week. In my view, the best explanation is to seek its ultimate source in the Old Testament Decalogue and the first account of creation. A major reason for the widespread adoption of the pattern is undoubtedly the influence of the Roman Empire, where the seven-day week gradually replaced the ancient Roman eight-day cycle, Constantine even making Sunday an official holiday in AD 321.

A ten-day week was introduced during the French Revolution but was discontinued after twelve years; in Soviet Russia the seven-day week was abolished in favor of continuous production with staggered days of rest, but it also was reinstated after eleven years. One aim in both cases was to remove religious influences from daily life, and the effect would certainly have been to make things very difficult for faithful Jews, Christians, and Muslims. As Voltaire once wrote, "If you want to kill Christianity, you must abolish Sunday." In many societies today there are renewed moves to abolish sabbaths and Sundays, these driven by the pressures of secularism and consumerism.

A *"palace in time."* The most profound reflection on the meaning of the sabbath I have come across is by Abraham Heschel (1951a).[23] This section is based on his insights and includes several extracts so readers can appreciate his inimitable style.

> He who wants to enter the holiness of the day must first lay down the profanity of clattering commerce, of being yoked to toil. He must . . . learn to understand that the world has already been created and will survive without the help of man. Six days a week we wrestle with the world, wringing profit from the earth; on the Sabbath we especially care for the seed of eternity planted in the soul. . . . Six days a week we seek to dominate the world, on the seventh day we try to dominate the self. (214)

The Jewish philosopher Philo says the sabbath is intended to give human beings relaxation and refreshment so they can go back renewed to their daily work. Thus relaxation is for the sake of activity, to build up our strength for new efforts. But is that really true? No, in the Bible it is the opposite. The sabbath is not designed to recover lost strength and become fit for another

---

[23]I quote from his article, which is a shortened form of his book (Heschel 1951b). For other reflections from a variety of perspectives, see Bacchiocchi 1980; Moltmann 1985: 276-96; Ratzinger 1994; Lowery 2000: 79-152; Klagsbrun 2002; Bass 2005; Bockmuehl 2005; Sherman 2005; Instone-Brewer 2013.

week's work. Human beings are not beasts of burden, and the sabbath is not for the purpose of making us work more efficiently:

> The Sabbath is not for the sake of the weekdays; the weekdays are for the sake of Sabbath. It is not an interlude but the climax of living. . . . Labor is a craft, but perfect rest is an art. It is the result of an accord of body, mind, and imagination. . . . The seventh day is a *palace in time* that we build. It is made of soul, of joy and reticence. In its atmosphere, a discipline is a reminder of adjacency to eternity. . . . The seventh day is a mine where the spirit's precious metal can be found with which to construct the palace in time, a dimension in which the human is at home with the divine, a dimension in which man aspires to approach the likeness of the divine. . . . The art of keeping the seventh day is the art of painting on the canvas of time the mysterious grandeur of the climax of creation: as He sanctified the seventh day, so shall we. . . . What would be a world without Sabbath? It would be a world . . . without the vision of a window in eternity that opens into time. (Heschel 1951a: 215-16, emphasis original)

So how should we celebrate the Sabbath? On the one hand, it is "an opportunity to mend our tattered lives," to rest and be renewed (Heschel 1951a: 217). On the other hand, it should be something delightful in itself. To keep the seventh day holy does not mean we have to be miserable. On the contrary, it means we make it a special day, employing all of our heart, mind, soul, and senses. We can enjoy good food, spend time with family and friends, breathe fresh air, and listen to our favorite music. Best of all, we can spend time with God, our heavenly Father and Friend.

A Jewish interpretation of Genesis 2:2 asks, "After the six days of creation—what did the universe still lack?" (Heschel 1951a: 220). And the answer is *rest*! Rest is not just stopping work and chilling out. Rest is not something negative but something real and positive. "What was created on the seventh day? *Tranquillity, serenity, peace* and *repose*" (221, emphasis original).

Sabbath and Sunday. One of the most important similarities between Judaism and Christianity is the celebration of sabbath, yet there is a notable difference concerning whether the sabbath should be celebrated on Saturday or Sunday. It is unsurprising that Jews choose the former, which is commonly—though not universally—regarded as the seventh day, the continuation of the Old Testament method of counting days. Most Christians choose the latter, with the notable exception of Seventh-day Adventists, though some who celebrate Sunday as the Lord's Day distinguish this from the sabbath as a Jewish institution.

Three New Testament texts are commonly cited with reference to the Christian practice of meeting for worship on Sundays. First, Luke references early Christians meeting "on the first day of the week . . . to break bread" and listen to Paul (Acts 20:7). It is the "earliest unambiguous evidence" for Christian worship on that day, "a stage in the growing consciousness of, and ecclesiastical importance of, the 'first day of the week.'"[24] The meeting was probably held on Sunday evening, following the Roman reckoning of a day from midnight to midnight (not Saturday evening, which would be the first day of the week according to Jewish reckoning). This is evident from John 20, where the resurrection takes place early in the morning on the first day of the week (Jn 20:1) and Jesus appears to his disciples that evening, still the first day of the week (Jn 20:19). The evening would have been a practical time to meet because most people were working during the day.

Second, at least in Corinth and Galatia Paul implies a regular meeting for worship on Sundays ("on the first day of every week," 1 Cor 16:2).[25] Third, the "Lord's Day" in Revelation 1:10 probably also refers to the first day of the week, which gradually took the place of the sabbath as a day of worship for Christians, as we see in several early Christian writings (e.g., Didache 14:1; Ignatius, *Magnesians* 9:1; Gospel of Peter 35, 50).[26]

How and when Christians began to observe the Lord's Day instead of the Jewish sabbath has been much debated. Beckwith and Stott (1978) argue for continuity between the sabbath and the Lord's Day as a weekly day of memorial, worship, and rest. The sabbath commemorated creation and exodus; the Lord's Day commemorated resurrection. In their view, observance of the Lord's Day began in New Testament times, initially alongside the sabbath and in due course taking its place. Quite differently, Bacchiocchi (1977) disputes the claim that the three texts mentioned above are the basis for Christian observance of Sunday as sabbath, arguing that the transition took place in the second century due to Roman influence and anti-Judaism among the church fathers. Whether Constantine's motivation for choosing Sunday as a day of rest was out of respect for the Christian day of worship

---

[24]The first quote is from Bruce 1962: 407, the second from Turner 1982: 132.
[25]Thiselton 2000.
[26]Bauckham 1982; Beale 1999.

or related to sun worship is debated.[27] Interestingly, according to international standard ISO 8601, Monday is now the first day of the week, so Sunday has become the seventh day!

On a personal note, I have always kept to the principle of resting on Sunday, even if occasionally it has meant working late on Saturday night or getting up early on Monday to meet a deadline. It has been a tremendous blessing to have a day when there is no obligation to do this or that, when the stresses and strains of regular work can be put aside for a while. But I must admit I sometimes tend to feel like Philo, that the sabbath is a good way of refreshing body, mind, and soul so that I can work more effectively the next week. Perhaps I still need to learn what Heschel means when he describes the sabbath as a "palace in time." Certainly I shall need to learn it at some point if I am to appreciate the sabbath rest promised by God in Hebrews 4 (something I am expected to enter) and enjoy the eternal sabbath described in Revelation 14:13.

Christians are often reminded of Jesus' great commission to go and make disciples of all nations (Mt 28:18-20), and that is plenty to keep them fruitfully occupied for six days a week. However, the fourth commandment points to Jesus' great invitation:

> Come to me, all you who are weary and burdened, and I will give you rest. Take my yoke upon you and learn from me, for I am gentle and humble in heart, and you will find rest for your souls. (Mt 11:28-29)

[27]The former is argued by Beckwith and Stott (1978: 81-82), the latter by Rordorf (1962: 162-66), who mentions the possibility that Constantine may also have hoped to boost support among the sizeable Christian minority by means of this policy. For further discussion of the relationship between sabbath and Sunday, with various conclusions, see Rordorf 1962; Lee 1966; Jewett 1971; Bacchiocchi 1977; Beckwith and Stott 1978; Carson 1982b; Swartley 1983: 65-95; Eskenazi et al. 1991; Sales 1994; Greene-McCreight 1995; Beckwith 1996: 10-50; Sturcke 2005.

5 FAMILY

The first group of commandments concludes with a principle for families. Some rabbis consider the fifth commandment most important of all, and there is little doubt it has molded Jewish traditions of family life in the past and continues to do so today.[1] Motyer (2005: 227) treats it as a rule for children, instructing them to respect and obey their parents. Children are told to obey their parents in Proverbs (e.g., Prov 1:8) and Ephesians (Eph 6:1-3), and in the latter case the fifth commandment is cited in support. However, it does not follow that this is the primary concern of the commandment in its Old Testament context. Rhee (1965) views it as an exhortation to filial piety comparable to the teaching of Confucius. Others have questioned its relevance to those with absent or abusive parents.[2]

HONORING PARENTS

Ancient Near East. Respect for the elderly in general, and parents in particular, was normal in ancient Near Eastern societies, at least in principle. Of course, people do not always do what their societies expect them to do, so laws and wisdom sayings encourage people to remember and follow principles in practice.

   Dignity. One of the prime concerns of respect for the elderly in the ancient Near East was dignity. Younger people were expected to maintain

---

[1]Goldman 1956: 177; Sherwin 2007: 89-99.
[2]This chapter is expanded from a previously published article of mine (Baker 2011) by permission of the publisher, all rights reserved.

the older person's status in society. Literary and royal inscriptions from the Old Babylonian period show that children were expected to honor and revere their parents.[3] An Egyptian example is the administrative arrangement called "the staff of old age," by which an elderly person who cannot continue to work effectively retains their position but has a younger assistant to carry out the work. Westbrook (1998: 12-13) compares this with the respect for senior citizens in Leviticus 19:32, in contrast to the compulsory retirement and preference for younger workers that is common in modern societies.

A similar concern is apparent in the Assyrian story of Ahiqar, an elderly sage who has no son of his own and who passes on his wisdom to his nephew Nadin instead.[4] However, Nadin is treacherous and plots against his uncle, almost causing his death. In one version of the story, he justifies his behavior on the basis of his uncle's senility:

> My father Ahiqar is grown old, and stands at the door of his grave; and his intelligence has withdrawn and his understanding is diminished.[5]

Several pieces of wisdom in the Words of Ahiqar counteract such an attitude, emphasizing the responsibility of younger people for maintaining the dignity of parents and elders:

> My son, when thou seest a man who is older than thee, rise up before him.[6]

> Whoever takes no pride in his father's and mother's name may Shama[sh] not shine [on him], for he is an evil man.[7]

---

[3]Stol 1998: 60, 62. For examples, see *CAD* 8: 17b-18a; 12: 45b-46a. The Akkadian terms are *kubbutu* ("honor") and *palāḫu* ("revere"); the Hebrew equivalents are כבד and ירא respectively. A son who showed disrespect to his father by striking him was liable to severe punishment (CH §195); for a recent discussion of this law, see Roth 2006.

[4]The oldest extant version is an Aramaic papyrus of the fifth century BC from Elephantine. The text is incomplete, and fuller but later versions have survived in Syriac, Armenian, and other languages. For a detailed introduction, plus translation and notes on the Aramaic text, see *OTP* 2: 479-507. For a synopsis of several different versions, see *APOT* 2: 715-84. There are several references to Ahikar (i.e., Ahiqar) and Nadab (i.e., Nadin) in the book of Tobit (Tob 1:21-22; 2:10; 11:18; 14:10), which also assumes the concept of honoring parents, though it does not contain specific sayings.

[5]Syriac version, §3.1 (*APOT* 2: 740).

[6]Syriac version, §22 (*DOTT*: 273); cf. Armenian version, §2.80 (*APOT* 2: 739).

[7]Aramaic version, §49 (*OTP* 2: 504); cf. *ANET*: 429.

Son, love the father who begat thee, and earn not the curses of thy father and mother; to the end that thou mayst rejoice in the prosperity of thy own sons.[8]

Support. Another major issue concerning family relationships in ancient Near Eastern laws and wisdom is practical care and support for aging parents. For example, the Sumerian king Lipit-Ishtar, in the prologue to his twentieth-century BC laws, states the following:

With a . . . decree (?) I made the father support his children, I made the child support his father. I made the father stand by his children, I made the child stand by his father.[9]

Sumerian family laws that stipulate harsh punishments for a son who repudiates his parents may also have this concern in mind (AI §§A1-2; cf. CH §§192-93; SLET §4). Legal texts from the Old Babylonian period refer to the obligation to support parents economically and stipulate how much is expected from children.[10]

The Egyptian Instruction of Any gives advice about proper treatment of one's mother:

Double the food your mother gave you,
Support her as she supported you;
She had a heavy load in you,
But she did not abandon you.
When you were born after your months
She was yet yoked [to you],
Her breast in your mouth for three years.
As you grew and your excrement disgusted,
She was not disgusted, saying: "What shall I do!"
When she sent you to school,
And you were taught to write,
She kept watching over you daily,
With bread and beer in her house.[11]

---

[8]Armenian version, §2.18 (*APOT* 2: 732). §2.78 is almost identical (*APOT* 2: 738).
[9]Lines ii.16-24 (*COS*: 2.154, p. 411).
[10]Stol 1998: 60, 62.
[11]§7 (*COS*: 1.46, p. 113); cf. Sir 7:27-28; Tob 4:4.

Duties of a son in the Aqhat Legend, one of the Ugaritic texts, include practical care for a father:

To shut up the jaws of his detractors,
to drive out anyone who would do him in;
To take his hand when [he is] drunk,
to bear him up [when he is] full of wine;
To eat his grain [offering] in the temple of Baʿlu,
his portion in the temple of ʾIlu;
To resurface his roof when rain softens it up,
to wash his outfit on a muddy day.[12]

As well as these specific laws and instructions, various other documents provide information about the care of the elderly in the ancient Near East.[13] This care includes provision of basic needs (especially grain, oil, and clothing) plus practical help with daily living when required.

Worship. Clearly parents, and elderly people in general, were considered worthy of special honor and respect in the ancient Near East. There is also evidence that the duty of honor continued after the death of the one who was honored. This was not simply a matter of providing an appropriate burial, though that would certainly have been included.[14] Ancestor worship was apparently common in Egypt, Ugarit, and Mesopotamia, probably with a view to obtaining blessings from the deceased and to ensuring they do not return to haunt the living.

One Ugaritic passage that seems to imply ancestor worship is found in the Aqhat Legend, already mentioned in connection with support of parents, here recording the duties of a son:

Someone to raise up the stela of his father's god,
in the sanctuary the votive emblem of his clan;
To send up from the earth his incense,
from the dust the song of his place.[15]

---

[12]*COS*: 1.103, p. 344; tr. from *CTA*: 17, i.27-34. On this text, see also Loretz 1979.
[13]Stol and Vleeming 1998; Westbrook 1998: 10-14.
[14]E.g., a second-millennium contract from Nuzi states, ". . . as long as A. lives, B. shall give him food and clothing and honor him. When he dies, he shall mourn him and bury him" (Westbrook 1998: 13).
[15]*COS*: 1.103, p. 344; tr. from *CTA*: 17, i.27-34. Lines 3 and 4 may be referring to ancestor worship at the family vault, which was located under the house in Ugaritic custom, according to Pardee (*COS*: 1.103, n. 8). Cf. Healey 1979; Pope 1981: 159-61.

There is also an accession liturgy from Ugarit in which departed kings are summoned to bestow blessings on the new king:

> Summon Ammishtramru, the King!
> Summon, as well, Niqmaddu, the King![16]

There is evidence from Ugarit and elsewhere of drinking feasts held for and with departed ancestors, for which the term *marzéakh* was used.[17]

Likewise in Mesopotamia, it was considered essential to maintain a mutually beneficial link with one's ancestors.[18] For example, the Akkadian word *kispu* referred to funeral rites as well as to a ritual banquet in memory of the dead that involved contacting ancestors and offering them food and drink. Something similar seems to be implied in an inscription of Panamuwa, an eighth-century king in northern Syria, who hopes his son will include him in the feast when making an offering to the god Hadad:

> May [the dead] spirit of Panamuwa [eat] with you (i.e., Hadad),
> and may the dead spirit of Panamuwa [drink] with you.[19]

Fifth commandment. This commandment also comes in slightly different forms in Exodus and Deuteronomy.

Exodus 20:12	Deuteronomy 5:16
Honor your father and your mother;[20]	Honor your father and your mother, *as the LORD your God has commanded you;*
so that you may live long[21]	so that you may live long *and so that it may be good for you*[22]

---

[16]Patrons of the Ugaritic Dynasty (*COS*: 1.105, esp. lines 11-12). This is the majority interpretation of the text (e.g., Levine and de Tarragon 1984; Pardee 2002: 85-88), though Schmidt (1994: 100-120) sees it as a coronation ritual that incorporates mourning rites for the deceased king, one having no implications of an ancestor cult.

[17]Pope 1981: 176-79; King and Stager 2001: 379-80.

[18]Bayliss 1973; Skaist 1980; Hallo 1992; van der Toorn 1996: 48-65; King and Stager 2001: 380.

[19]*COS*: 2.36, lines 15-18.

[20]LXX inserts "so that it may be good for you and" before "so that you may live long," probably because of the presence of this phrase in the Deuteronomic parallel.

[21]Lit. "that your days may be long." The intransitive *hiphil*, as in Deut 6:2; 25:15; and 1 Kings 8:8, means "to be long" rather than "to lengthen" (Houtman 1996; Propp 2006).

[22]The order of the clauses "so that you may live long" and "so that it may be good for you" is reversed in LXX and the Nash Papyrus.

on[23] the land that the LORD your God is giving to you.	on the land that the LORD your God is giving to you.

The fifth commandment is the fundamental principle for family life in the Old Testament.[24] Like all the commandments, it is addressed to the whole people of God, including both adults and younger people.[25] Everyone has or has had parents, and those who are separated from birth parents generally have others who fill that role in their lives.

The commandment is expressed positively,[26] similar to the preceding commandment on honoring the sabbath, though prohibition of the negative is certainly included (cf. Deut 27:16). To harm, curse, or persistently disobey a parent is treated as a particularly serious crime in Old Testament law, one leading to capital punishment (Ex 21:15, 17; Lev 20:9; Deut 21:18-21).[27] But the basic commandment here is formulated positively, making it much broader than simply a prohibition of parent abuse. It is assumed that to honor parents is natural and proper (cf. Deut 32:5-6, 18-19), and to treat them in any other way would be unacceptable behavior for God's people.

Keeping the fifth commandment has its own reward—long life in the land given by God. This expression can refer to both individual (Deut 6:2; 22:7) and corporate (Deut 11:8-9; 30:16-20) longevity, in the latter case focusing on the length of time Israel is granted to live in the Promised Land. Both

---

[23] So NJPS (cf. KJV), which follows the usual meaning of the Hebrew עַל. Most translations have "in," which is more idiomatic in English.

[24] Jungbauer 2002: 130-35; cf. Gamberoni 1964.

[25] Albertz 1978; Harrelson 1997: 78-88; Portier-Young 2007: 100-101; Miller 2009: 174-75.

[26] Some scholars suppose that the "original" form of the commandment was negative (e.g., Sellin 1924: 83-84; Harrelson 1997: 34), but there is no evidence for this, and it is unnecessary to insist that the original author must have expressed all ten sentences in a uniform way (cf. Phillips 1970: 66, 80; Childs 1974; Durham 1987). Gerstenberger (1965b: 43-50) also argues for the originality of the positive form, suggesting that it arose in clan instruction. Whether or not wisdom circles are to be seen as the place of *origin* for this commandment, there is no doubt that its sentiments would be at home there (cf. Prov 1:8; 15:5; 19:26; etc.). On the "original" form of the Decalogue, see pp. 16-18 above.

[27] Cf. Deut 27:16. For discussion, see Bellefontaine 1979; Callaway 1984; Hagedorn 2000; Willis 2001: 163-85. It appears the death penalty was not always implemented in practice (at least in later times), because Philo criticizes those who reduce the penalty to cutting off the hand (*Special Laws* 2:243-48). Cf. CH §195: "If a child should strike his father, they shall cut off his hand."

may be in view here.[28] Israelites who honor those who have given them life will be blessed by extension of their own lives on earth (cf. Prov 4:10). Later on the commandment will be referred to as "the first commandment with a promise" (Eph 6:2). The Deuteronomic version of the commandment expands the promise of longevity with the characteristic words "so that it may be good for you" (cf. Deut 4:40; 5:29; 6:3, 18; 12:25, 28; 22:7), and adds a further motive clause: "as the LORD your God has commanded you" (cf. Deut 4:23; 5:12; 13:6; 20:17).

As mentioned above (see p. 8), Philo suggests the fifth commandment stands at the border between two groups of commandments just as parents stand at the border between the mortal and the immortal. Although fully human, they have the privilege of partnering with God—the Creator and Giver of Life—in the marvelous processes of conception and birth.

The rationale of the commandment and its position in the Decalogue may be related to the concept of parents as God's image bearers and therefore his representatives in bringing children into the world (Gen 1:26-28; 5:1-3). In any case, in the Decalogue honoring parents is a duty that follows naturally from honoring God, his Name, and his Day. Honoring parents is also associated with honoring God and keeping the sabbath in Leviticus:

> Each of you must respect your mother and father, and you must observe my Sabbaths. I am the LORD your God. (Lev 19:3)

> Stand up in the presence of the aged, show respect for the elderly and revere your God. I am the LORD. (Lev 19:32)

The same Hebrew verb is used here for showing an attitude of *respect* toward parents (Lev 19:3) and *reverence* toward God (Lev 19:32).[29]

Ancestor worship. As we have seen, in ancient Near Eastern thought the duty of honoring parents continued after their death, often involving religious ceremonies and ritual banquets. In the Old Testament, however,

---

[28]Cf. Houtman 1996: 57-58; Miller 2004c: 140-43.

[29]The Hebrew is ירא ("fear," "revere," "respect"). It may be noted that the Hebrew verb translated "honor" in the fifth commandment (כבד) is also used with reference to God (e.g., 1 Sam 2:30; Is 25:3; 43:20, 23) and is related to the noun "glory" (כָּבוֹד).

ancestor worship is mentioned only rarely and always as something to be avoided.

While a decent burial was considered necessary (Gen 23:4; 47:29-30; 2 Sam 21:10-14; cf. Jer 22:19), it is notable that tombs are of relatively little importance in biblical Israel compared with many other cultures, both ancient and modern. Jacob marks Rachel's tomb with a pillar (Gen 35:20), and Absalom and Shebna make advance preparations for their own memorials (2 Sam 18:18; Is 22:15-16), but there is no record of pilgrimages or worship in connection with ancestral tombs. The dead are lamented (e.g., 2 Sam 1:17-27; 1 Kings 13:30; Jer 34:5; Amos 5:16-17; 8:10), but the biblical laments do not include any religious element. Laceration and shaving the forehead in mourning, though common elsewhere, are not acceptable for Israelites (Lev 19:27-28; Deut 14:1).[30] Those who offer the triennial tithe make a formal declaration that none of it has been offered to the dead (Deut 26:14), implying that some people do make offerings to the dead (though this certainly does not authorize the practice).[31] Consultation of the dead is strictly forbidden (Lev 19:31; 20:6, 27; Deut 18:10-14; cf. 2 Kings 21:6; 23:24), and the one recorded attempt to do this ends in disaster (1 Sam 28).

It seems ancient Israel was significantly different from neighboring nations in its attitude toward the dead, at least in principle. The word *marzéakh* occurs twice in the Old Testament, denoting a funeral meal (Jer 16:5-7) and excessive feasting (Amos 6:4-7), but in neither case is there any indication that the dead were worshiped. While it is possible ancestor worship occurred from time to time, there is no doubt the practice would have been contrary to Israelite faith as advocated in the law and prophets.[32]

---

[30]The former is associated with worship of other gods in 1 Kings 18:28 and Hos 7:14. Similar practices are mentioned in Lev 21:5; Is 15:2; 22:12; Jer 16:6; 41:5; 47:5; 48:37; Ezek 7:18; Mic 1:16.

[31]Cf. Ps 106:28; Sir 30:18; Jubilees 22:17. The practice may be viewed more positively in Tob 4:17, though some interpret this as a reference to funeral meals rather than offerings to the dead. For discussion, see Moore 1996; Bullard and Hatton 2001.

[32]Several scholars argue for the existence of ancestor worship in ancient Israel (e.g., Spronk 1986; Lewis 1989; 1991; Bloch-Smith 1992; van der Toorn 1996: 206-35; cf. Brichto 1973; Kennedy 1992; Arnold 1999: 414-15). Others deny it (e.g., Kaufmann 1961: 311-16; de Vaux 1961: 56-61; Schmidt 1994; Johnston 2002: 167-95). For Christian reflections on ancestor practices in Asia today, see Ro 1985.

REFLECTION

Two of the ancient Near Eastern concepts discussed above are important in Old Testament teaching on attitudes toward parents and elders—namely, *dignity* and *support*. There is also a distinctive feature that emerges from a study of the fifth commandment in its canonical context—respect for *tradition*. These three concepts are the basis for our reflection.

Dignity. The first concern of the commandment is respect for parents and maintenance of their dignity. The word translated "honor" here elsewhere denotes an attitude of worship toward God (Ps 86:9; Prov 3:9; Is 24:15) and also God's attitude of care toward human beings (Ps 91:15). This two-way honoring is explicit in the word of God to Eli: "those who honor me I will honor" (1 Sam 2:30). The same word is used of submission to human authority (1 Sam 15:30). To quote Barth (1951: 243), "To honor some one really means to ascribe to him the dignity which is his due." In contrast, Genesis records several examples of disrespect to parents (Gen 9:22; 27:18-27; 35:22).

It is notable that mothers and fathers are due equal respect from their children. Perhaps to emphasize this point in a patriarchal society, the version of the commandment in Leviticus 19:3 puts the mother before the father.[33] Virtually every time the Bible mentions attitudes toward parents, whether in law, wisdom, or prophecy, both mother and father are mentioned. This is distinctive compared with other parts of the ancient Near East, where the status of women is generally lower and where most extant texts are concerned only with respectful attitudes toward one's father or older men in general. The main exception is the Egyptian Instruction of Any (see p. 86 above), which advises support for one's mother.

Honoring mother and father is emphasized repeatedly in Proverbs.[34] This includes obeying their teaching (Prov 1:8-9; 6:20; 15:5; 23:22; 30:17), bringing them joy by becoming wise (Prov 10:1; 15:20; 23:23-25; cf. Prov 17:21, 25; 28:4), and not hurting or cursing them (Prov 19:26; 20:20; 28:24; 30:11). The point is expanded further in the Dead Sea Scrolls and the deuterocanonical wisdom literature, where it includes duties of giving practical help in old age

---

[33]Though LXX, Peshitta, and Vulgate reverse the order.
[34]Barth (1951: 249) describes the book of Proverbs as "a large-scale commentary on the fifth commandment."

and conducting a proper burial.[35] The prophets say relatively little about honoring parents, though it is assumed to be a fundamental virtue (Is 1:2; 3:5; Ezek 22:7; Mic 7:6; Mal 1:6).[36] In the New Testament we read that Jesus was obedient to his parents (Lk 2:51) and that Christian children are encouraged to do likewise (Eph 6:1-3; Col 3:20).

It is important to distinguish between dignity and authority. Often the fifth commandment is thought to be concerned with parental authority.[37] But the Bible emphasizes responsibility, focusing on the duty of children to honor rather than the right of parents to exercise authority.[38] Unlike modern laws that tend to focus on rights, biblical laws are more concerned with responsibilities.[39]

Support. In Israel, as elsewhere in the ancient Near East, to honor one's parents includes practical care and support. In his detailed study of the fifth commandment and its development throughout the Bible, Jungbauer (2002: 80-82) argues that responsibility for care of elderly parents is one of its most basic concerns. Several examples of care for parents are recorded in Old Testament narratives (Gen 45:9-11; 47:12; 1 Sam 22:3-4). The story of Ruth and Naomi (Ruth 1) concerns care of a mother-in-law by her daughter-in-law after the death of her sons and may also be seen as an illustration of the fifth commandment in practice.[40]

In the New Testament, Jesus criticizes people who offer to God what they should have used to support their parents (Mt 15:1-6; Mk 7:9-13)[41] and ensures provision for his own mother when he dies (Jn 19:25-27). He restores a widow's only son to life (Lk 7:12-15), so ensuring she would have someone to support her. Instructions to honor widows in the Pastoral Epistles are concerned with providing for their needs (1 Tim 5:3-8; cf. Acts 6:1). Care for parents is presumably motivated, at least in part, by gratitude for the care that parents give to children in their early years.[42]

---

[35]Tob 4:3-4; 6:15; cf. Tob 14:11-13; Sir 3:1-16; 7:27-28; 4Q416 Instruction, frag. 2, col. III: 15-19.

[36]Cf. Mal 4:6. Deuteronomy makes the same assumption (Deut 32:5-6, 18-20).

[37]Jungbauer 2002: 82-84; cf. Albertz 1978: 348-49.

[38]Blidstein 1975: xi-xii, 20. Barth (1951: 242) comments, "The authority of parents proclaimed in the fifth commandment is not that of a power posited and exercised as a right, but that of a spiritual power."

[39]Miller 2004c: 141-43; Fishbane 2009: 182-83.

[40]Miller 2009: 185-88. Cf. Mic 7:6, where it is assumed that the same duty of honor applies to in-laws as to blood parents.

[41]On "vowing away the fifth commandment," see Bailey 2000.

[42]Blidstein 1975: 8-19; Portier-Young 2007: 102-5.

Sometimes it will seem a burden to care for elderly parents, though it is probably rare that children have to do *more* for their parents in their later years than was done for them in their childhood. In one of the rabbinic writings we read,

> A man who can afford it and does not support his aged parents is a murderer. God is bitterly disappointed in such a man. "I made respect of them of equal importance with respect of Me," He thunders against him. "If I had lived with this man, he would have treated Me as he did them. It is good that I did not come near him."[43]

Of course, there are enormous cultural differences in the way human beings relate across the generations. For example, to put aging parents in a nursing home rather than accommodating them in one's own home would be a scandalous idea in some cultures. In another culture, however, provision of professional nursing care may be a good way of honoring parents, so long as it is done for their genuine good and not just to relinquish responsibility. Today's world is very different from that of the ancient Hebrews, and it would be unrealistic for us to simply model our family life on theirs. Nevertheless, the fifth commandment challenges the attitude of many today who show little concern for their parents when at home and seem to forget them after they leave.

Tradition. A further matter addressed by the fifth commandment is the value of tradition, especially the religious education given by one's parents.[44] Barth (1951: 242-49) expresses it like this: "The honoring of parents required of children does not mean the outward and formal subjection of the will of the younger to that of the older generation, but the respecting of the latter as the bearer and mediator of the promise given to the people with regard to its existence." This fits with the conclusion reached above (see pp. 8-9) that the fifth commandment belongs to the first group and that it is primarily concerned with respect for God. As Phillips (1970: 81) points out, this should also help ensure children maintain the faith of their parents. Religious education was primarily the responsibility of parents in ancient Israel, as we see in Deuteronomy (Deut 6:6-7; 11:18-19; 32:7) and Proverbs (Prov 1-7).

---

[43]*Seder Eliyahu Rabba*, quoted by Goldman 1956: 178.
[44]Jungbauer 2002: 84-87.

Medieval rabbis refer to the significance of the fifth commandment for preserving religious tradition, each new generation accepting the teachings of their elders and passing it on to the next.[45] Honoring parents leads to respect for ancestral tradition and so has a stabilizing effect on society. This is evident in the theological questions young people ask their parents about the past (Ex 12:24-27; 13:14-15; Deut 6:20-25; Josh 4:6-7). Another biblical example is the Rechabites and their faithfulness to the principles of their founding father (Jer 35).

This may be compared to the idea of filial piety, considered the root of all virtue in Confucian ethics.[46] Honoring parents is fundamental and includes respect for their authority and obedience to their instruction. However, this does not mean absolute obedience to one's immediate father, especially when it comes to moral matters, but should be understood more generally as respect for tradition. The father is not an independent authority figure, because he also defers to his own father and so to the ongoing tradition of knowledge and wisdom. It is therefore assumed that parents who stand within the tradition are able to guide their children in the Way. But if a father should be out of line with his ancestors, filial piety may require the child *not* to follow him, seeking rather a better path in accordance with the ancestral tradition.

There was disagreement among the medieval rabbis as to whether the fifth commandment required a child to honor a morally deficient parent.[47] While some considered the rule to be unconditional—irrespective of the parent's behavior—others pointed out that if a parent taught their child to disobey the Torah, then the child ought to obey God rather than their parent. This reminds me of the first time I preached on the fifth commandment: there was a young woman in the congregation whose father was in prison for murdering her mother. I wondered what she was thinking as I spoke about honoring parents.

In most cases, however, honoring parents includes acknowledging their maturity and wisdom. Younger people often prefer their own way of doing things, but they should be careful not to act as though it is easy to do better than one's forebears or assume that new ideas are automatically an

---

[45]Blidstein 1975: 19-24; cf. Sherwin 2007: 95-98.
[46]Rhee 1965: 212-13; Nuyen 2004.
[47]Sherwin 2007: 90-93.

improvement on old ones. No one starts life in a vacuum. Everyone belongs to a historical and cultural context and has much to learn from the experience of others, even when choosing to differ.[48]

Family life. Just as Israel's relationship with God is the foundation of the covenant community (first commandment), so relationships between the generations are foundational to human society (fifth commandment). In many traditional societies, those who honor the old may expect to enjoy such honor themselves in due course. In contrast, modern Western society tends to glorify youth and dread old age. Young, energetic people are appointed to jobs in preference to older people with experience and maturity. People do their best to stay young—or at least look young—as long as possible, viewing time as the enemy. Tradition is outmoded; innovation is the watchword.

Some view the fifth commandment as easy to keep, while others find it the most difficult of all, no doubt depending on their own experiences of family life. In this broken world, some parents have done little that is positive for their children apart from bringing them into the world, and children from such homes inevitably have greater difficulty in honoring their parents than those blessed with happy homes. Victims of child abuse are likely to struggle with the fifth commandment. In such a situation, disturbed parental behavior has to be resisted, and blind obedience is clearly not required. Nevertheless, to honor one's parents might mean to avoid exposing them to unnecessary shame even while taking appropriate action to deal with the issues. Intergenerational family therapy can be helpful here in bringing together the values of honoring parents and the need for personal authenticity, enabling clients to respect their parents while still respecting themselves.[49] There is also teaching in the Bible that may help them come to terms with pain and find strength in God, the divine parent who demonstrates to his children true love, expressed in both fatherly (Deut 1:30-31; Ps 103:13) and motherly (Is 49:15; 66:12-13) terms.[50]

The validity of the fifth commandment is not dependent on having perfect parents but on the role of parents as God's representatives in giving life.[51]

---

[48]Cf. Lochman 1979: 81-82; Fishbane 2009: 175-78.
[49]Fishbane 2009: 180-91.
[50]Scott 1988.
[51]Barth 1951: 251-57.

Like other commandments—such as those prohibiting homicide, adultery, and theft—it applies to all, whether or not one's parents are good or deserve respect. It is natural to treat well those who treat us well, as Jesus points out in the Sermon on the Mount (Mt 5:46-47), but the Decalogue challenges the people of God to go further than that. We may find the fifth commandment easy or hard or almost impossible to keep. Nevertheless, it reminds us of our origins ("your father and your mother") while pointing us to the future ("so that you may live long"), encouraging us to value the family as the core of human society.[52]

---

[52]On the family in the Bible and its historical context, see further Harrisville 1969; de Boer 1974; Wright 1992; Cohen 1993; Barton 1996; Blenkinsopp 1997; Moxnes 1997; Perdue et al. 1997; Dearman et al. 1998; van Henten and Brenner 2000; Sanders 2002; Balch and Osiek 2003; Hess and Rodas 2003; Garland and Garland 2007; Blessing 2010.

LOVING NEIGHBOR

6 LIFE

The second group of commandments is concerned with relationships within the people of God, beginning with the most important matter of all—protecting human life. It is expressed concisely as prohibition of killing (homicide). This is an ancient principle, stated clearly in God's covenant with Noah: "Whoever sheds human blood, by humans shall their blood be shed" (Gen 9:6). Even before that, the principle is implicit in the story of Cain and Abel (Gen 4:7-12). God gives life to human beings, and only God has the right to take it away.

HOMICIDE

Ancient Near East. In most civilized nations, ancient and modern, homicide is considered wrong in principle, though the way the principle is applied varies. It is stated explicitly in the first clause of the Sumerian Laws of Ur-Namma, the oldest law collection known to us from the ancient Near East:

> If a man commits a homicide, they shall kill that man. (LU §1)

Though no Egyptian laws survive from the Old Testament period, homicide is condemned in stories, wisdom literature, religious texts, and royal records.[1] For example, the Book of the Dead includes a repeated declaration in the presence of the gods that the deceased has not killed or commanded others to kill.[2]

---

[1]Hoch and Orel 1992: 87-111.
[2]Chapter 125 (*ANET*: 34-35, §§A14-15, B5; *COS*: 2.12, pp. 60-61).

Three main categories of homicide may be distinguished in ancient and modern law, though the details vary and we should not assume the ancients understood them in exactly the same way as we do today:

- premeditated killing (murder)
- unintentional/non-premeditated killing (manslaughter)
- accidental killing (negligence)

Punishment for homicide took two main forms in the ancient Near East: death or compensation. Capital punishment for murder is required in Ur-Namma's law mentioned above and the Babylonian Laws of Hammurabi (CH §153). Various kinds of unintentional and accidental killing are also mentioned by Hammurabi, specifying punishment by death or compensation depending on the circumstances and the social class of the victim (CH §§116, 206-14, 218-19, 229-31, 250-52). Similar principles apply in the Sumerian Laws of Eshnunna, noting that a capital case is to be decided by the king (LE §23-24, 47A-48, 54-58). One Sumerian homicide trial ends with execution and another with compensation.[3] The death penalty for murder is demanded in royal letters from Larsa and Babylon and in a treaty from Eshnunna, whereas treaties from Syria and Ugarit stipulate compensation.[4] It appears capital punishment was common for murder in Egypt.[5]

The Hittite Laws specify compensation in the shape of slaves, silver, or land for all cases of homicide (HL §§1-6, 43-44a). The amount of compensation depends on the status of the person killed and whether the death occurs in a quarrel or by accident. There are indications that the Hittites replaced an older practice of capital punishment with compensation.[6] Recorded homicide trials from Ugarit and Assyria are concluded with compensation.[7]

In a report from Mari (Mesopotamia, eighteenth century BC), we read about negotiations offering compensation to the brother of a murder victim who rejects this and chooses instead to punish the murderer with mutilation, humiliation, and death. The Middle Assyrian Laws give a victim's family the choice between killing the killer or accepting monetary

---

[3]*ANET*: 542; Jacobsen 1959; Westbrook 1988: 47-49; Greengus 2011: 160.
[4]Westbrook 1988: 47, 49; Greengus 2011: 66, 166.
[5]Hoch and Orel 1992: 112-18.
[6]HL §§92, 121, 166-67; cf. Greengus 2011: 164-67. On homicide in Hittite law, see also Haase 2003: 644-47.
[7]*ANET*: 547; Roth 1987; Greengus 2011: 160, 163-64; cf. Wiseman 1974: 259-60.

compensation (MAL §§A10, B2), and a neo-Assyrian contract provides an example of this choice in practice.[8] There is also a case of a Hittite king allowing the heir of a murdered man to choose between execution of the murderer and compensation.[9]

Sixth commandment. The prohibition of homicide is evidently not distinctive to Israel, but the terse form of the sixth commandment (just three syllables in Hebrew) is unique:

> You shall not commit homicide.[10] (Exodus 20:13/Deuteronomy 5:17)

The Hebrew verb is relatively rare.[11] It refers to the killing of one person by another, whether intentional or otherwise. Elsewhere this word is used for both "murder" and "manslaughter."[12] It is not generally used for capital punishment[13] and never for killing in war, self-defense, suicide, or slaughtering animals. In other words, it is concerned with illegal killing by individuals rather than killing authorized by the state in execution or war. The most precise translation in English is "commit homicide," though in everyday language it may be preferable to use the word *kill* or *murder*. Other kinds of killing like abortion and euthanasia are not in view here, though the commandment implies the sanctity of human life and may influence our views on these matters.

The negative form of the commandment is worth mentioning. In fact, altogether eight of the commandments are negative, while the fourth and fifth alone are positive, and there is even a negative element in the expansion of the fourth. Such juxtaposition is characteristic of all Old Testament law, as Childs (1974: 394) points out, and there is no need to argue that one of the two types has priority over the other. The predominantly negative format

---

[8]Westbrook 1988: 50-51. In MAL §A50, however, capital punishment is specified for homicide without mentioning an alternative.

[9]Telipinu Edict §49 (*COS*: 2.19, p. 119). See Westbrook 1988: 49; Greengus 2011: 167.

[10]The translation "kill" (NJB; RSV; Childs 1974; Durham 1987; Simpson 2004) is too broad, while "murder" (NRSV; NIV; REB; NJPS; ESV; NET; NLT2; Cole 1973; McConville 2002a) is too narrow. See further discussion below.

[11]The verb רצח is used only 47 times in Old Testament, much less frequently than other words for "kill," such as הרג (167 times) and מות (*hiphil, hophal,* and *polel*; 214 times). On this verb, see Hossfeld 1992; 2003; Becking 2011.

[12]For examples of the word used for murder, see Num 35:16-21; 1 Kings 21:19; Job 24:14; Ps 94:6; Is 1:21; Hos 6:9. For manslaughter, see Num 35:11-12, 22-28; Deut 4:41-42; 19:3-6; Josh 20:3-6. Either of these would lead to blood vengeance (as shown in Num 35, etc.).

[13]E.g., Ex 21:12, 15-17, where the expression מוֹת יוּמָת is used, though Num 35:30 is an exception to this.

is not a deficiency, as if the emphasis was on banning pleasurable activities. On the contrary, Mendenhall (1954a) argues that it allows a maximum of self-determination to the semi-nomads recently freed from slavery, whereas positive commands would be more restrictive. The prohibitions mark the outer limits to be observed so the relationship between God and his people is not disturbed and the community is protected from behavior that could destroy itself.[14]

In any case, "all the Commandments, either explicitly or implicitly, have both a positive and a negative meaning" (Miller 2009: 7). For example, the first commandment is reiterated in Deuteronomy in a positive form (Deut 6:13; 13:4), and its well-known counterpart in the Shema follows suit (Deut 6:4-5). Homicide is prohibited in order to preserve human life, adultery is prohibited out of respect for marriage, the prohibition of stealing recognizes the legitimacy of property ownership, and so on.

Murder and manslaughter. The sixth commandment itself is concise, simply stating that homicide is wrong, prophetic allusions to the commandment being similar (Jer 7:9; Hos 4:2; cf. Is 1:21). However, the principle is elaborated more fully in several other laws (Ex 21:12-14; Num 35:15-28; Deut 19:4-13).

These laws distinguish between murder (premeditated killing) and other kinds of killing (those resulting from an accident, those without calculated malice, etc.). All are wrong, but murder is much more serious and carries the death penalty. As we have seen above, some other ancient laws allow for compensation to the family as an alternative to capital punishment, but in Israel the death penalty for murder is non-negotiable (Num 35:31-33; cf. Lev 24:17, 21). Human life is sacred, and its loss cannot be compensated with a bag of gold, though a monetary settlement is allowed when death occurs because of negligence rather than intent (Ex 21:29-30). In the case of manslaughter or negligence, the law protects someone who kills accidentally or without premeditation from blood vengeance by the family of the deceased, if this person seeks safety at God's altar (Ex 21:13-14; cf. 1 Kings 1:50-53; 2:28) or in a city of refuge (Num 35:6-15; Deut 19:1-13; Josh 20).[15]

---

[14]Cf. von Rad 1957: 194-95; Childs 1974: 398; Fretheim 1991; Houtman 1996.

[15]For a discussion of blood vengeance and places of refuge, see Willis 2001: 89-144; Barmash 2005: 20-93.

Incidentally, a similar distinction is made in the laws on theft:

> If a thief is caught breaking in at night and is beaten to death, it is not murder.
> If it happens after sunrise, it is murder. (Ex 22:2-3a, DLB)

The underlying principle is that the owner of a burgled property does not have the right to kill the burglar. If the burglary occurs at night, this may be excused, presumably because of the need for self-defense (cf. Job 24:14, 16). During the day, however, the owner can more easily call for help, and can see the intruder clearly and thus identify him to the authorities, so there should be no need for violence. This may be compared with a Babylonian law that requires a burglar caught in the day to pay compensation of ten silver shekels, whereas he may be executed if the burglary takes place at night (LE §13).

REFLECTION

The sixth commandment is relevant in many ways in our day, not least in its original meaning as a prohibition of homicide. It may also provoke us to broader reflection on how we treat other human beings, ranging from the controversial topics of abortion and war to attitudes toward those we dislike and those who dislike us.

License to kill. The first biblical law to deal with homicide is found in the early chapters of Genesis:

> For your lifeblood I will surely demand an accounting. I will demand an accounting from every animal. And from each human being, too, I will demand an accounting for the life of another human being.
>
> Whoever sheds human blood,
> by human beings shall their blood be shed;
> for in the image of God
> has God made mankind. (Gen 9:5-6)

Several points are made. God the giver of life asserts his authority over human life (cf. Ezek 18:4) and warns that an animal or person who kills will be held accountable. Anyone who takes another person's life is to be punished with death, following the principle that punishment should fit the crime (cf. Ex 21:12-14, 23-25). The same penalty applies to an animal that kills a human being (cf. Ex 21:28-32), though the reverse does not apply, because this same text permits humans—in some circumstances—to kill animals (Gen 9:3-4). Finally, there is a theological basis for the law: human beings have made in the image of God (cf. Gen 1:26-27; 5:1). A double logic is apparent here. On the one hand, human beings have a special status among God's creatures, and their lives are to be preserved, not destroyed. On the other hand, human beings are God's representatives on earth, and they are entrusted with the task of executing murderers if and when required.[16]

The act of killing itself is not the heart of the problem, for God brings all human lives to an end at some point and occasionally commands people to kill (e.g., capital punishment, Old Testament holy wars). Rather, the problem is unauthorized killing—that is, any killing *not* commanded by God. The nub of the matter is *who* has authority over life and death, and the Bible—including the sixth commandment—makes it clear that God alone has that authority. Yet in our postmodern world, it is not politically correct to say this. To kill in the name of God, as proposed by some religious fundamentalists, is considered outrageous, while to kill in the name of democracy or justice or for the defense of one's country may be thought necessary and even meritorious. On an individual level, if we believe that God alone has the right to determine whether a person lives or dies, this will inevitably influence our attitudes toward abortion and euthanasia.[17]

Killing in war. As explained above, warfare is not the primary concern of the sixth commandment in its original context. Nevertheless, the commandment is the fundamental principle behind the concept of a "just war," in the sense that war and killing are presumed to be wrong unless there is strong evidence to indicate that justice and compassion would be better served by waging war than by not doing so.[18] It follows that war can only be justified in exceptional circumstances.

So what does this mean for our attitudes toward war today? First, it is important to note that the Bible as a whole is more concerned with making peace than waging war. While holy war does have a limited place in Old

---

[16]For further discussion of this important text, see von Rad 1972; Westermann 1974; Hamilton 1990. It is also one of the key texts discussed by Cavanaugh (2005) in his article, "Killing in the Name of God," which has stimulated my thoughts in the following paragraph.

[17]These are big issues that cannot be dealt with here. For a thought-provoking article that reflects on them in relation to the sixth commandment, see Tinker 2003.

[18]Simpson 2004. The same principle motivates pacifism, but I will not discuss that here.

Testament history, many recorded wars are quite *un*holy. Neither wisdom literature nor prophecy glorifies war, and the New Testament emphasizes love of enemies rather than their destruction. To quote William Cavanaugh (2005: 144),

> Christian reflection on war must go beyond merely ticking off the just-war criteria as a preliminary step to supporting the military adventures of the nation-state. Radical obedience to God's command must be the beginning and end of Christian reflection on war. Specifically, we must take seriously the teaching of Jesus that love of enemies is the fulfillment of the Law, that the prohibition against killing has been extended to the prohibition of anger and hatred, that the *lex talionis* has been fulfilled in the commandment to turn the other cheek.

In my view, this does not mean Christians should never take part in war, but it must always be seen as a last resort and only entered into if it really is the lesser of two evils. To put it theologically, one should only go to war if convinced it is the will of God and not merely the will of the state.

Having said that, I am aware that the practical implications are far from straightforward. Presidents or generals who believe in God may be in a position to allow that belief to influence their military decisions, but the majority of ordinary soldiers have little choice except to obey orders. Nevertheless, in most democratic nations there are opportunities for ordinary citizens to give input to their leaders and to vote them out of office if they do not listen. According to a survey on the Iraq War, however, only 10 percent of Americans said that their religious beliefs were the most important factor. "The overwhelming opposition of church leaders to the war" was ignored, while the majority of ordinary "Christians" were in favor, "apparently content to place the judgment of the state over that of the church regarding the justifiability of the war" (Cavanaugh 2005: 147).

Hatred and anger. While the specific prohibition of the sixth commandment concerns acts of murder and manslaughter, the attitude that underlies such acts is implicitly wrong as well. This is clear in Leviticus 19, a passage based substantially on the Decalogue. The sixth commandment is not mentioned explicitly, but it is covered by the prohibition of hating and taking vengeance:

> Do not hate a fellow Israelite in your heart. Rebuke your neighbor frankly so
> you will not share in their guilt. Do not seek revenge or bear a grudge against
> anyone among your people, but love your neighbor as yourself. I am the LORD.
> (Lev 19:17-18)

People who follow these principles will obviously not be killing each other.
If a neighbor is going astray, they should be rebuked and warned (Lev 19:17;
cf. Ezek 3:17-21; Mt 18:15-17), but that does not entitle others to hate or insult
them. In fact, it is quite the reverse: they are to be loved (Lev 19:18). Jesus
also extends the commandment to include our attitudes:

> You have heard that it was said to the people long ago, "You shall not murder,
> and anyone who murders will be subject to judgment." But I tell you that
> anyone who is angry with a brother or sister will be subject to judgment.
> Again, anyone who says to a brother or sister, "Raca," is answerable to the
> court. And anyone who says, "You fool!" will be in danger of the fire of hell.
> Therefore, if you are offering your gift at the altar and there remember that
> your brother or sister has something against you, leave your gift there in front
> of the altar. First go and be reconciled to them; then come and offer your gift.
> (Mt 5:21-24)

Followers of Jesus should not be satisfied with merely refraining from
murder (Mt 5:21). They should restrain their anger and be careful in what
they say when upset with someone else (Mt 5:22). Moreover, if someone is
angry with them, they should take the initiative to bring about reconcili-
ation (Mt 5:23-24).

Paul gives a practical suggestion for anger management: "Do not let the
sun go down while you are still angry" (Eph 4:26), following this with an
encouragement to replace anger and verbal abuse with kindness and compassion (Eph 4:31-32). Perhaps remembering Jesus' reflection on the sixth
commandment, John equates hatred with murder (1 Jn 3:15) and points to
the example of Jesus as a better way to treat brothers and sisters—the way of
sacrificial love (1 Jn 3:16; cf. Rom 13:8-10).

According to Pope John Paul II (1993: §15), Jesus fulfilled God's commandments by bringing out their fullest meaning, so the sixth commandment is
not merely a prohibition of killing but "a call to an attentive love which
protects and promotes the life of one's neighbor." The Word of God emphasizes the sanctity of human life as a gift of God and points in the direction

of a radical love for neighbor and enemy—the sort of love demonstrated uniquely in the cross. It is not just a matter of avoiding harm to neighbors but rather actively promoting their good, valuing their lives, and protecting them from danger.

7 MARRIAGE

If protecting human life is the first principle of relationships for the people of God, the second is protecting marriage—the most fundamental relationship in almost every human society. Sadly, for many people this is a painful subject, especially if they are single and would prefer to be married or if they have been divorced or widowed. Even so, families form the core units in most societies and begin traditionally with marriage. Of course, the nature of marriage varies greatly between different cultures and at different times, ranging anywhere from a legal bond recognized and protected by civil and religious authorities to common-law marriages and domestic partnerships. The principle of protecting marriage is expressed in the seventh commandment as prohibition of adultery. Since this is a legal category, it applies primarily to legally recognized marriages, but it may also apply implicitly to other relationships where the partners have made a long-term commitment to each other.

ADULTERY

Ancient Near East. One of the oldest legal records that refers to adultery is a Sumerian court case. The circumstances are described as follows:

> Ishtar-ummi the daughter of Ili-asu was taken in marriage by Erra-malik. In the first place she broke into his granary. In the second place she opened his pots of sesame-oil and covered them with cloths. In the third place he caught her on top of a man; he bound her on the body of the man in the bed (and) carried her to the assembly.[1]

---

[1] *COS*: 3.140; cf. Greengus 1969–1970; Roth 1988: 195-97; Westbrook 1990: 557-59, esp. n. 64.

It is then recorded that the assembly set an amount for divorce money and authorized public humiliation for the woman. The focus of the case is adultery, and the first two offenses committed by Ishtar-ummi are relatively trivial, probably mentioned only to emphasize her bad character. It seems Erra-malik was concerned primarily with his wife's behavior and her punishment, and this does not necessarily imply that her lover was left unpunished, even though no punishment is specifically stated.

Many ancient Near Eastern laws deal with adultery. The fundamental principles are expressed succinctly in the Laws of Hammurabi:

> If a man's wife should be seized lying with another male, they shall bind them and cast them into the water; if the wife's master allows his wife to live, then the king shall allow his subject [i.e., the other male] to live. (CH §129)

Both the man and woman who commit adultery are subject to capital punishment, but if the wife is released by her husband, the man is also to be released. Similar rules are found in the Hittite Laws, noting that the king may overrule the husband's decision but that the principle of parity still applies (HL §§197-98). Likewise, in the Middle Assyrian Laws capital punishment is standard, but the offended husband may determine a lesser punishment for his wife, in which case the man with whom she committed adultery is to be treated in a comparable way (MAL §§A13-15).[2]

Several qualifications and exceptions to these fundamental principles are made. First, in cases of rape, only the man is to be executed (LU §6; LE §26; CH §130; HL §197a; MAL §A12).[3] Second, if the woman seduces the man or conceals the fact that she is married, the man is exempt from punishment (LU §7; MAL §§A14b, 16). In determining whether an incident is counted as rape or seduction, location is critical. If the woman is walking along a street or through the mountains—perfectly legitimate activities—there is a

---

[2]LE §28 stipulates that a wife caught in the act of adultery is to die, but it does not mention what is to be done with the man in question, though the interpretation of this clause is disputed (see Westbrook 1990: 553-54; COS: 2.130, n. 4). The Neo-Babylonian Laws do not deal with adultery, but a number of marriage agreements from this period include a clause specifying capital punishment for a wife who is discovered in the act (Roth 1988). This does not imply that the wife's lover would be immune from punishment as well, but a marriage agreement cannot involve him in advance since his identity is not yet known.

[3]In MAL §A16, however, it appears that a husband whose wife has been raped may punish her, perhaps suspecting that she has played some part in initiating the relationship. In that case, the man concerned receives identical punishment. For further discussion, see Driver and Miles 1935: 37, 40-41, 50-52.

presumption of rape, so the man is punished (HL §197a; MAL §A12). If the incident takes place in the man's house, it is likely the woman agreed to be there, and both are executed (MAL §A13).[4] If the incident takes place in the woman's house, however, it is assumed she initiated the relationship, thus becoming "the woman's offense" (HL §197b). The law stipulates capital punishment for the woman in this case, though the following sentence permits the husband to kill both of them on the spot if he discovers them in the act (cf. MAL §15). If the incident takes place in an inn, the guilt depends on whether the man knows the woman is married, in which case both are punished as adulterers, or assumed her to be unattached, in which case only the woman is punished (MAL §A14).[5]

Third, monetary compensation is stipulated if a man deflowers another man's slave woman (LU §8; LE §31). Fourth, there are procedures for dealing with false accusations of adultery. When a man and woman have not been caught in the act, there is generally recourse to the gods to establish the truth (LU §14; CH §§131-32; MAL §17). If the accusation proves false, the accuser is punished with a fine (LU §14) or flogging and humiliation (CH §127)—or all of these plus a month's hard labor (MAL §A18).

Fifth, there are regulations to cover adultery in various specific situations, such as the wife of a prisoner of war (LE §29; CH §133), a father who is attracted to his son's fiancée (CH §155-56), a married woman who is recruited by an unrelated man for a trading venture (MAL §A22), a female procurer who employs a married woman for sexual services (MAL §A23), and a married woman who leaves her husband to live elsewhere (MAL §A24). Harsh punishments are stipulated for the guilty party in most cases, these varying from drowning to substantial fines to mutilation.

It is striking that most of the laws for adultery show gender equality in the punishment administered, regarding both partners as equally guilty unless one has forced, seduced, or deceived the other. However, there is gender imbalance in the perception of adultery itself. The essence of adultery in the ancient Near East is a sexual relationship between a married woman and someone other than her husband. It is considered a threefold offense against the following:

---

[4]The phrase "knowing that she is the wife of a man" may indicate that the man could claim exemption from punishment if the woman had concealed her marital status.
[5]For further discussion, see Finkelstein 1966: 362-65.

- the woman's husband (who has exclusive marital rights)
- the gods (who are liable to be enraged by human sin)
- society (which is structured on the basis of patrilineal families and would be destabilized if adultery were to take place freely due to uncertainty about the paternity of heirs)[6]

In contrast, a married man who has a sexual relationship with a single woman would not be committing adultery, though it seems that this was also considered morally wrong. It could result in legal sanctions (LL §30),[7] divorce (CH §142), forcible taking of his wife (MAL §55), or a hefty fine (MAL §56).[8]

We have no laws from ancient Egypt or Canaan, but other documents describe adultery as "a great sin."[9] Similar terminology is used in the Egyptian stories of the Two Brothers and the Instruction of Any.[10] In the Book of the Dead, at the entry examination for the next world the deceased affirms he has not slept with another man's wife.[11] Mesopotamian literature has comparable references in the Hymn to Ninurta and the Shurpu Incantations.[12]

Seventh commandment. Like the sixth commandment, the seventh is expressed concisely:

> You shall not commit adultery. (Exodus 20:14/Deuteronomy 5:18 DLB)

At first sight this sounds quite straightforward, but to understand the implications it is important to clarify what exactly is meant by adultery in the context. Adultery is commonly understood today as voluntary sexual intercourse between a married person and someone other than their spouse. In

---

[6]Loewenstamm 1962: 146-48; Tigay 1996: 71; Marsman 2003: 168-71; Wells 2009: 235.

[7]For a study of LL §30 together with two legal texts that reflect similar thinking, see Westbrook 1984.

[8]LL §33 deals with an accusation that an unmarried girl has had sexual relations, implying serious consequences if the accusation should prove true. Another text that disapproves of such relationships is The Women's Oath, a Sumerian love poem in which the girl asks her lover to swear that he has not had any previous love affairs (*COS*: 1.169A, lines 13-26). CH §143 complements §142 by emphasizing the importance of chastity for a betrothed woman (Westbrook 1990: 572-73).

[9]Moran 1959; Rabinowitz 1959; Eyre 1984; Márquez Rowe 2000.

[10]*COS*: 1.40, p. 86, column 1 (§4.1); 1.46, p. 111, column 1.

[11]Chapter 125 (*ANET*: 35 §B19; *COS*: 2.12, p. 61, column 2). Further Egyptian references are given by Jasnow 2003: 343-44.

[12]Ninurta lines 3-4 (*BWL*: 119); Shurpu tablets 2:47-48 and 4:6 (Reiner 1958: 14, 25; Beyerlin 1975: 132).

the context of ancient Israel, as elsewhere in the ancient Near East, two qualifications to this definition are necessary. First, the primary concern is with a man (either married or single) having intercourse with a married woman other than his wife (Lev 18:20;[13] 20:10; Deut 22:22). Second, adultery laws apply to betrothed couples as well as to those who are already married (Deut 22:23-24).

Although most Old Testament laws about adultery are formulated from a male perspective, both men and women who break them are considered adulterers (Lev 20:10; Deut 22:22). The seventh commandment is addressed to both sexes, and the verb translated "commit adultery" is elsewhere used of both men and women (Prov 6:32; 30:20; Jer 29:23; Ezek 16:32). This principle is in line with other ancient Near Eastern laws, though it seems to be ignored in some societies today, where a woman who commits adultery may be publicly humiliated and severely punished but her "partner in crime" remains invisible.

Adultery is distinguished from fornication, which is also considered wrong but is not a capital crime (Ex 22:16-17; Deut 22:28-29).[14] The reason for this distinction is that the seventh commandment is not so much concerned with sex as with maintaining the sanctity of marriage as the fundamental unit of society instituted by God. So if two single people had intercourse, the remedy was for them to get married, so long as the girl's father agreed.[15] The same would probably have applied if a married man had intercourse with a single woman, for the culture allowed—and the law tolerated—polygamy and concubinage.

---

[13]The usual verb meaning "commit adultery" (נאף) is not used here, and Westbrook (1990: 568) suggests that this refers to a man sleeping with a neighbor's wife with the husband's permission in order to provide offspring for a childless couple. However, there is no evidence for such a custom of surrogate fatherhood (Milgrom 2000: 1550). In any case, such an arrangement would be forbidden by the law even if permitted by the husband.

[14]These two laws differ in that Exodus is concerned with seduction and Deuteronomy with rape, but neither are equivalent to adultery and therefore neither punished by death (cf. Pressler 1993: 35-41; Edenburg 2009: 55-56). Prostitution is condemned too (Lev 19:29; 21:7, 9; Deut 23:17-18; Prov 7; 23:27-28). There are various other laws on sexual relationships in Lev 20 and Deut 22–25. See also Sir 23:16-27.

[15]Interpreters differ on how to translate Deut 22:29. As I have argued elsewhere (Baker 2007: 96), the verb ענה (piel) denotes "taking advantage of a woman by having intercourse without granting her the rights of marriage or concubinage, or ignoring culturally-approved patterns for sexual relationships" (cf. van Wolde 2002). On this basis I suggest the following translation: "The man who lay with her shall give fifty silver shekels to the young woman's father. She shall become his wife because he has had intercourse with her. He can never divorce her as long as he lives."

According to some scholars, the purpose of the adultery laws was to safeguard paternity rather than sexual ethics due to the cultural importance of perpetuating one's family name through children.[16] Wright (1979: 120-24) disputes this, pointing out that the death penalty would be an excessive punishment if this were the only concern. He argues that adultery was "a crime against the relationship between God and his people" because the stability of the household was essential to Israel's relationship with God. Just as the fifth commandment promotes family stability by establishing domestic authority and the eighth commandment upholds its economic viability by protecting property, so the seventh commandment guards the sexual integrity of the marriage at the heart of the household.

A great sin. According to Kornfeld (1950), adultery was understood differently in biblical law than in other ancient Near Eastern laws. Elsewhere it was seen as a family matter, he argues, and the wronged husband had the right to decide what action to take against offenders. Israel took a similar view prior to Moses, but after him adultery became a sin against God, not simply an offense against the husband. However, this contrast should not be overemphasized. On the one hand, as already mentioned, adultery in the ancient Near East did not only offend the woman's husband but also the gods and society. On the other hand, in the Old Testament, adultery is a sin against God and also an offense against the husband and society.[17]

When Abimelech takes Sarah without realizing she is Abraham's wife (Gen 20:6, 9), and when Joseph refuses to be seduced by Potiphar's wife (Gen 39:9), the adultery that might have taken place is described as a great sin (or words to that effect). This is consistent with the understanding of adultery in ancient Egypt and Canaan. The same terminology is used for idolatry elsewhere in the Old Testament (Ex 32:21, 30-31; 2 Kings 17:21), which was seen by the prophets as spiritual adultery (e.g., Is 57:1-13; Jer 3:6-9; Ezek 23:37; Hos 1-3).[18] Adultery is treated as a sin against God (Ps 51:4), an "outrageous thing" (Jer 29:23; cf. Gen 34:7; Deut 22:21), and a "detestable offense" (Ezek 22:11; 33:26). It defiles the man and woman

---

[16]Mace 1953: 242; Phillips 1970: 117; 1981: 7-8; Goodfriend 1992; cf. Niditch 1979: 146.

[17]Kornfeld's proposal is accepted and elaborated by Greenberg (1960: 12-13; 1986: 1-4) but rejected by Loewenstamm (1962), Jackson (1975b: 59-62), and Westbrook (1990: 543-47).

[18]On the analogy between adultery and idolatry, see Bosman 1988; Winiarski 2006.

concerned (Lev 18:20; Num 5:13; Ezek 18:6; 23:13, 17; 33:26) and also pol-
lutes the whole community so that it needs to be purged of evil (Deut
22:22-24; cf. Lev 18:20, 24-30).

The seriousness of adultery is evident from its prominent position in
the Decalogue (following homicide[19]) as well as the stipulation of the
death penalty for both the man and woman involved (Lev 20:10;
Deut 22:22, 24). In practice, it seems the death penalty was not always
enforced for adultery. This is explicit in other ancient Near Eastern laws
and perhaps implied in Proverbs 6:32-35, where a potential adulterer is
warned that the offended husband may not be satisfied with compensation. Several prophetic texts suggest lenience: for example, Jeremiah 3:8
and Hosea 2:2 imply divorce rather than death for an adulteress, while
Ezekiel mentions humiliation (Ezek 16:36-39; 23:26-30; cf. Jer 13:26-27;
Hos 2:2-3). However, it should be noted that in the context of these proph-
ecies adultery is a metaphor for Israel's unfaithfulness to her covenant
partner, and it is uncertain how far the penalties mentioned represent actual
legal practice. In any case, none of the incidents of adultery recounted in the
Bible actually end with execution.[20]

In the case of rape, or if the woman is a slave, the woman is exempt from
punishment (Lev 19:20-22; Deut 22:25-27). There is no corresponding exemption from punishment for the man on the grounds that the woman seduced him or concealed her marital status, unlike in some ancient Near
Eastern laws. Numbers 5:11-31 deals with the case of a wife whose husband
suspects her of being unfaithful but has no proof, and the focus is on proving
her guilt or innocence. Nothing is said about punishment for the man with
whom she has committed adultery (if she is proved guilty) or for the ac-
cusing husband, if it turns out that he has falsely accused his wife, though it
does not follow that there would not have been any punishment (cf.
Deut 22:13-19).[21] According to the principle that there must be two or three
witnesses to convict someone of a capital crime (Num 35:30b; Deut 17:6),

---

[19]As mentioned above (see p. 9), the order of these two commandments is reversed in the LXX, followed by the Nash Papyrus and Philo. As a result, the prohibition of adultery is at the beginning of
the second group, giving it even greater prominence.

[20]On sanctions against adultery in ancient Israel, see further McKeating 1979. For a critique of
McKeating's argument, see Phillips 1981.

[21]For discussion of this passage, see Brichto 1975; Frymer-Kensky 1984; Milgrom 1985. For comparison with CH §131-32, see Fishbane 1974; Greengus 2011: 53-55.

adulterers should only be executed with adequate proof, so the provision in Hittite and Assyrian law that a husband may kill his wife and her lover on the spot if caught in the act of adultery is not included in Israelite law.

The story of David and Bathsheba (2 Sam 11) is well known. Their adultery had far-reaching consequences for David's family (not to mention Bathsheba's husband). What is striking here is not so much the adultery itself as the prophet Nathan's boldness in confronting the king with his sin and David's repentance (2 Sam 12). The latter becomes the basis for one of the greatest Old Testament psalms (Ps 51). David escaped the death penalty but was doubly punished by the death of the child born as a result of the liaison (2 Sam 12:14-18) and later by Absalom committing adultery with his wives (2 Sam 12:11-12; 16:21-22; cf. Job 31:9-10; MAL §§A55-56). Bathsheba is not blamed, presumably because she would have had little choice but to obey when summoned to the king's palace.

Job puts adulterers together with murderers (Job 24:14-15; cf. Jas 2:11), in Psalm 50:18 they are grouped with thieves, and Jeremiah couples adultery with idolatry (Jer 5:7; 23:13-14; cf. Jer 7:9; 1 Cor 6:9). Proverbs repeatedly emphasizes the folly of adultery (e.g., Prov 2:16-19; 5:1-20; 6:23-35; 7:4-27; 30:20). Hosea, whose own wife was unfaithful (Hos 2:4; 3:1), is outspoken on the evil of adultery (Hos 4:2, 13-14; 7:4), and Malachi also condemns the practice (Mal 3:5; cf. Mal 2:14-15).

REFLECTION

Marriage. From the beginning of the Bible to its end, marriage is presented as the closest relationship possible between a man and a woman. Normally— and ideally—this is monogamy (Gen 2:24; Ex 20:17; Deut 24:5; Ps 128; Prov 5:15-20; 12:4; 18:22; Eccles 9:9; Mal 2:14), though polygamy is tolerated in some circumstances.[22] Marriage has three main purposes according to

---

[22]Lamech is the first person mentioned with two wives (Gen 4:19), and polygamy seems to be quite common in the patriarchal period (Gen 22:20-24; 25:6; 29:21-30; 36:2-3, 12; 1 Chron 7:14), but after that most marriages of commoners are monogamous. There are several references to multiple wives and to concubines in the period of the judges, specifically Caleb (1 Chron 2:18, 46, 48), Gideon (Judg 8:30-31), a Levite (Judg 19), and Elkanah (1 Sam 1:1-2), but that was a period when "everyone did as they saw fit" (Judg 21:25), so we need not assume that these are examples intended to be followed by others. Three kings are reported to have numerous wives and concubines—in spite of the prohibition in the law of the king (Deut 17:17)—namely, David (1 Sam 25:39-44; 2 Sam 5:13; 1 Chron 3:1-9), Solomon (1 Kings 11:3), and Rehoboam (2 Chron 11:21).

Genesis: continuance and expansion of the human race (Gen 1:28; cf. Gen 4:1-2), companionship and mutual support (Gen 2:18, 23; cf. Gen 24:67), and sexual intimacy (Gen 2:23-25; cf. Gen 26:8; Song; 1 Cor 7:3-5).

Prohibition of adultery is crucial for protection of marriage because marriage is designed to be an exclusive and intimate relationship between husband and wife, which plainly rules out intimate relationships with other people. Faithfulness in marriage is important for stability in the family, the primary place where economic security and personal safety are found. So the Bible expects married couples to be faithful to each other and single people not to interfere with other people's marriages.

The Bible often compares marriage with the relationship between God and his people (Deut 7:6-11; 32:21; Is 54; Jer 3; Ezek 16; Hos 1–3; cf. Eph 5), emphasizing God's faithfulness and the danger of human unfaithfulness. The comparison tells us something about God and our relationship with him—and it also tells us something about marriage. If we wish to be imitators of God (Lev 19:2), those who are married should love their spouses and be faithful to them just as God is faithful to his people.

Marriage laws provide a framework to facilitate this, but they will only be effective if they are obeyed in spirit and truth. It is not the legality that counts but the stable relationship which the laws are designed to reinforce. On the one hand, it is possible for someone to have a series of marriages and divorces and never technically commit adultery. On the other hand, it is possible for a couple to live together faithfully all their lives without any legal bond at all. In terms of traditional Christian ethics, they would be "living in sin," but morally it is arguable that they would be doing better than those who treat marriage as a purely temporary arrangement. C. S. Lewis (1952: 106-7) writes,

> If people do not believe in permanent marriage, it is perhaps better that they should live together unmarried than that they should make vows they do not mean to keep. It is true that by living together without marriage they will be guilty (in Christian eyes) of fornication. But one fault is not mended by adding another: unchastity is not improved by adding perjury.

Joy Davidman (1953: 94) complements his statement when she writes that marriage is "a union of two into one, not a tentative bargain between warily sparring antagonists." At the time, she was estranged from her unfaithful husband despite her attempts to save the marriage. Eventually Davidman agreed to divorce, and she later married Lewis.[23]

Divorce. So what about divorce? The Old Testament permits divorce in some circumstances (Deut 24:1-4; cf. Is 50:1; Jer 3:1) but certainly does not encourage it (Mal 2:14-16). Jesus considers divorce followed by remarriage as equivalent to adultery:

> It has been said, "Anyone who divorces his wife must give her a certificate of divorce." But I tell you that anyone who divorces his wife, except for sexual immorality, makes her the victim of adultery, and anyone who marries a divorced woman commits adultery. (Mt 5:31-32)

At the same time, he implies that divorce is justifiable if one's spouse has committed adultery. The teaching is developed further in a debate with the Pharisees (Mt 19:3-9; Mk 10:2-12; Lk 16:18). It is mostly formulated from the perspective of the husband, though Mark 10:12 adds that a wife who initiates a divorce and marries another man is guilty of adultery. Paul assumes adultery is against the law (Rom 2:22; 7:3; 13:9) and repeats Jesus' prohibition of divorce followed by remarriage (1 Cor 7:10-11). He supplements this with his own recommendation that Christians with unbelieving spouses should not initiate divorce but should accept it if initiated by the non-Christian partner (1 Cor 7:12-16).[24]

Divorce is easier and much more common in many societies today than it used to be. It has been claimed that the divorce rate in the United States is as high as 50 percent, though this is disputed by Feldhahn and Whitehead (2014), who point to statistics from the US Census Bureau which indicate that 72 percent of those who have ever been married are still with their first spouse. In other words, most marriages still last a lifetime. This is particularly true for Christians, they argue, since studies show that regular church attendance lowers the divorce rate. However, two other social trends impinge on these statistics. First, an increasing number of couples live together as partners without getting married, since the traditional stigma of "living in sin" has largely disappeared, allowing couples to separate without the legal

---

[23]For two thorough studies of marriage from a biblical and Christian perspective, see Ash 2003; Köstenberger and Jones 2010. See also Hamilton and Collins 1992.

[24]For a thorough study of divorce and remarriage in the Bible, see Instone-Brewer 2002. The same author has also written a more popular book that deals with pastoral issues faced by churches in this area (Instone-Brewer 2003). See also Wall 1992; Cornes 1993; Wenham and Heth 2002.

implications of divorce. Second, the age at which men and women get married in modern Western societies is higher than in previous generations. Both of these trends, together with the increase in divorce, result in a much smaller proportion of the adult population being legally married than at any time in the past.

As we have seen, biblical writers are consistent in condemning adultery as a great sin and divorce as highly undesirable. Nevertheless, that is not the final word on these matters. When the scribes and Pharisees drag a woman who has broken the seventh commandment to Jesus (Jn 8:3-11), he does not dispute their accusation. Nor does he provoke a legal argument by pointing out that their quote from Moses is inaccurate—the laws of adultery emphasize equal punishment for both the man and woman involved. Rather, he takes an entirely different approach, avoiding further embarrassment to the woman by looking away from her and challenging her accusers to realize that they are sinners too. Then Jesus turns to the woman as Savior rather than Judge and sends her away forgiven. Amazing grace!

Purity. Jesus assumes the prohibition of adultery as a basic requirement for his followers (Mt 5:27; cf. Mt 19:18) and challenges them to reflect on their thoughts and motives with respect to sexuality (Mt 5:28-29):

> I tell you that anyone who looks at a woman lustfully has already committed adultery with her in his heart. If your right eye causes you to stumble, gouge it out and throw it away. It is better for you to lose one part of your body than for your whole body to be thrown into hell.

It is good to keep the legal requirements of the Ten Commandments but better still to go beyond legalistic obedience to purity of heart and mind.

The essence of the law concerns the internal. Jesus does not forbid women from appearing in public, nor does he criticize contemporary sporting events that focus on lithe male bodies. His words do not mean we should never look at anyone of the opposite sex and appreciate them, for that would go against the very positive view of human beauty in the Old Testament (e.g., 1 Sam 16:12; 25:3; not to mention the Song of Songs). But they certainly are very much to the point in today's sex-obsessed society, in which whole magazines and shops are devoted to ways of making oneself physically attractive to the opposite sex, and so many people dress and behave in such a way as to invite us to ignore this teaching of Jesus.

So what can we do to think pure thoughts and live pure lives? One well-tried way is to withdraw from the world to the monastery or desert, though that way of life does not guarantee mental chastity, even if it makes it more difficult to commit physical adultery. It is not enough to simply decide *not* to think about something. William Barclay (1975: 149-50), a reliable source of practical advice, suggests two positive things that may help defeat forbidden thoughts. One is action: filling our lives with service so there is no time for wrong thoughts, focusing on others rather than ourselves. Another is filling our minds with good thoughts. Paul says something similar to the second point:

> Whatever is true, whatever is noble, whatever is right, whatever is pure, whatever is lovely, whatever is admirable—if anything is excellent or praiseworthy—think about such things. (Phil 4:8)

Such a positive approach to purity would affect the books and magazines we read, the films we watch, the Internet sites we visit, and the way we relate to those we meet in everyday life.

Each of us might benefit from reflecting on our own lives and reviewing how we can progress beyond minimal obedience to the seventh commandment to a positive appreciation of the beautiful people God has created around us—in purity of heart and mind.

8 PROPERTY

The ownership of property is of fundamental importance in most societies. This is clear from the cruel penalties for infringing property rights thought necessary in ancient Assyria and Babylonia and still practiced in some cultures today. It is also clear in a quite different way in the obsessive materialism of modern Western society, where "what you have is who you are." So what does the Bible have to say about property? As with the two preceding commandments, the Decalogue expresses a principle by means of a prohibition, in this case protecting property by prohibiting theft. First, however, let us consider the ancient Near Eastern context.[1]

THEFT

Ancient Near East. Several of Israel's ancient neighbors had laws about theft. The oldest known are in the Laws of Lipit-Ishtar:

> If a man enters the orchard of another man and is seized there for thievery, he shall weigh and deliver 10 shekels of silver.
>
> If a man cuts down a tree in another man's orchard, he shall weigh and deliver 20 shekels of silver. (LL §§9-10)

The first law is also in the Laws of Eshnunna, extended to cover fields and houses and adding that if the theft takes place at night, then the punishment will be death (LE §§12-13). Compensation of ten silver shekels is also decreed

---

[1]This chapter reuses some previously published material in a revised form (Baker 2009: 16-28) by permission of the publisher, all rights reserved.

for theft of a boat (LE §6). The second law also occurs in the Laws of Hammurabi, but with a higher penalty of thirty silver shekels (CH §59).[2]

Hammurabi's laws are generally much stricter than the earlier law collections, demanding capital punishment for robbery (CH §§21-22) and compensation by the local authorities if the robber is not arrested (CH §§23-24). However, it appears the punishment is negotiable, since one clause allows for tenfold restitution and thirtyfold in the case of temple or royal property; it only insists on the death penalty if the thief is unable to pay this sum (CH §8).

Looting also counts as theft and is to be punished ruthlessly:

> If a fire breaks out in a man's house, and a man who came to help put it out covets the household furnishings belonging to the householder, and takes household furnishings belonging to the householder, that man shall be cast into that very fire. (CH §25)

The culprit in this case may have justified his action as a reasonable reward for helping to extinguish the fire, but the law still considers it an infringement of property rights.

Several laws deal with indirect theft—for example:

> If a man should purchase . . . anything . . . from a son of a man or from a slave of a man without witnesses or a contract—or if he accepts the goods for safe-keeping—that man is a thief, he shall be killed. (CH §7)

> If the buyer could not produce the seller who sold [the lost property] to him or the witnesses before whom he made the purchase, but the owner of the lost property could produce witnesses who can identify his lost property, then it is the buyer who is the thief, he shall be killed; the owner of the lost property shall take his lost property. (CH §10; cf. CH §§9, 11-13; LE §40)

According to the first law, a person who obtains property illegally from someone within a household, such as a minor or a slave, is guilty of theft. According to the second law, a purchaser of stolen goods who is unable or unwilling to identify the thief is reckoned to be the thief. In both cases the death penalty applies. A receiver of goods stolen from the temple or palace is liable to the death penalty as well as the thief (CH §6).

---

[2]Whether this concerns damage or theft is not stated, but it seems likely that someone who goes to the trouble of felling a tree would take away the wood, which was a valuable commodity in Babylonia (cf. Driver and Miles 1952: 160-62).

A much lighter penalty—namely, compensation of three or five shekels of silver (CH §§259-60)—is decreed for stealing agricultural implements. It is possible this case refers to an unauthorized loan rather than theft, though the usual Akkadian verb for stealing is used (*šarāqu*). An employee who is corrupt, resulting in the loss of his employer's property, is punished severely but not by death (CH §§253-56, 265).

The Middle Assyrian Laws contain several clauses dealing with theft by women, who are generally penalized by death or mutilation (MAL §§A1, 3-6). For example,

> If a man is either ill or dead, and his wife should steal something from his house and give it either to a man, or to a woman, or to anyone else, they shall kill the man's wife as well as the receivers [of the stolen goods]. (MAL §A3)

> If . . . a slave . . . should receive something from a man's wife, they shall cut off the slave's . . . nose and ears; they shall restore the stolen goods; the man shall cut off his own wife's ears. But if he releases his wife and does not cut off her ears, they shall not cut off [the nose and ears] of the slave . . ., and they shall not restore the stolen goods. (MAL §A4)[3]

On the other hand, the punishment for a man who steals (MAL §§B14-15; C5, 8; F1), receives stolen property (MAL §C9), or is involved in corruption (MAL §§C10-11; F2) is relatively lenient, generally consisting of a beating plus restitution.

The most detailed treatment of theft is found in the Hittite Laws. More than fifty clauses specify precise penalties for theft, these varying based on what is stolen and—in some cases—the status of the thief. For example,

> If anyone steals a bull—if it is a weanling calf, it is not a "bull"; if it is a yearling calf, it is not a "bull"; if it is a 2-year-old bovine, that is a "bull." Formerly they gave 30 cattle. But now he shall give 15 cattle: 5 two-year-olds, 5 yearlings and 5 weanlings. He shall look to his house for it. (HL §57)

> If they seize a free man at the outset, before he enters the house, he shall pay 12 shekels of silver. If they seize a slave at the outset, before he enters the house, he shall pay 6 shekels of silver. (HL §93)

---

[3]Note that both the thief and the receiver of the stolen goods are to be punished, and if the punishment is waived, it must be waived for both of them (cf. CH §129; HL §198).

Multiple restitution is required for stealing of animals, varying from fifteenfold for a bull to threefold for an ox or horse (HL §§57-70). A different rule applies in the case of pigs or bees, where a monetary payment is required, the amount depending on the circumstances (HL §§81-85, 91-92). Monetary compensation also applies in the case of stolen plants, trees, clay, birds, or implements (HL §§101-4, 108-10, 113, 119-26, 129-33, 142-43), while stolen bricks or foundation stones are to be replaced twofold or fivefold respectively (HL §128). If a door should be stolen, the thief is liable for any consequential loss in the house as well as compensation of forty silver shekels (HL §127). Burglary or attempted burglary is punished by a monetary payment in addition to full restitution, the figure depending on the status of the offender: twelve shekels for a free man, six shekels plus mutilation for a slave (HL §§93-97). The only instance of the death penalty is for theft of a bronze spear from the palace (HL §126).[4]

Eighth commandment. The simplicity of the eighth commandment is unparalleled in all other ancient Near Eastern laws on theft:

> You shall not steal. (Exodus 20:15/Deuteronomy 5:19 DLB)

The prohibition is addressed to the whole people of God without distinction of status. In Hebrew, it takes the second-person singular form, often used in the Old Testament for the whole nation but at the same time indicating the personal responsibility of each individual to obey.

The Hebrew verb translated "steal" is generally concerned with material things or animals, but it can also refer to stealing a person in the sense of kidnapping (Ex 21:16; Deut 24:7; cf. Gen 40:15) or taking someone away for their own safety (2 Sam 19:41; 2 Kings 11:2; 2 Chron 22:11).[5] There are also various figurative senses, such as to steal someone's heart (2 Sam 15:6; cf. 2 Sam 19:3; Job 4:12; 21:18; 27:20; Jer 23:30).

---

[4]For further references, see Baker 2009: 16-19.

[5]The verb is גנב. It occurs forty times in the Old Testament, and the related nouns "thief" and "stolen object" occur another nineteen times in narrative, law, wisdom, and prophecy. The verb גנב may be distinguished from לקח ("take," "seize") and גזל ("rob," "take by force") by the element of secrecy, though there is not a rigid distinction (Hamp 1974; cf. Jackson 1972: 1-19; Westbrook 1988: 15-38). In any case, we should not make too much of this, keeping in mind the uniformly brief form of the commandments in the second group. One of the three verbs has to be chosen, and it is likely that it was intended to express the whole semantic range covered by the English words "steal," "rob," "seize," and "take by force."

A distinctive interpretation of this commandment was proposed by Alt (1949), who argued that it was originally concerned not with material possessions but rather with the stealing of free citizens (that is, kidnapping) in order to sell or enslave them (as in Ex 21:16 and Deut 24:7; cf. CH §14; HL §19). However, it is much more likely that the eighth commandment is deliberately broad in scope, including all kinds of action that deprive other people of property that is rightfully theirs. Although kidnapping is a serious crime and carries the death penalty, it is probably not common enough to justify a place in the Decalogue.[6]

The commandment, "You shall not steal," is repeated in the Holiness Code (Lev 19:11a) with a short expansion: "You shall not defraud or rob your neighbor" (Lev 19:13a). The Deuteronomic Laws do not mention theft directly, though there is social legislation concerning property rights and responsibilities. Theft is implicitly condemned by the psalms (e.g., Ps 35:10; 50:18; 62:10) and wisdom literature (e.g., Job 24:2; Prov 22:22-23; 30:9) and treated as a crime by the prophets (e.g., Jer 7:9; Ezek 18:7, 12, 16, 18; Hos 4:2; 7:1; Mic 2:2; Zech 5:3-4). It is prohibited no less strongly in the New Testament (Mt 19:18; Mk 10:19; Lk 18:20; Rom 2:21; 13:9; 1 Cor 5:10-11; 6:10; Eph 4:28).

Crime and punishment. The brevity of the commandment leaves open the question of punishment for those who break it. In comparison with the extensive coverage of theft in ancient Near Eastern laws, biblical law treats the subject quite briefly. This does not mean it is a trivial offense, for its presence in the Decalogue indicates an action that fundamentally disrupts the life of God's people. But the Old Testament does not trouble to define every possible kind of theft and appropriate punishment, and simply mentions a few sample cases. The Book of the Covenant specifies multiple restitution as punishment for burglary, stealing animals, negligent damage to crops, and careless loss of a neighbor's property (Ex 22:1-12). Leviticus 6 is more concerned with how a thief may not merely put things right with the person from whom he stole but also obtain God's forgiveness.

It is significant that biblical penalties for theft are more humane than elsewhere, never involving mutilation, beating, or death. The relative leniency of Old Testament law in punishing property offenses may be contrasted with its severity in dealing with homicide, ruling out compromise

---

[6]For further discussion and references, see Baker 2009: 20-21.

between the murderer and the victim's next of kin.[7] A property offense is paid for in terms of property by restoration of the stolen property to its owner plus an extra amount as compensation to the owner and as a deterrent to other thieves.[8] The Bible places a much higher value on human life than on material possessions, so property offenses are punished less severely than offenses against the life and dignity of other human beings, such as homicide and adultery.

As we progress through the Ten Commandments, it is apparent that the penalties decrease in severity just as the seriousness of the crime decreases. For example,

- in cases of murder (deliberate homicide), capital punishment is non-negotiable;

- in cases of adultery, capital punishment is standard, but leniency and forgiveness are possible;

- in cases of theft, capital punishment is never used.

REFLECTION

Interested parties. Who is this commandment intended to protect? Clines (1995: 42) suggests prohibition of theft is in the interest of the rich, who have possessions they want to hold on to, whereas McConville (2002a) points out that it is particularly important for the protection of the poor, who have only limited property that is necessary for survival.

A striking feature of the biblical laws is that one rule applies for all, whereas other ancient laws sometimes stipulate different punishments depending on the status of the thief (e.g., HL §§93-99) and the owner of the stolen property (e.g., CH §8). The Middle Assyrian Laws differentiate between stealing by men and women, with women being punished much more harshly. In a later period, Roman law prescribes crucifixion for a poor thief, while successful politicians are assigned provinces to be looted for personal gain.[9]

---

[7]Greenberg 1960: 13-20; cf. Finkelstein 1981: 37-41.

[8]In this the biblical laws are comparable to the Hittite Laws, though the rate of restitution is lower: fivefold for an ox (cf. tenfold in HL §63) and fourfold for a sheep (cf. sixfold in HL §69). If the original animal can be returned to its owner, double restitution is sufficient (cf. threefold in HL §70; according to Hoffner 1997, contra Paul 1970: 85-86). Neither in the Bible nor the other laws is such payment to be understood as a "fine" in the modern sense of a penalty paid to the state; rather, it is compensation paid to the person who has suffered loss by theft.

[9]Davidman 1953: 98.

In the Bible, however, even the king is subject to the law (Deut 17:18-20) and expected to respect the property rights of his citizens (cf. 1 Kings 21). This would have been a revolutionary idea in the ancient world, where rulers tended to regard the property of their people as their own.[10] Samuel warns Israel that kings tend to behave in this way (1 Sam 8:11-17) while affirming that he himself is innocent of such theft (1 Sam 12:1-5).

We may have sympathy for those who steal in order to eat, like Jean Valjean in *Les Misérables*, who spends nineteen years in prison for stealing a loaf of bread (cf. Prov 6:30-31). But I suspect poverty is not the most frequent reason for theft. My experience of poor people in Indonesia suggests that they are just as honest as the rich, and most will work day and night to earn what they need to survive rather than steal from others. Many thieves are well off, and there is no evidence that increasing wealth makes people more honest. In fact, it is arguable that rulers and the extremely wealthy tend to be the most corrupt. This is obvious in some of the notoriously corrupt societies of the developing world, but it is also true in many societies that consider themselves more civilized.[11]

Indirect theft. The Bible also forbids various kinds of indirect theft, such as taking possession of lost property (Ex 23:4-5; Deut 22:1-4), moving boundary markers (Deut 19:14), charging interest on loans to the poor (Ex 22:25; Lev 25:35-38; cf. Deut 23:19-20), late payment of wages (Lev 19:13; Deut 24:14-15), and using false weights and measures (Lev 19:35-36; Deut 25:13-16).[12] In today's world too, this commandment is not only for burglars and pickpockets—if it were, most of us could claim we have kept it without fail. Rather, it prohibits all kinds of improper gain, whether by marketing inferior-quality goods, charging excessive prices, being involved in financial corruption, filing dishonest tax returns, profiting from others' ignorance, giving and receiving bribes, pilfering at work, traveling on trains without a ticket, ignoring copyright laws, or buying and selling unfairly traded goods.

Let us reflect briefly on the last point—fair trade. The Deuteronomic law of weights and measures instructs as follows:

---

[10]Landes 1998: 31-36; Sacks 1999: 14-15; cf. Gnuse 1985: 60-65.

[11]Recent research in psychology suggests that wealthy people are more likely to be unethical than the poor (Piff et al. 2010; 2012).

[12]For discussion of biblical laws on these matters, see Baker 2009: 36-43, 97-102, 253-66, 296-304.

> Do not have two differing weights in your bag—one heavy, one light. Do not
> have two differing measures in your house—one large, one small. You must
> have accurate and honest weights and measures, so that you may live long in
> the land the LORD your God is giving you. For the LORD your God detests
> anyone who does these things, anyone who deals dishonestly. (Deut 25:13-16)[13]

In the everyday activities of buying and selling, weights and measures are to
be "accurate and honest" (lit. "full and just"). Both adjectives have theological
overtones. The former includes the ideas of wholeness, prosperity, and peace;
the latter denotes righteousness and justice. God's people are not to take advantage of others in business but should deal fairly and honestly with all.

Two theological incentives are given for keeping this law. Positively, the
people are assured that honesty will lead to prosperity (Deut 25:15). For Old
Testament Israel, this means long life in the Promised Land. Negatively, corruption is abhorrent to God (Deut 25:16). As a result, people who act dis-
honestly will face divine judgment, just like those who indulge in idolatry
(cf. Deut 7:25-26).

In some developing countries, there are market sellers who take advantage of customers by doctoring their scales or using nonstandard weights
and measures. Products are sometimes diluted, for example, mixing roasted
corn into ground coffee or plastic pellets into rice. This may seem outrageous to foreign visitors, who expect consistent trading standards in markets.
But if we reflect a little more, we may realize that marketing tactics in "developed" countries are often far from honest. For example, much modern
advertising and packaging is designed to make products look bigger and
better than they really are. Though not literally breaking the law on weights
and measures, the intention is much the same. Worse still, in sourcing
produce from poorer countries, powerful companies often exert leverage on
suppliers, forcing prices below fair levels, with disastrous consequences for
the local workers. The law quoted above is relevant to all these situations:
from individual traders using traditional weights and measures to international businesses with sophisticated technology and thousands of employees.

---

[13]Similar principles are emphasized throughout the Old Testament (e.g., Lev 19:35-36; Prov 11:1;
20:10, 23; Ezek 45:10; Hos 12:7-8; Amos 8:5; Mic 6:10-11). The references to traders in Zeph 1:11
and Zech 14:21 may imply that they are frequently corrupt (Kidwell 2014). Note that the word
כְּנַעֲנִי in Zech 14:21 is translated "trader" by most modern English versions (except NIV and
NET, which have "Canaanite"). The same word in Job 41:6 and Prov 31:24 and similar expressions
in Ezek 17:4 and Zeph 1:11 are translated "trader" or "merchant" almost without exception.

Another Old Testament law deals with wages, stressing that they must be paid on time:

> Do not defraud or rob your neighbor. Do not hold back the wages of a hired
> worker overnight. (Lev 19:13)

Jesus' parable of the laborers in the vineyard assumes the principle of fair wages for employees and goes further by emphasizing generosity to a person in need by paying more than he is entitled to (Mt 20:1-16; cf. Jas 5:1-6).

So how are these laws to be applied today? They have particular relevance to people involved in business, serving as a reminder to follow biblical principles of justice and generosity. It is becoming increasingly clear that the standard of living considered normal in the developed world has been made possible in part through exploitation of poorer people elsewhere. In response to this, the fair-trade movement aims to give a better deal for producers and to make consumers more aware of the working conditions of those who produce the goods they enjoy.[14] This may be seen as a contemporary implementation of biblical law. Choosing fair-trade goods when they are available and supporting shops with fair business practices can be one way of following Paul's advice: "As we have opportunity, let us do good to all people" (Gal 6:10).[15] Sadly, however, there is evidence that in some cases a relatively small part of the extra amount paid for fair-trade goods actually reaches producers in the developing world. It would be naive to assume the motives of all fair-trade promoters are altruistic.[16]

Economic structures. The eighth commandment rules out all kinds of theft, whether direct or indirect, but it should not be seen as merely a defense of private property. It may also be taken as a challenge to reflect on larger economic structures. Such structures within and between nations can make robbery an institution and ensure the rich stay rich while others are permanently poor.[17]

---

[14]For further information, see websites like those of Fairtrade International (www.fairtrade.net), Fair Trade USA (www.fairtradeusa.org), and the Trade Justice Movement (www.tjm.org.uk).

[15]For further reflection on how modern trading practices conflict with biblical ideals, with particular reference to Zech 14:21, see Kidwell 2014. On business ethics, see the websites of the Institute for Business Ethics (www.ibe.org.uk) and Transforming Business (www.transformingbusiness.net).

[16]On the scholarly debate about fair trade, see Steinrücken and Jaenichen 2007; Smith 2009; Griffiths 2011; Salvador et al. 2013; Cater et al. 2015.

[17]Brueggemann 1994. A bit differently, Gnuse (1985: 5-9) argues that the eighth commandment does not serve to protect private property, because important possessions belong to the community and

During the 1980s in Britain, for example, real household income increased by almost 3 percent per year, suggesting that plenty of resources were available. But a breakdown of the distribution of this income shows that the richest 10 percent of the population enjoyed an increase of over 4 percent per year, whereas the income of the poorest 10 percent actually *decreased* by more than 1 percent per year during the same period.[18] This redistribution of wealth from the poor to the rich was a result of Tory economic policies under the leadership of Margaret Thatcher, policies sometimes called "Thatcherism." Since 1990, inequality stabilized for most of the population in Britain, while the share of income going to the top 1 percent continued to increase.[19] This inequality may also be one of the reasons for the enormous growth in personal debt in Britain, at times increasing by 10 percent per year, several times higher than inflation. Perhaps it is not coincidental that the increase in economic disparity in contemporary Britain has taken place alongside a downturn in belief in God and church attendance, and the marginalization of the Bible and its laws.

On an international level, it was calculated that developing countries transferred almost $200 billion to wealthier countries in 2002, four times more than they received in international aid.[20] More recently, development aid was about $165 billion per year, while $100 billion or more was *lost* by developing countries due to tax avoidance by multinational companies, not to mention billions of dollars in interest on debts, patent licensing fees for technologies and pharmaceuticals, and losses due to the protectionist policies of many donors.[21] Overall, it seems likely that poor countries are still contributing to the development of rich countries rather than vice versa.

Another modern issue is inflation, which may be seen as the creation of excess currency or credit beyond the real wealth of a country, as suggested by Larkin (1982). Biblical laws relating to economics assume payment in silver or goods, which are relatively stable in value, but a new issue arises when the value of the currency itself varies due to inflation or devaluation. This is particularly relevant when money takes the form of banknotes, where it is possible

---

ultimately to God. So the focus of the commandment is on the appropriation of communal possessions for private use and is designed to protect persons, especially the poor, rather than property.
[18]Alcock 1997: 17.
[19]The top 1 percent of individuals took 5.7 percent of total household income in 1990; this increased to 8.7 percent in 2009–2010, then dropped slightly to 8.3 percent in 2013–2014 (Belfield et al. 2015: 27-34).
[20]See UN News 2003.
[21]UNDP 2011: chap. 5; Canuto and Halland 2013; Hickel 2013; Provost and Tran 2013.

to create extra money by simply printing more of it. Printing money effectively reduces the value of a currency, thus infringing the principle of justice in buying and selling. It is particularly serious for the poor, who live at subsistence level, and the elderly, who rely on their savings for retirement income.

Property ownership. In reflecting on property, one question that has often been asked is whether we ought to own property at all. Communal ownership of property was practiced in the early days of the Jerusalem Christian fellowship (Acts 4:32-37), though it should be noted this was voluntary (Acts 5:4) and apparently not repeated in other New Testament fellowships. Monasticism has played an important role throughout Christian history, especially in the Roman Catholic and Eastern Orthodox traditions, and usually involves commitment to a simple lifestyle and taking vows of chastity, poverty, and obedience. The Kibbutz Movement has been influential in modern Judaism, its ideology embracing equality as communal enterprise and ownership.

The founders of communism argued for the benefits of shared ownership of property as an alternative to oppressive systems where the elite owned and controlled almost everything. Communism as a political system is largely discredited now, of course, as it seems the whole world turns to capitalism. The result is that the elite own and control almost everything! Shin (2014) reports that the eighty-five wealthiest people in the world own as much as the 3.5 billion poorest people put together. For most readers of this book—somewhere between those extremes—life is probably quite comfortable, and we may be happy enough with the present system on a personal level. However, those who profess belief in a God of truth and love should surely base their lifestyle on what is good and right rather than what is comfortable. So what does the Bible actually say?

At the beginning, we learn that everything God made is good and is here for us to enjoy and use responsibly (Gen 1–3). Property is God's gift to his people (Deut 8:17-18), as in the idyllic picture of the Israelites living in peace, "everyone under their own vine and under their own fig tree" (1 Kings 4:25; cf. 2 Kings 18:31; Mic 4:4; Zech 3:10). In fact, even the nomadic ideal, perpetuated by the Rechabites (Jer 35), does not mean a complete refusal to own property. Abraham, for example, is wealthy by the standards of his time (Gen 13:2), and his nomadic lifestyle does not prevent him purchasing a cave to bury his wife (Gen 23). The New Testament also acknowledges the right to own and enjoy material things (1 Tim 6:17) so long as it is accompanied by a generous attitude toward others (1 Tim 6:18). But sadly, there are people who accumulate far too much for themselves at the expense of the poor, and the prophets do not hesitate to condemn them for their greed (Is 3:14-15; 5:8; Amos 2:6-8; 5:11; Mic 2:2).

The biblical understanding of ownership is more like stewardship than an absolute right of disposal over something. God is recognized as the ultimate owner of the land (Lev 25:23). Real estate is a sacred trust to be kept in the family and passed on to descendants, and the produce of the land is not only for the benefit of the owner but to be shared with others. On this view, property is a resource for the common good, with an emphasis on responsibility and compassion rather than possession and power. This does not mean renunciation of all individual property rights, but the people of God should have a radically different approach to property ownership than that which is common in today's world.

Although the Bible does not condemn property as bad in itself, the dangers of materialism are frequently pointed out (e.g., Ps 52:7; Mt 6:24; Lk 6:24-25; 12:16-21; 1 Tim 6:9-10; Rev 3:17), and the willingness to give up material goods in the pursuit of a higher good is commended (Lk 6:20-21; 18:18-30). In any case, Jesus encourages his followers to view property from a long-term perspective. He advises them to store up treasure in heaven, safe from theft and decay, rather than here on earth:

> Do not store up for yourselves treasures on earth . . . where thieves break in and steal. But store up for yourselves treasures in heaven . . . where thieves do not break in and steal. For where your treasure is, there your heart will be also. (Mt 6:19-21)

To do this requires single-mindedness, for it is impossible to serve both God and money (Mt 6:24). But if serving God is top priority, there is no need to worry about food and clothing, for the heavenly Father knows the material needs of his children and will take care of them (Mt 6:25-33).

$\mathcal{9}$ TRUTH

Human beings long to know the truth, as shown, for example, in the extended and expensive efforts to discover what happened to Malaysia Airlines Flight 370 that went missing in March 2014. A Russian proverb says, "Better to be slapped with the truth than kissed with a lie." At the same time, the truth can be dangerous to those who have vested interests in keeping it from being known, and people sometimes go to great lengths to hide or deny the truth. One of the most important ways of discovering the truth is to call witnesses, who can testify to what they have seen and heard, and this is the focus of the ninth commandment and related laws in the ancient Near East.[1]

PERJURY

Ancient Near East. The use of witnesses to establish the truth in legal cases was widespread in the ancient Near East, and perjury (false testimony in court) was a very serious offense. The Laws of Ur-Namma include the following clauses:

> If a man presents himself as a witness but is demonstrated to be a perjurer, he shall weigh and deliver 15 shekels of silver. (LU §28)

> If a man presents himself as a witness but refuses to take the oath, he shall make compensation of whatever was the object of the case. (LU §29)

---

[1]This chapter reuses some previously published material in a revised form (Baker 2009: 201-8) by permission of the publisher, all rights reserved.

According to Hammurabi, a false witness in a trial for a capital offense is liable to capital punishment (CH §§1-3) and a lesser punishment where the penalty for the crime is compensation in grain or silver (CH §4). This follows the principle of talion (that is, the punishment must fit the crime), in which the false accuser receives the punishment intended for the accused (LL §17).[2] Witnesses are also used to ensure the veracity of property and financial transactions in order to avoid a possible charge of theft (CH §§7, 9-11, 13, gap z, 106-7, 122-24) and to confirm that a warning has been given to someone whose wall is in a state of disrepair (CH § gap e).

The Middle Assyrian Laws require witnesses to prove charges of rape (MAL §A12), slander (MAL §A17), unauthorized wearing of a veil (MAL §A40), and witchcraft (MAL §A47). No doubt they would be used in other cases too, but the testimony of witnesses would be particularly important for offenses such as these, which cannot be proved after the event. (This is unlike a case of theft, for example, where property may be found in someone's possession.)

Although there are no extant laws from ancient Egypt and the Levant, there is considerable evidence concerning the role of witnesses in legal practice.[3] The Egyptian Amenemope advises, "Do not bear witness with false words," and warns against using false oaths to steal land or other property.[4] Perjury is also mentioned as a serious offense in literature from Assyria,[5] Babylonia,[6] and the Hittites.[7]

Ninth commandment. There are minor differences between the wording of the ninth commandment in the Hebrew of Exodus and Deuteronomy, but this does not affect the English translation:

> You shall not testify[8] against your neighbor as a false[9] witness. (Exodus 20:16/Deuteronomy 5:20)

---

[2]The same principle applies in other contexts too: CH §§116, 196-97, 200, 229-32; MAL §§A50, 52.

[3]See Baker 2009: 202, n. 6.

[4]Instruction of Amenemope, chapters 6, 11, 13 (*COS*: 1.47, lines vii.18, xiv.9, xvi.1). See also Prayer Stele of Nefer-abu to Ptah (Beyerlin 1975: 36).

[5]E.g., Shurpu Incantations, tablet 2, lines 14-15 (Reiner 1958: 13; Beyerlin 1975: 132).

[6]E.g., "I Will Praise the Lord of Wisdom," tablet 2, line 22 (*ANET*: 597; Beyerlin 1975: 139).

[7]E.g., Prayer of Kantuzilis (*ANET*: 400; Beyerlin 1975: 168) and one of the state archive catalogues (*COS*: 3.38, line A, ii 18).

[8]Lit. "answer."

[9]Exodus and Deuteronomy use two different Hebrew words, both meaning "false" (שֶׁקֶר and שָׁוְא respectively). The latter literally means "vain," using the same word as the third commandment. Durham (1987) suggests this is intended to extend the meaning to any sort of evasive or worthless testimony, but the meaning is not substantially different.

The traditional translation is, "You shall not bear false witness against your neighbor" (RSV).[10] I have translated it somewhat differently above, because the Hebrew word for "witness" actually refers to the person who testifies rather than their testimony, though this does not greatly affect the meaning of the commandment in practice. "Your neighbor" refers to a fellow member of God's people,[11] each of whom is bound by the Decalogue, though that does not mean it would be acceptable to testify falsely against a foreigner.

In the legal context of ancient Israel, the commandment is concerned with witnesses who give false testimony in court. Following the prohibition of homicide, adultery, and theft, the insistence that witnesses speak the truth is vital to the process of ensuring justice for those accused of crimes as well as victims of crime. Witnesses might be called by the prosecution (e.g., 1 Kings 21:10, 13; Is 43:10, 12) and the defense (e.g., Prov 14:25; Is 43:9). In the absence of professional lawyers, a witness would often act as accuser (e.g., Ps 27:12; 35:11). In some cases, forensic evidence could be produced (e.g., Ex 22:13; Deut 22:17), but generally the testimony of witnesses would be the main evidence in bringing a conviction, making their responsibility to tell the truth correspondingly great.

Witnesses. Several laws expand the ninth commandment; for example,

> You shall not make a false statement; you shall not join hands with the wicked, by acting as a malicious witness. You shall not follow the crowd in wrong-doing; and you shall not testify in a lawsuit, diverting from the truth to follow the crowd, so as to pervert justice. (Ex 23:1-2, DLB)[12]

There are three main issues. First, witnesses are not to make false statements, whether based on unsubstantiated hearsay or as a deliberate distortion of the truth (Ex 23:1a). Second, they must withstand any pressure to cooperate with the wicked, whether to convict someone who is innocent or free someone who is guilty (Ex 23:1b). Third, it is often easier to follow the crowd than to stand for the truth (Ex 23:2; cf. 1 Kings 19:10; Jer 11:19), but the

---

[10]So also NRSV; NJPS; ESV. The equivalent in more modern language is, "You shall not give false testimony against your neighbor" (NIV), or, "You shall not give false evidence . . ." (NJB; cf. REB). The traditional translation is supported by LXX. On this, see Simian-Yofre 1986; Propp 2006.

[11]Childs 1974; Durham 1987; Brueggemann 1994; contra Cassuto 1951.

[12]For notes on this translation, see Baker 2009: 204.

majority is not always right. "Even if you are a minority of one, the truth is the truth" (Mahatma Gandhi).

The matter of witnesses is elaborated further in Deuteronomy. In order to reduce the risk of false accusations, a minimum of two witnesses is required to convict someone of a crime (Deut 17:6; 19:15; cf. Num 35:30). This sensible rule does not always guarantee justice, of course, as exemplified in the trial of Naboth (1 Kings 21:10, 13). In this case, the legal minimum of two witnesses is followed, but the requirement of truth telling ignored—as also in the trials of Jesus (Mt 26:59-60), Stephen (Acts 6:11-14), and Susanna (Dan 13:28-41[13]).

If it is suspected that someone has given false testimony (Deut 19:16), there is to be a thorough investigation (Deut 19:18a; cf. Deut 13:14; 17:4). This is to take place "in the presence of the LORD" (Deut 19:17), represented by the priests and judges, presumably at the central sanctuary.[14] If the witness proves to be false, he suffers the punishment the accused would have suffered if proved guilty (Deut 19:18b-19a). Such punishment is designed to cleanse the community of evil (Deut 19:19b) and deter others who might be tempted to give false testimony (Deut 19:20).

The principle of talion applies, here expressed by the phrase "life for life, eye for eye, tooth for tooth" (Deut 19:21; cf. Ex 21:23-25; Lev 24:18-20), as in the ancient Near Eastern laws mentioned above. This should not be seen as a list of specific punishments but rather a vivid way of expressing the principle that punishment should fit the crime. The precise application of the principle would presumably be decided by the judges in a particular lawsuit. Far from encouraging vengeance, as it is sometimes misunderstood, the principle is intended to ensure justice. On the one hand, by punishing those who kill or abuse other human beings, it maintains the sanctity of life (cf. Num 35:31-34). On the other hand, it limits vengeance and rules out punishment disproportionate to the offense, as in Lamech's boast that he killed someone who merely wounded him (Gen 4:23-24).[15]

One way to avoid giving false testimony is by substituting silence for speech. Witnesses may be reluctant to speak out if they know what they say

---

[13]In the deuterocanonical Additions to Daniel.

[14]Cf. Deut 17:8-13. So Driver 1902; Wilson 1995: 144-45, 173-77; contra Tigay 1996.

[15]For further discussion of talion, see Daube 1947: 102-53; Frymer-Kensky 1980; Crüsemann 1987; Otto 1991; Nel 1994; Piattelli 1995; Haase 1997; Jackson 2002; Barmash 2005: 154-77.

will be unwelcome (cf. Amos 5:10), so another law makes it clear that members of the community have a duty to testify if they have seen a crime (Lev 5:1; cf. Prov 29:24). Wrongdoing is not to be covered up, even by simply keeping quiet. Witnesses are expected to tell the truth in court—the whole truth, and nothing but the truth.

REFLECTION

Speaking the truth. Truthful testimony in court is emphasized by the ninth commandment, in other laws mentioned above, and throughout the Bible (e.g., Ps 27:12; Prov 6:19; 12:17; 14:5, 25; 24:28; 25:18; Jer 7:9; Mt 19:18; Mk 10:19; Lk 18:20). But although it is primarily concerned with perjury, the ninth commandment has been understood from early days to cover other kinds of lying and deceitful speech as well.

In Leviticus 19, which recapitulates most of the commandments, the people are told, "Do not lie. Do not deceive one another" (Lev 19:11b), followed immediately by a recap of the third commandment on swearing falsely by the name of God (Lev 19:12) and soon after by a prohibition of slander (Lev 19:16). In Hosea's summary of the Decalogue, false witness is broadened to become lying (Hos 4:2; cf. Hos 7:1-4).[16]

Like the other negative commandments, the ninth does not simply prohibit a crime. It can also be understood positively to affirm the importance of truthful speech—and writing—for the people of God and indeed for society as a whole. This is clear in Psalm 15, where God welcomes "the one whose walk is blameless, who does what is righteous, who speaks the truth from their heart . . ." (Ps 15:2; cf. Ps 51:6; 119:43). Flattery and boasting are ruled out (Ps 5:5, 9; 12:3-4), as are slander, deceit, and lies (Jer 9:4-5; Mic 6:12). Lies and falsehood are contrasted with the truth to be found in God's law (Ps 119:29, 69, 104, 128, 163).[17]

In view of this strong emphasis on speaking the truth, it is puzzling that the Old Testament contains several stories about characters who lie or deceive for various reasons. Often there appears to be little or no condemnation of their behavior, for example in the cases of Abram and Sarai (Gen 12:10-20), Rebekah and Jacob (Gen 27:5-24), the Hebrew midwives

---

[16]For a very thorough study of lying in the Old Testament, see Klopfenstein 1964.

[17]See also Ps 50:19-20; 52:1-5; Prov 6:17; 10:18-21; 12:6, 13-22; 13:3; 14:3; 18:6-8; 26:18-28; 30:8; Is 59:12-15; cf. Mt 5:33-37; 15:19; Jn 8:31-32, 44; Eph 4:25; Col 3:9; Jas 3:1-12.

(Ex 1:15-19), Rahab (Josh 2:1-7), Ehud (Judg 3:16-23), Jael (Judg 4:17-21), and Michal (1 Sam 19:11-17). There are several approaches to this issue. The traditional Christian approach, which may be traced back as far as Augustine, is to assume lying is always wrong and therefore condemn biblical characters who lie or try to explain that they are not really lying. However, a number of recent scholars argue that biblical authors do not always view such behavior as wrong.[18]

Careful reading of the texts reveals subtle hints in many narratives indicating a moral judgment, though stopping short of outright approval or condemnation. Genesis has clues that point to a negative assessment by the author: for example, Abraham's silence when challenged by Pharaoh implies his guilt (Gen 12:18-20), and Jacob's attempt to make amends with Esau is probably an indirect admission of past sins (Gen 33:1-11).[19] In contrast, God blesses the midwives for their scheme to save the Hebrew babies (Ex 1:20-21), Israel protects Rahab and her family in return for her protection of the spies (Josh 2:8-14; 6:17, 25), Ehud's wily killing of the Moabite king is attributed to the LORD (Judg 3:15, 28), and Jael is extolled as the "most blessed of women" (Judg 5:24-27). From the incidents mentioned above, only in the case of Michal is there no explicit comment, but in the flow of the story it is clear that she plays a positive role in shielding the future king from jealous Saul.

Many of the accounts of deception involve women. Fuchs (1988) takes this as a negative portrayal of the women concerned on the part of the male author of the text, whereas Craven (1989) seeks to justify their behavior by showing that they acted in faith to preserve the covenant community. Prouser (1994) argues that in the Bible it is often the underdog who lies, and deception is considered acceptable and even praiseworthy if it enables a weaker party to succeed against one that is stronger. She sees the reason for this in the fact that Israel as a nation was generally in a weak position and so had sympathy for those who could succeed in the face of adversity. In her view, the reason why female characters often use deception is because they are disadvantaged persons, not because they are women.[20]

---

[18]For reflections on lying in the teaching of Augustine, see Griffiths 2004; Meilaender 2006: 47-76. On recent approaches to deception in the Hebrew Bible, in addition to the footnotes in the following paragraphs, see Freund 1991; Friedmann 2002: 42-68.

[19]Wenham 2000: 75-77.

[20]Cf. Williams (2001), who argues that deception is only evaluated positively in Genesis when it is a response to someone who has previously wronged the deceiver.

Rowe (2014) draws on insights from anthropological research, suggesting that lying does not necessarily indicate that truth is unimportant but shows the value of true knowledge and the need to distinguish between those who have the right to that knowledge and those to whom it is denied. Truthfulness is unquestionably important, but it sometimes has to be balanced with other moral obligations, such as preservation of life, loyalty to family, and faith in God. This definition is quite different from acquiescing in the common practice of balancing truthfulness with political expedience and personal advantage, as is only too common today.

Augustine's rejection of lying does not fit easily with a number of Old Testament incidents in which deception serves a positive purpose and is not condemned by the biblical author. In reflecting on this today, I suggest that occasionally it may be right to conceal the truth with a lie, as was done by those who hid Jews from Nazis during the Second World War. In some circumstances, it may be appropriate to not tell the whole truth, gradually reveal it, or subtly change the subject. But if this seems necessary, we need to be careful that our motives are genuinely for the sake of a moral obligation that is more important than speaking the truth; otherwise, we are telling a lie simply to get ourselves out of a sticky situation.

Truth in public. The law against perjury is one of the few commandments in the Decalogue that is still generally accepted in postmodern societies. The 1970s Watergate scandal began with a burglary but grew into a major attempt by President Nixon and his men to cover up the truth, leading eventually to Nixon's resignation. Bill Clinton was impeached and Jeffrey Archer, a member of Parliament, sent to prison not for their sexual immorality but because they gave false evidence in the attempt to cover it up. An Australian judge, Marcus Einfeld, was convicted of perjury and sentenced to three years in prison for making false statements in connection with a $77 driving fine.

Strangely, though, this does not mean that truth is generally considered important. It seems many politicians and journalists routinely lie, and, even though people moan about it, little is actually done to stop it. To give just one example, Tony Blair remained prime minister of Britain in spite of substantial evidence he misled the nation about the Iraq War. A recurring theme in the BBC political satire, *Yes, Prime Minister*, is the way characters tend to say and do what is expedient rather than what is true.

The Old Testament affirms the importance of truth in public life, with particular condemnation of religious leaders who use their positions to propagate lies (Jer 6:13-14; 8:10-11; 23:21-32; Ezek 13) and pander to their audiences with smooth talk (cf. Is 30:9-11). Mendacity brings iniquity (Is 5:18) and causes confusion by pretending to be virtue (Is 5:20).

Another kind of untruth that is pervasive today is the use of moral euphemisms designed to make what is wrong appear right or at least unobjectionable.[21] Instead of committing adultery, people have an affair. Instead of having an abortion, they terminate a pregnancy. Instead of killing innocent citizens, there is collateral damage. Instead of unemployment, there is downsizing. Instead of lying, there are "terminological inexactitudes" (Winston Churchill, 1906).

What about us? Are we habitually truthful? When we speak and write, it is often easier to say what we think people want to hear—or what we want them to hear—than what is actually true. Sometimes it is tempting to keep quiet and not say anything at all rather than speaking up when we ought to. The Bible encourages us to go beyond the rejection of false testimony, to become people who speak the truth from our hearts.[22]

"What is truth?" Pilate's famous words are spoken in response to Jesus' claim, "The reason I was born and came into the world is to testify to the truth" (Jn 18:37-38). Jesus fulfills the ninth commandment by testifying to the truth, and he promises those who accept his teaching and become his disciples, "You will know the truth, and the truth will set you free" (Jn 8:32). At the same time, he warns those who reject the truth that they belong to the devil, the father of lies (Jn 8:44). In contrast, his own father is the "God of truth" (Ps 31:5; Is 65:16).[23]

Jesus encourages his followers to make a habit of truthfulness so that their integrity is well known and they don't need oaths to persuade people to believe them:

Again, you have heard that it was said to the people long ago, "Do not break your oath, but fulfill to the Lord the oaths you have made." But I tell you, do

---

[21]Strozier 1966; Brueggemann 1997b: 294-96; Hütter 2005: 199-200.

[22]For reflections on truthfulness and falsehood in public life today, with particular reference to the ninth commandment, see Andrew 1963a; Brueggemann 1997b; Harrelson 1997: 119-23; Braaten 2005; Hütter 2005.

[23]So the traditional translation in KJV, followed by NJB; cf. Anderson 1972; Craigie 1983; Oswalt 1998; Watts 2005. See also Num 23:19; 1 Sam 15:29.

not swear an oath at all: either by heaven, for it is God's throne; or by the earth, for it is his footstool; or by Jerusalem, for it is the city of the Great King. And do not swear by your head, for you cannot make even one hair white or black. All you need to say is simply "Yes" or "No"; anything beyond this comes from the evil one. (Mt 5:33-37)

James emphasizes the same point (Jas 5:12), as does Philo (*Decalogue* 84-91). This is similar to the old motto of the London Stock Exchange—"My word is my bond"—where gentlemen kept to their agreements without the need for written contracts.

Some Christians take Jesus' words as prohibiting oaths in any circumstance. However, his main point is to emphasize telling the truth rather than prohibiting oaths. If a Christian is summoned to court as a witness, it may be appropriate to fulfill the legal requirement and take an oath. After all, the purpose of this is to help the judge and jury establish the truth in a situation where the life and welfare of the accused is at stake. For witnesses to take oaths may be helpful to this end, especially in societies today where untruth is rampant but perjury is still considered wrong.

Finally, it is worth reflecting that Jesus is not simply a witness to the truth and teacher of the truth; he embodies the truth in his very nature. At the beginning of John's gospel, we learn about "the glory of the one and only Son, who came from the Father, full of grace and truth" (Jn 1:14). Further, "the law was given through Moses; grace and truth came through Jesus Christ" (Jn 1:17). Later, Thomas asks a question that gives Jesus the opportunity to make his unforgettable statement: "I am the way and the truth and the life. No one comes to the Father except through me" (Jn 14:6). In one sense, then, Jesus *is* the truth.

Toward the end of his life, as Jesus prepares his disciples for life without their teacher, he makes another promise: "When he, the Spirit of truth, comes, he will guide you into all the truth" (Jn 16:13). So also today, if we are open to his inspiration, the Holy Spirit confirms and illuminates the truths recorded in the Bible, focusing on Jesus—the Truth—to the glory of God the Father (Jn 5:39; 15:26; cf. Phil 2:9-11; 2 Pet 1:2-21).

10 LAST BUT NOT LEAST

"You shall not covet!" The last of the ten commandments has puzzled Jews and Christians throughout the centuries. Does it really mean what it appears to say, that the desire for other people's possessions is a serious offense in the sight of God—just like idolatry and blasphemy, homicide and adultery? If so, how could a law that deals with thoughts rather than actions be put into effect? And why is it included in the Decalogue along with capital crimes and other actionable offenses rather than in the exhortations of Deuteronomy or the preaching of the prophets? Or does the tenth commandment perhaps mean something different, something more concrete, such as, "You shall not take steps to acquire possessions that do not rightfully belong to you," which might include various kinds of corruption and intrigue?[1]

COVETING

Ancient Near East. None of the ancient Near Eastern laws refer to coveting except a clause in the Laws of Hammurabi that mentions coveting goods in a burning house and taking them (CH §25). It is not the coveting itself that is the problem here, but the theft.

In non-legal materials, however, there are various references to coveting. The Babylonian Shamash Hymn (or Hymn to the Sun God) mentions it briefly:

---

[1]This chapter reuses some previously published material in a revised form (Baker 2009: 28-36) by permission of the publisher, all rights reserved.

A man who covets his neighbor's wife

Will [. . .] before his appointed day . . .[2]

In an Assyrian confession of sins, the penitent admits, "I lifted my face to your extensive possessions, to your precious silver went my desire."[3]

Coveting is considered foolish in Egyptian wisdom literature, such as the Instruction for Merikare.[4] It is also mentioned in the Book of the Dead, which includes a declaration of innocence before a tribunal of forty-two gods. The deceased addresses each god in turn, and to the third god he claims,

O Beaky, who has come forth from Hermopolis, I have not been envious.[5]

This declaration ranges from the sublime to the ridiculous, from murder and robbery to winking and blabbering, so the denial of coveting here does not necessarily mean it is considered a serious wrongdoing.

A treaty between the Hittite king Mursili II and his vassal Kupanta-Kurunta of Mira-Kuwaliya requires, "You shall not desire any border district of Hatti,"[6] with a similar formulation to the tenth commandment. No doubt the suzerain is concerned with potential seizure of territory rather than simply the desires of the vassal (as is explicit in the subsequent clause), so the prohibition is directed against both wanting and attempting to take land.[7] Such desire combined with action is also implied in one of the Amarna letters, where Abdihiba of Jerusalem reports to the Egyptian king that "Milkilu does not break with the sons of Lab'aya and the sons of Arzayu, in order to covet the land of the king for themselves."[8]

A Phoenician inscription from Karatepe pronounces a curse on someone who covets a city, using the same Semitic word as in the tenth commandment:

---

[2]Lines 88-89. *COS* does not include this section of the hymn, so I have quoted it from *BWL* (130-31); cf. Foster 2005: 631.

[3]Text in Ebeling 1916: 297; 1919: no. 45:12-13; tr. by Moran 1967: 547; cf. Seux 1976: 207.

[4]Lines 40-41 (*COS*: 1.35). Cf. Instruction of Ptah-hotep, lines 300-315 (*ANET*: 413); Eloquent Peasant, lines 165, 290-93 (*ANET*: 409).

[5]Chapter 125 (*COS*: 2.12, p. 61, column 1). *ANET*: 35 §B3 translates this as "I have not been covetous." A later clause may also refer to coveting, but its meaning is uncertain: "O Serpent-Whose-Head-Is-Erect, who has come forth from the cavern, my possessions have not increased except by my own property" (*COS*: 2.12, p. 62, column 1; cf. *ANET*: 35 §B41).

[6]Part of §10 of the treaty; see Beckman 1999: 76; cf. Mendenhall 1954a: 30.

[7]Moran 1967: 546.

[8]Letter 289:5-8 in Knudtzon 1915, tr. by Moran 1967: 547.

Now if a king among kings or a prince among princes,

if a man, who is a man of renown . . . ,

if indeed he shall covet this city, and shall tear away this gate . . . ,

if from covetousness he shall tear [it] away—

if from hate or from evil he shall tear away this gate

then shall Ba'al Shamem and El, creator of the earth . . .

erase that kingdom, and that king, and that man who is a man of renown.[9]

Here too it is clear that an external act is involved, not just covetous thoughts, and the additional verb "tear away" makes this explicit.[10]

Tenth commandment. The wording of the tenth commandment is slightly different in Exodus and Deuteronomy, but the essence is the same.

Exodus 20:17	Deuteronomy 5:21
You shall not covet your neighbor's *household:* you shall not *covet* your neighbor's *wife*, or his male or female slave, *or* his ox or donkey, or anything else of your neighbor's.	You shall not covet your neighbor's *wife;* you shall not *desire* your neighbor's *house, his field,* or his male or female slave, his ox or donkey, or anything else of your neighbor's.

As mentioned above, Roman Catholic and Lutheran tradition divides this commandment in two, so it is actually the ninth and tenth commandments.

There is in fact a double prohibition, each part beginning with the words "you shall not . . ." In Exodus the verb "covet" is repeated, whereas in Deuteronomy a pair of synonymous verbs is used: "covet" and "desire."[11] These two verbs also occur elsewhere in parallel (e.g., Gen 3:6; Prov 6:25 and Ps 45:11; Ps 68:16 and Ps 132:13-14) and are very close in meaning. Both are used in positive and negative contexts. Both are commonly used with reference to human desire but can also be used of the divine. Desire is ethically neutral, neither commanded nor prohibited in itself. It is assumed that people—and God—will have desires, and the ethical issues concern whether the object

---

[9]The Azatiwada Inscription, lines iii.12-iv.1 (*COS*: 2.31). For the original text, with translation, see *KAI* no. 26; Gordon 1949: 111-12.

[10]Cf. Alt 1949: 334, n. 1; Marcus and Gelb 1949: 120; Moran 1967: 544. For a comparative study of covetousness and desire in Egyptian and biblical wisdom literature, see Shupak 1993: 105-16.

[11]The Hebrew verbs are חמד (*qal*) and אוה (*hithpael*). For a detailed discussion of these verbs, see Baker 2005b: 7-13. Cf. Mayer 1971; Wallis 1977.

of desire is good and whether it may be obtained legitimately without harm to others.

Apart from the use of these different verbs, there are two interrelated differences between the canonical versions of the tenth commandment:

- change of order between "house[hold]" and "wife"
- addition of the word "field" in Deuteronomy[12]

To understand the reason for the first change, it is important to be aware that the Hebrew word *bayit* means both "house" and "household" and that it has the second meaning in Exodus and the first in Deuteronomy. Admittedly, it is often translated "house" in Exodus 20, but I suggest it really means "house*hold*" and includes all of a man's possessions that are economically significant.[13] The main contents of the household are specified in decreasing order of importance: wife, slaves, working animals, and material things. An obvious reason why a wife might be coveted would be sexual attraction (cf. Prov 6:25), but another would be her economic significance. The dowry was capital that the wife brought to the marriage,[14] and Proverbs 31:10-31 emphasizes the major role of Israelite wives in the family economy. Children are noticeably absent from the list. This may be because their function in a family is not primarily economic and thus not as likely to be objects of coveting.

In Deuteronomy 5, however, the word *bayit* means "house" rather than "household." This is probably why it is transposed with the word "wife" and follows the second verb. The effect is to create two parallel clauses rather than a summary clause followed by a detailed list as in Exodus. The first clause prohibits coveting a neighbor's wife, while the second clause prohibits desire for his house or field, male or female slave, ox or donkey, or any other possessions. The addition of "field" makes three pairs and a concluding phrase, a total of seven items.[15] Thus the two clauses forbid the coveting of family and property, "the kernel of a man's existence" (Weinfeld 1991). The first

---

[12]LXX harmonizes these differences, so the form in Exodus is the same as in Deuteronomy, and the same word is used to translate both חמד and אוה. It also adds "or any of his livestock" after "ox or donkey," probably influenced by Deut 5:14.

[13]Cf. Gen 7:1; Deut 11:6. See Jepsen 1967: esp. 295; Durham 1987; Houtman 1996.

[14]E.g., Gen 31:14-16; Josh 15:16-19; 1 Kings 9:16; cf. Vasholz 1987; Westbrook 1991; 2003a: 60-62; Matlock 2007: 303-4.

[15]Cf. Gen 39:5; 2 Kings 8:3, 5; Is 5:8; Mic 2:2 for the pairing of "house" and "field."

relates to the seventh commandment (adultery), while the second relates to the eighth (theft).

It has been suggested the change in the order of the words "house[hold]" and "wife" in the two versions of the commandment is due to the higher status of women in the thought of the Deuteronomic editors.[16] Moran (1967) disputes this, arguing that the last part of the commandment reflects a traditional type of list of possessions in the ancient Near East, especially at Ugarit, so the version in Deuteronomy could be as old as that in Exodus. Whatever the precise social status of women may have been in ancient societies, a man's wife is not included in such lists of possessions because neither in Israel nor at Ugarit was she regarded as a saleable item. Concerning the lists in the two versions of the tenth commandment, "what the items have in common is not that they are pieces of property, but that they are typical of what may be the object of a neighbor's coveting" (Wright 1990: 197).

Apart from the Decalogue, Old Testament law makes little reference to coveting, and it never appears in the Book of the Covenant or Holiness Code and rarely in Deuteronomy. In his second sermon, Moses warns that pagan images seized in battle could lead to idolatry: "Do not covet the silver and gold on them, and do not take it for yourselves, or you will be ensnared by it, for it is detestable to the LORD your God" (Deut 7:25). But the only specific biblical law on coveting is the tenth commandment in its two versions.

Intention or action? A crucial issue for interpretation is whether the tenth commandment is concerned with intention or action. At first sight, most modern readers would probably assume the former, that the commandment prohibits desiring something that belongs to someone else. But quite a few interpreters, ancient and modern, have understood it to be concerned with attempts to acquire another person's property, not merely desire or covetous thoughts. For example, Rabbi Simeon Bar Yokhai defined coveting as "when one exerts pressure to obtain possession," and Rabbi Ishmael argued on the basis of Deuteronomy 7:25 that what was forbidden was not mere desire, nor even its verbal expression, but acting on that desire.[17] A similar interpretation of the tenth commandment as concerned with action, not just intention, was proposed in the nineteenth century by Ernst Meier

---

[16]E.g., Phillips 1983: 6; Weinfeld 1991. There may be some truth in this, but Wright (1990: 90-92) points out the weaknesses in Phillips's extreme version of the theory.

[17]Greenberg 1985: esp. 107-8; Rofé 1985: 45-46.

(1846) and in the early twentieth century by Johannes Herrmann (1927), apparently unaware of the rabbinic precedent. In my view, however, there is no adequate reason to depart from a straightforward reading of the text, that the tenth commandment is concerned with thoughts and intentions, as I have argued in detail elsewhere.[18] In this way it complements the first eight commandments that focus on deeds and the ninth that deals with words.

Thoughts are significant. It is not just that good or bad thoughts can lead to words and deeds that affect other people. God is concerned with the whole of life, including those parts that are invisible to other people (cf. Gen 6:5; 1 Sam 16:7; Ps 139; Jer 1:5; Jn 2:24-25; Rom 8:27). Wrong thoughts are wrong in themselves and are therefore to be avoided whether or not they lead to wrong deeds. No punishment is specified for coveting because just punishment can only be carried out when there is adequate proof of an offense, which is impossible in this case. Nevertheless, the people of God are encouraged to be satisfied with nothing less than the best (cf. Lev 19:2; Deut 18:13; Mt 5:48; Jas 1:4), even if there are no penalties to enforce obedience. So the tenth commandment indicates that God desires not only faithful worshipers, nor those who avoid gross sins against other human beings, but people who are pure in heart and mind (cf. Ps 24:3-4; 51:6-10; Mt 5:8; Rom 12:2; Phil 4:8).

It seems the tenth commandment has been deliberately formulated to indicate the importance of thoughts in the life of God's people. In general, the Decalogue lists serious offenses, and it should be possible to refrain from committing these with determined effort. In fact, were it not for the tenth commandment, some people might conclude that they have kept the law perfectly. Jesus meets a rich man who seems to think this: "All these I have kept since I was a boy," he claims (Lk 18:21). Interestingly, the selection of commandments Jesus mentions does not include the tenth, and the man's answer might have been different if it had. The ensuing conversation indicates that material possessions have an excessive importance in his life.

To return to the question posed at the beginning of this chapter, the tenth commandment really does mean what it says. The sixth to ninth commandments concern relationships with neighbors, forbidding us to deprive others

---

[18]Baker 2005b: 13-20. See also Moran 1967; Jackson 1971; Durham 1987; Weinfeld 1991; Houtman 1996; Levine 2000: 141-59; Christensen 2001; McConville 2002a; Biddle 2003; Botica 2014. For a different view, see Chaney 2004.

of their legitimate rights to life, marriage, property, and reputation. The tenth moves from deeds and words to intentions: "Don't even think about it!"

REFLECTION

A unique law. As we have seen, the tenth commandment is unique among the laws of the ancient Near East. No other known law refers to coveting except the clause about theft in the Laws of Hammurabi, which mentions coveting and looting goods in a burning house (CH §25). Even there it is not said that coveting would be a problem in itself if it did not lead to theft. Clearly Old Testament law is distinctive in counting coveting as an offense— indeed a serious offense, judging by the fact it is included in the Decalogue.

The same is true in most modern societies, where no laws against coveting exist.[19] On the contrary, coveting is actively encouraged by popular culture and peer pressure. Once upon a time, social status depended on one's family name or profession; now it depends more on status goods and behavior—wearing designer clothes, driving luxury cars, eating at expensive restaurants. We are bombarded by advertisements promoting conspicuous consumption. Companies use increasingly aggressive techniques to persuade us to part with our money: ongoing "sales," half-price offers, interest-free credit, and so-called "free" gifts. Whole television channels are sustained by advertising, and bundles of junk mail are delivered to mailboxes each week.

One of my favorite companies is Google, though sometimes I feel uneasy because it knows so much about me. The power of its search engine, scope of its maps, storage of incredible amounts of data, and countless other innovative projects are simply astonishing. On a trivial level, did you know they once rented two hundred goats for a week to trim the grass at Googleplex, their headquarters in California? On a bigger issue, the annual carbon emissions from people googling at their computers has been calculated as equivalent to the weight of twenty thousand African elephants.[20] But my point

---

[19]Though Burnside (2010c: 285-88) explains that the modern English law of theft tends to be subjective, so that a person who intends to steal goods may be said to have appropriated them even if the owner has not yet been deprived of their property or has consented to property being taken.

[20]Jackson Chung, "Exactly How Big IS Google?," MakeUseOf, January 31, 2014, www.makeuseof .com/tag/exactly-big-google.

here is simply to note that virtually all of this is paid for by advertising—taking advantage of our natural instinct to covet.

Coveting is the essence of "keeping up with the Joneses," an idiom popularized by an American comic strip in the early part of the twentieth century (1913–1938) that highlighted comparison with one's neighbor as the motivation for accumulation of material goods. However, according to the Bible, we should *love* the Joneses rather than try to keep up with them or covet their possessions. As Craigie (1976: 164) expresses it, "The neighbor's world is not one to be coveted, but the neighbor is to be loved as a fellow member of the family of God."

Danger! Coveting is dangerous. Often it is the first step toward breaking other commandments: lust leads to adultery, greed leads to stealing, and so on. Several examples are given in the Old Testament of people who covet and the consequences that follow. Lot covets the fertile valley of the Jordan and leaves the Promised Land to live in sinful Sodom, later losing both his wife and his dignity (Gen 14:10-13; 19). Achan covets the silver and gold of Jericho (Josh 7:21), bringing disaster on his family and the whole nation. David covets his neighbor's wife and sets in motion a train of events that leads to adultery, murder, and eventually the death of his son (2 Sam 11–12).

In the New Testament, Jesus warns more than once about the danger of covetous and impure thoughts:

> Out of the heart come evil thoughts—murder, adultery, sexual immorality, theft, false testimony, slander. (Mt 15:19)

> Be on your guard against all kinds of greed; life does not consist in an abundance of possessions. (Lk 12:15)

Likewise, Paul urges Christians to "put to death . . . whatever belongs to your earthly nature: sexual immorality, impurity, lust, evil desires and greed, which is idolatry" (Col 3:5; cf. Rom 1:29; Eph 5:3, 5). His later counsel is well known though sometimes incorrectly quoted as "money is the root of all evil":

> For the love of money is a root of all kinds of evil. Some people, eager for money, have wandered from the faith and pierced themselves with many griefs. (1 Tim 6:10)

The most common reasons for breaking almost any of the commandments are probably greed and self-interest (often expressed more politely as "self-fulfillment" or "realizing one's potential"). In contrast, God's people are called to worship him and serve others (Mk 12:28-34, quoting Deut 6:5 and Lev 19:18). Their priorities should be loving God and neighbor rather than self-fulfillment or personal desires. This does not necessarily mean living in poverty or discomfort, for—as Jesus promises in the Sermon on the Mount—God will supply the needs of those who put his kingdom first (Mt 6:33). But the bottom line is a choice between God and mammon, for we cannot serve two masters (Mt 6:24).

Contentment. Coveting is a serious matter, by no means least among the laws of Israel. Probably no other commandment has greater theological and ethical importance except the first. For the first is fundamental to a relationship with God, the last to our attitude toward fellow human beings. This attitude may be summed up as contentment with what God gives us rather than desiring things he gives to others. In today's materialistic world, such an attitude is countercultural and certainly not economically correct, but it is what the tenth commandment requires of the people of God.

On this last point, the tenth commandment is applicable to economics, condemning greed and exploitation and advocating gratitude and contentment.[21] It counteracted the Canaanite economic system, where a small proportion of the population controlled the majority of the goods produced, a system that increasingly influenced Israelite life during the monarchy. Even though the methods used by the wealthy to acquire land at the expense of smallholders may not be illegal, they are fundamentally unacceptable for the people of God, stemming from ambitions that are opposed to the tenth commandment.[22] It would not be difficult to apply these prophetic critiques to many situations in the modern world.

How can we achieve such contentment? Agur's answer is to pray, and his prayer is recorded toward the end of Proverbs:

Two things I ask of you, LORD;
do not refuse me before I die:

---

[21]On greed and exploitation, see also Mic 2:1-2 (cf. Is 5:8), where the same idea is expressed without using the word "covet." On gratitude and contentment, see Deut 8:10-14; Ps 62:10; Prov 30:7-9; Phil 4:11-12; 1 Tim 6:6-8; Heb 13:5. For theological reflections on consumerism, see Bartholomew and Moritz 2000.

[22]Wright 1990: 139; cf. Premnath 1988; Ceresko 1988.

Keep falsehood and lies far from me;
>   give me neither poverty nor riches,
>   but give me only my daily bread.
Otherwise, I may have too much and disown you
>   and say, "Who is the LORD?"
Or I may become poor and steal,
>   and so dishonor the name of my God. (Prov 30:7-9)

Paul gives his testimony. For him, contentment is something learned in the varied experiences of life:

> I have learned to be content whatever the circumstances. I know what it is to be in need, and I know what it is to have plenty. I have learned the secret of being content in any and every situation, whether well fed or hungry, whether living in plenty or in want. (Phil 4:11-12; cf. 1 Tim 6:6-8)

And the letter to the Hebrews reminds its readers that, because God is and will always be with them, they should be content with his provision for their needs:

> Keep your lives free from the love of money and be content with what you have, because God has said,
> "Never will I leave you; never will I forsake you." (Heb 13:5)

THE DECALOGUE TODAY

LIVING AS THE PEOPLE OF GOD

Some people think of law as boring or burdensome, but that is not how it is perceived in the Bible. It is a blessing rather than a burden, bringing wisdom and joy (Ps 19:7-11). The people of God are given laws for life (Deut 4:1; 6:1-2; 30:16; cf. 1 Kings 3:14; Neh 9:29; Prov 4:4; 7:2; Mt 19:17). These laws are for their "own good" (Deut 10:13) because obedience will lead to a good life in the Promised Land (Deut 4:40; 5:16, 29; 6:3, 18).

LAWS FOR LIFE

The purpose of the law for God's people is summed up toward the end of Deuteronomy. As he prepares the people for entering the Promised Land, Moses' last sermon has the theme "choose life":

> See, I set before you today life and prosperity, death and destruction. For I
> command you today to love the LORD your God, to walk in obedience to him,
> and to keep his commands, decrees and laws; then you will live and increase,
> and the LORD your God will bless you in the land. . . . But if your heart turns
> away and you are not obedient, and if you are drawn away to bow down to
> other gods and worship them, I declare to you this day that you will certainly
> be destroyed. . . . I have set before you life and death, blessings and curses.
> Now choose life, so that you and your children may live and that you may love
> the LORD your God, listen to his voice, and hold fast to him. For the LORD is
> your life. (Deut 30:15-20)

God has saved his people by grace and granted them new life. Moses has now given them God's laws to guide them in living this new life. He invites them to respond by choosing life in relationship with God rather than the alternative: death and destruction. To quote von Rad (1957: 193-94):

> Israel understood the revelation of the commandments as a saving event of the first rank, and celebrated it as such. Israel . . . recognized [the Decalogue] as a revelation vouchsafed to her at a particular moment in her history, through which she was offered the saving gift of life. The proclamation of the commandments and the promise of life were obviously closely connected. . . . With the commandments [God] has offered to his people life; with the hearing of the commandments Israel was placed in the position of decision for life or death.

It is crucial to remember the distinction between salvation by obedience to the law and obedience to the law as a response to salvation. The Old Testament—like the New—affirms that salvation is received by faith, not achieved by works. So when God calls Israel to make a decision for life or death, the commandments are not conditions for the covenant. The covenant does not come into effect on the basis of Israel's obedience. On the contrary, Israel has already become the people of God (Deut 27:9), and on this basis they are called to keep his commandments (Deut 27:10).

As the constitution of God's people, the Decalogue states vital principles for maintaining a good relationship with God and other members of the community and gives reasons why it is important to do so. In the words of Childs (1974: 398), "the Decalogue provides the basis for the covenant with all of Israel," so "to transgress is not to commit a misdemeanor but to break the very fiber of which the divine-human relation consists." Thus it is not human sanctions that are specified but warnings of punishment and promises of blessing from God.

The Decalogue was not only significant in the formative period of Israel's history but also in its ongoing life. It expresses ethical principles that underlie more detailed laws in Exodus, Leviticus, and Deuteronomy, and it was a source of inspiration for worship, wisdom, and prophecy in ancient Israel. Since then it has had an extensive influence on law, religion, and ethics in many parts of the world. However, the fact that the Decalogue was originally addressed to Israel, the Old Testament people of God, raises the question of how far it should apply to Christians—or indeed anyone else—today. So I turn to Jesus' teaching on the subject.

JESUS AND THE DECALOGUE

In his Sermon on the Mount, Jesus has strong words about the lasting value of Old Testament law:

> Do not think that I have come to abolish the Law or the Prophets; I have not come to abolish them but to fulfill them. For truly I tell you, until heaven and earth disappear, not the smallest letter, not the least stroke of a pen, will by any means disappear from the Law until everything is accomplished. Therefore anyone who sets aside one of the least of these commands and teaches others accordingly will be called least in the kingdom of heaven, but whoever practices and teaches these commands will be called great in the kingdom of heaven. (Mt 5:17-19)

Jesus does not interpret the law legalistically, as we see from his debates with the Pharisees and other Jewish groups in the Gospels, but neither does he abrogate it. Immediately after the words quoted above, Matthew records Jesus' contemporary reflections on several laws. Jesus begins by quoting the commandments on homicide and adultery, implying their validity, and encourages his followers to go beyond the letter of the law by obeying it in their words and thoughts as well as deeds (Mt 5:21-30). He then interprets the law of divorce in the light of the commandment on adultery, implying the priority of the commandment over the concession Moses granted, which permitted divorce in some circumstances (Mt 5:31-32; cf. Mt 19:3-9; Deut 24:1-4).[1]

At one point Jesus appears to disagree with the law:

> You have heard that it was said, "Love your neighbor and hate your enemy." But I tell you, love your enemies and pray for those who persecute you, that you may be children of your Father in heaven. He causes his sun to rise on the evil and the good, and sends rain on the righteous and the unrighteous. (Mt 5:43-45)

So does Jesus change Old Testament law here? No! In fact, the Old Testament doesn't tell people to hate enemies at all. If anything, they are to love

---

[1]For a detailed study of the relationship between the Decalogue and the Sermon on the Mount, see Lioy 2004.

them (Ex 23:4-5; Prov 25:21; cf. 1 Sam 24:4, 10, 18-19). Jesus is rejecting a popular misquotation of the law, not what it actually says. Once again, Jesus takes up an Old Testament law ("love your neighbor as yourself"; cf. Lev 19:18) and extends it further. He encourages his followers to go beyond loving their neighbors to loving enemies as well.

There are debates in New Testament times about circumcision and about clean and unclean foods, but there are no disputes about the authority of the Decalogue. Jesus interprets the sabbath law more flexibly than the Pharisees, provoking them to wrath, but he does not dispute its ongoing validity (Mk 2:23–3:6). When he sees Jewish tradition taking priority over the commandment about honoring parents, he affirms the authority of the commandment rather than the tradition (Mt 15:1-6).

Probably most readers of this book keep most of the commandments most of the time. However, Jesus encourages his followers not merely to keep the letter of the law but to follow its spirit, aiming for perfection as imitators of God (Mt 5:48). They are to be satisfied with nothing less than wholehearted love for God and neighbor—the real goal of the law (Mt 22:40; cf. Rom 13:8-10; Jas 2:8).

As we have seen, the Decalogue is the basis for Old Testament ethics, supplemented by the detailed laws, wisdom teaching, and prophetic addresses. It indicates how God intended his people to live in relationship with him and each other. Likewise, along with Jesus' Sermon on the Mount and other ethical teaching in both the Old and New Testaments, I believe the Decalogue should be the starting point for Christian ethics. We have no authority to annul or alter it, even though new laws, wisdom, and prophecy may be required to apply it in the new situations we face these days.[2]

To sum up, the Decalogue is the constitution of the people of God, written in stone by the supreme Lawgiver. In Old and New Testament times it provided the basis for life in the covenant community and has continued to do so for many Jews ever since. Christians too, grafted into the people of

---

[2]Several works on Christian ethics begin with, or make substantial use of, the Decalogue: e.g., Verkuyl 1978; Frame 2008. Many books on the Decalogue, both Jewish and Christian, include reflection on its ethical relevance in the world today: e.g., Davidman 1953; Goldman 1956; Wallace 1965; Lochman 1979; Jefferson 1982; Davies 1990; Field 1992; Briscoe 1994; Lehmann 1995; Harrelson 1997; Hauerwas and Willimon 1999; Mikva 1999; Tomasino 2000; Ryken 2003; Brown 2004; Braaten and Seitz 2005; Harrelson 2006; Clowney and Jones 2007; van Harn 2007; Klinghoffer 2007; Leininger 2007; Packer 2007; Miller 2009; Rooker 2010; Porter 2011.

God by faith (Rom 11:11-24), recognize the Decalogue as God's gift to them. Indeed for all who have ears to hear, whatever their creed, this unique and fascinating set of laws still has a great deal to say about relationships with God and other people. It contains essential principles for living as the people of God that are as relevant in the twenty-first century as when they were first given.

BIBLIOGRAPHY

DECALOGUE (GENERAL)

Aaron, David H. 2006. *Etched in Stone: The Emergence of the Decalogue*. New York: T&T Clark.

Addis, W. E. 1899. "Decalogue." In *Encyclopaedia Biblica*, edited by T. K. Cheyne and J. Sutherland Black, 1:1049-51. London: Black.

Albeck, Shalom. 1985. "The Ten Commandments and the Essence of Religious Faith." In *The Ten Commandments in History and Tradition*, edited by Ben-Zion Segal and Gershon Levi, 261-89. Publications of the Perry Foundation for Biblical Research. Jerusalem: Magnes Press, 1990. Translated from Hebrew, 1985.

Amir, Yehoshua. 1985. "The Decalogue According to Philo." In *The Ten Commandments in History and Tradition*, edited by Ben-Zion Segal and Gershon Levi, 121-60. Publications of the Perry Foundation for Biblical Research. Jerusalem: Magnes Press, 1990. Translated from Hebrew, 1985.

Bailey, Ivor. 1991. "The Ten Commandments." *ExpTim* 102: 80-81, 114-15, 144-45, 175-76, 206-7, 237-38, 271-72, 307-8, 339-40, 370-71.

Bailey, Kenneth C. 1963. "The Decalogue as Morality and Ethics." *Theology Today* 20: 183-95.

Baker, David L. 2004. "Written in Stone? The Ten Commandments Then and Now." *Whitefield Briefing* 9, no. 3.

———. 2005a. "The Finger of God and the Forming of a Nation: The Origin and Purpose of the Decalogue." *TynBul* 56, no. 1: 1-24.

———. 2005c. "Ten Commandments, Two Tablets: The Shape of the Decalogue." *Themelios* 30, no. 3: 6-22.

Block, Daniel I. 2011. "Reading the Decalogue Right to Left: The Ten Principles of Covenant Relationship in the Hebrew Bible." In *How I Love Your Torah, O Lord! Studies in the Book of Deuteronomy*, 21-60. Eugene, OR: Cascade.

Braaten, Carl E., and Christopher R. Seitz, eds. 2005. *I Am the Lord Your God: Christian Reflections on the Ten Commandments*. Grand Rapids: Eerdmans.

Braulik, Georg. 1991. *Die deuteronomischen Gesetze und der Dekalog: Studien zum Aufbau von Deuteronomium 12–26*. Stuttgarter Bibelstudien 145. Stuttgart: Katholisches Bibelwerk.

Briscoe, D. Stuart. 1994. *The Ten Commandments: Playing by the Rules*. Rev. ed. Foundations of the Faith. Carlisle: OM Publishing.

Brown, William P., ed. 2004. *The Ten Commandments: The Reciprocity of Faithfulness*. Library of Theological Ethics. Louisville, KY: Westminster John Knox.

Calvin, John. 1555. *John Calvin's Sermons on the Ten Commandments*. Edited by Benjamin W. Farley. Grand Rapids: Baker, 1980. Translated from French, 1555.

Cazelles, Henri. 1969. "Les origines du Décalogue." *Eretz-Israel* 9: 14-19.

Charles, R. H. 1926. *The Decalogue*. 2nd ed. Warburton Lectures, 1919-1923. Edinburgh: T&T Clark.

Clines, David J. A. 1995. "The Ten Commandments, Reading from Left to Right." In *Interested Parties: The Ideology of Writers and Readers of the Hebrew Bible*, 26-45. JSOTSup 205. Sheffield: Sheffield Academic.

———. 2015. "The Decalogue as the Prohibition of Theft." In *New Perspectives on Old Testament Prophecy and History: Essays in Honour of Hans M. Barstad*, edited by Rannfrid I. Thelle, Terje Stordalen, and Mervyn E. J. Richardson, 293-305. Leiden: Brill.

Clowney, Edmund P., and Rebecca Clowney Jones. 2007. *How Jesus Transforms the Ten Commandments*. Phillipsburg, NJ: P&R.

Cohen, Jeffrey M. 1994. "The Nature of the Decalogue." *JBQ* 22: 173-77.

Collins, Raymond F. 1992. "Ten Commandments." In *ABD*, vol. 6: 383-87.

Coogan, Michael. 2014. *The Ten Commandments: A Short History of an Ancient Text*. New Haven: Yale University Press.

Crüsemann, Frank. 1983. *Bewahrung der Freiheit: Das Thema des Dekalogs in Sozialgeschichtlicher Perspektive*. Kaiser Traktate 78. Munich: Kaiser.

Davidman, Joy. 1953. *Smoke on the Mountain: An Interpretation of the Ten Commandments*. Philadelphia: Westminster.

Davies, Rupert E. 1990. *Making Sense of the Commandments*. London: Epworth.

Derby, Josiah. 1993b. "The Two Tablets of the Covenant." *JBQ* 21: 73-79.

Ebeling, Gerhard. 1973. *Die Zehn Gebote*. Tübingen: Mohr.

Eichrodt, Walther. 1957. "The Law and the Gospel: The Meaning of the Ten Commandments in Israel and for Us." *Interpretation* 11: 23-40.

Field, David 1992. *God's Good Life: The Ten Commandments for the 21st Century*. Leicester, England: Inter-Varsity Press.

Freedman, David Noel. 2000. *The Nine Commandments: Uncovering a Hidden Pattern of Crime and Punishment in the Hebrew Bible*. Anchor Bible Reference Library. New York: Doubleday.

Freund, Richard A. 1998. "The Decalogue in Early Judaism and Christianity." In *The Function of Scripture in Early Jewish and Christian Tradition*, edited by Craig A. Evans and James A. Sanders, 124-41. JSNTSup 154. Sheffield: Sheffield Academic.

Frevel, Christian, Michael Konkel, and Johannes Schnocks, eds. 2005. *Die Zehn Worte: Der Dekalog als Testfall der Pentateuchkritik*. Quaestiones Disputatae 212. Freiburg, Germany: Herder.

Gledhill, Ruth. 2004. "Ten Commandments Fall on Stony Ground." *The Times*, September 3. www.thetimes.co.uk/tto/news/uk/article1928630.ece.

Goldman, Solomon. 1956. *The Ten Commandments*. Edited by Maurice Samuel. Chicago: University of Chicago Press.

Graupner, Axel. 1987. "Zum Verhältnis der beiden Dekalogfassungen Ex 20 und Dtn 5: Ein Gespräch mit Frank-Lothar Hossfeld." *ZAW* 99: 308-29.

———. 2000. "Vom Sinai zum Horeb oder vom Horeb zum Sinai? Zur Intention der Doppelüberlieferung des Dekalogs." In *Verbindungslinien: Festschrift für Werner H. Schmidt zum 65. Geburtstag*, edited by Axel Graupner, Holger Delkurt, and Alexander B. Ernst, 85-101. Neukirchen-Vluyn, Germany: Neukirchener.

———. 2001. "Die Zehn Gebote im Rahmen alttestamentlicher Ethik: Anmerkungen zum gegenwärtigen Stand der Forschung." In *Weisheit, Ethos und Gebot*, edited by Henning Graf Reventlow, 61-95. Biblisch-Theologische Studien 43. Neukirchen-Vluyn, Germany: Neukirchener.

Greenberg, Moshe. 1985. "The Decalogue Tradition Critically Examined." In *The Ten Commandments in History and Tradition*, edited by Ben-Zion Segal and Gershon Levi, 83-119. Publications of the Perry Foundation for Biblical Research. Jerusalem: Magnes, 1990. Translated from Hebrew, 1985.

Greenman, Jeffrey P., and Timothy Larsen, eds. 2012. *The Decalogue Through the Centuries: From the Hebrew Scriptures to Benedict XVI*. Louisville, KY: Westminster John Knox.

Hakala, Diane Louise. 2014. "The Decalogue as a Summary of the Law: Jewish and New Testament Approaches." PhD diss., University of Cambridge.

Hamel, Édouard. 1969. *Les dix paroles: Perspectives Bibliques*. Essais pour notre temps, Section de théologie 7. Montreal: Bellarmin.

van Harn, Roger E., ed. 2007. *The Ten Commandments for Jews, Christians, and Others*. Grand Rapids: Eerdmans.

Harrelson, Walter J. 1997. *The Ten Commandments and Human Rights*. Rev. ed. Macon, GA: Mercer University Press.

———. 2006. *The Ten Commandments for Today*. Louisville, KY: Westminster John Knox.

Hauerwas, Stanley M., and William H. Willimon. 1999. *The Truth About God: The Ten Commandments in Christian Life*. Nashville, TN: Abingdon.

Himbaza, Innocent. 2004. *Le Décalogue et l'histoire du texte: Etudes des formes textuelles du Décalogue et leurs implications dans l'histoire du texte de l'Ancien Testament*. OBO 207. Göttingen: Vandenhoeck & Ruprecht.

Hossfeld, Frank-Lothar. 1982. *Der Dekalog: seine Späten Fassungen, die Originale Komposition und seine Vorstufen*. OBO 45. Göttingen: Vandenhoeck & Ruprecht.

Jackson, Bernard S. 1995. "Modelling Biblical Law: The Covenant Code." *Chicago-Kent Law Review* 70: 1745-1827.

Jacob, Benno. 1923. "The Decalogue." *JQR* 14: 141-87.

Jefferson, Philip, ed. 1982. *Voice from the Mountain: New Life for the Old Law*. Toronto: Anglican Book Centre.

Jepsen, Alfred. 1967. "Beiträge zur Auslegung und Geschichte des Dekalogs." *ZAW* 79: 275-304.

Johnstone, William. 1989. "The 'Ten Commandments': Some Recent Interpretations." *ExpTim* 100: 453-61.

Kapelrud, Arvid S. 1964. "Some Recent Points of View on the Time and Origin of the Decalogue." *Studia Theologica* 18: 81-90.

Kaufman, Stephen A. 1987. "The Second Table of the Decalogue and the Implicit Categories of Ancient Near Eastern Law." In *Love and Death in the Ancient Near East: Essays in Honor of Marvin H. Pope*, edited by John H. Marks and Robert M. Good, 111-16. Guilford, CT: Four Quarters.

Kline, Meredith G. 1960. "The Two Tables of the Covenant." *Westminster Theological Journal* 22: 133-46.

———. 1996. "Ten Commandments." In *New Bible Dictionary*, edited by D. R. W. Wood and I. Howard Marshall. 3rd ed. Downers Grove, IL: InterVarsity Press. Electronic edition.

Klinghoffer, David. 2007. *Shattered Tablets: Why We Ignore the Ten Commandments at Our Peril*. New York: Doubleday.

Köckert, Matthias. 2007. *Die Zehn Gebote*. Munich: Beck.

Koster, M. D. 1980. "The Numbering of the Ten Commandments in Some Peshitta Manuscripts." *VT* 30: 468-73.

Kratz, Reinhard Gregor. 1994. "Der Dekalog im Exodusbuch." *VT* 44: 205-38.

Kuntz, Paul Grimley. 2004. *The Ten Commandments in History: Mosaic Paradigms for a Well-Ordered Society*. Edited by Thomas D'Evelyn. Emory University Studies in Law and Religion. Grand Rapids: Eerdmans.

Lang, Bernhard. 1984. "Neues über den Dekalog." *Theologische Quartalschrift* 164: 58-65.

——. 1998. "The Decalogue in the Light of a Newly Published Palaeo-Hebrew Inscription (Hebrew Ostracon Moussaïeff no. 1)." *JSOT* 77: 21-25.

——. 2003. "Twelve Commandments—Three Stages: A New Theory on the Formation of the Decalogue." In *Reading from Right to Left: Essays on the Hebrew Bible in Honour of David J. A. Clines*, edited by J. Cheryl Exum and H. G. M. Williamson, 290-300. JSOTSup 373. London: Sheffield Academic.

——. 2006. "The Number Ten and the Iniquity of the Fathers: A New Interpretation of the Decalogue." *ZAW* 118: 218-38.

Lehmann, Paul L. 1995. *The Decalogue and a Human Future: The Meaning of the Commandments for Making and Keeping Human Life Human*. Grand Rapids: Eerdmans.

Leininger, David E. 2007. *God of Justice: A Look at the Ten Commandments for the 21st Century*. Lima, OH: CSS.

Lemaire, André. 1981. "Le Décalogue: Essai d'histoire de la redaction." In *Mélanges bibliques et orientaux en l'honneur de M. Henri Cazelles*, edited by André Caquot and M. Delcor, 259-95. Alter Orient und Altes Testament 212. Kevelaer: Butzon & Bercker.

Levin, Christoph. 1985. "Der Dekalog am Sinai." *VT* 35: 165-91.

Lioy, Dan. 2004. *The Decalogue in the Sermon on the Mount*. Studies in Biblical Literature 66. New York: Lang.

Lloyd, David. 2004. "Any Number of Commandments." *The Times*, September 13.

Lochman, Jan Milič. 1979. *Signposts to Freedom: The Ten Commandments and Christian Ethics*. Minneapolis: Augsburg, 1982. Translated from German, 1979.

Markl, Dominik. 2007. *Der Dekalog als Verfassung des Gottesvolkes: Die Brennpunkte einer Rechtshermeneutik des Pentateuch in Exodus 19–24 und Deuteronomium 5*. Freiburg, Germany: Herder.

——. 2013a. "The Ten Words Revealed and Revisited: The Origins of Law and Legal Hermeneutics in the Pentateuch." In *The Decalogue and Its Cultural Influence*, edited by Dominik Markl, 13-27. Hebrew Bible Monographs 58. Sheffield: Sheffield Phoenix.

——, ed. 2013b. *The Decalogue and Its Cultural Influence*. Hebrew Bible Monographs 58. Sheffield: Sheffield Phoenix.

Meier, Ernst. 1846. *Die Ursprüngliche Form des Dekalogs*. Mannheim, Germany: Bassermann.

Mikva, Rachel S., ed. 1999. *Broken Tablets: Restoring the Ten Commandments and Ourselves*. Woodstock, VT: Jewish Lights.

Millard, Alan R. 1994. "Re-Creating the Tablets of the Law." *Bible Review* 10, no. 1: 48-53.

———. 2007. "The Tablets in the Ark." In *Reading the Law: Studies in Honour of Gordon J. Wenham*, edited by J. Gordon McConville and Karl Möller, 254-66. New York: T&T Clark.

Miller, Patrick D. 1989. "The Place of the Decalogue in the Old Testament and Its Law." *Interpretation* 43: 229-42.

———. 2002. "The Good Neighborhood: Identity and Community Through the Commandments." In *Character and Scripture: Moral Formation, Community, and Biblical Interpretation*, edited by William P. Brown, 55-72. Grand Rapids: Eerdmans.

———. 2004b. "The Sufficiency and Insufficiency of the Commandments." In *The Way of the Lord: Essays in Old Testament Theology*, 17-36. FAT 39. Tübingen: Mohr Siebeck.

———. 2004c. "'That It May Go Well with You': The Commandments and the Common Good." In *The Way of the Lord: Essays in Old Testament Theology*, 136-63. FAT 39. Tübingen: Mohr Siebeck.

———. 2009. *The Ten Commandments*. Interpretation. Louisville, KY: Westminster John Knox.

Mowinckel, Sigmund. 1927. *Le Décalogue*. Études d'histoire et de Philosophie Religieuses 16. Paris: Félix Alcan.

Nicholson, Ernest W. 1977. "The Decalogue as the Direct Address of God." *VT* 27: 422-33.

Nielsen, Eduard. 1965. *The Ten Commandments in New Perspective: A Traditio-Historical Approach*. SBT 2.7. London: SCM, 1968. Translated from German, 1965.

Otto, Eckart. 1992. "Der Dekalog als Brennspiegel Israelitischer Rechtsgeschichte." In *Alttestamentliche Glaube und Biblische Theologie: Festschrift für Horst Dietrich Preuss*, edited by Jutta Hausmann and Hans-Jürgen Zobel, 59-68. Stuttgart: Kohlhammer.

Packer, James I. 2007. *God of Justice: A Look at the Ten Commandments for the 21st Century*. Lima, OH: CSS.

Phillips, Anthony. 1970. *Ancient Israel's Criminal Law: A New Approach to the Decalogue*. Oxford: Blackwell.

———. 1983a. "The Decalogue—Ancient Israel's Criminal Law." *JJS* 34: 1-20.

Porter, Daniel V. 2011. *Do the Ten Commandments Have a Universal Significance? God's Law as the Basis of a Global Culture*. Lewiston, NY: Mellen.

Reventlow, Henning Graf, and Yair Hoffman, eds. 2011. *The Decalogue in Jewish and Christian Tradition*. Library of Hebrew Bible/Old Testament Studies 509. New York: T&T Clark.

Rooker, Mark F. 2010. *The Ten Commandments: Ethics for the Twenty-First Century*. New American Commentary Studies in Bible & Theology. Nashville, TN: B&H.

Rowley, H. H. 1951. "Moses and the Decalogue." *BJRL* 34: 81-118. Reprinted with a few modifications in *Men of God*. London: Nelson, 1963: 1-36.

Ryken, Philip Graham. 2003. *Written in Stone: The Ten Commandments and Today's Moral Crisis*. Phillipsburg, NJ: P&R.

Schmidt, Werner H., Holger Delkurt, and Axel Graupner. 1993. *Die Zehn Gebote im Rahmen alttestamentlicher Ethik*. Erträge der Forschung 281. Darmstadt: Wissenschaftliche.

Segal, Ben-Zion, and Gershon Levi, eds. 1985. *The Ten Commandments in History and Tradition*. Publications of the Perry Foundation for Biblical Research. Jerusalem: Magnes, 1990. Translated from Hebrew, 1985.

Sivan, Hagith. 2004. *Between Woman, Man and God: A New Interpretation of the Ten Commandments*. JSOTSup 401. London: T&T Clark.

Slattery, Joseph A. 1979. "The Catechetical Use of the Decalogue from the End of the Catechumenate Through the Late Medieval Period." PhD diss., Catholic University of America.

Smith, Louis. 1991. "Original Sin as 'Envy': The Structure of the Biblical Decalogue." *Dialog* 30: 227-30.

Stamm, Johann Jakob, and Maurice Edward Andrew. 1967. *The Ten Commandments in Recent Research*. SBT 2.2. London: SCM.

Stevens, Marty E. 2004. "The Obedience of Trust: Recovering the Law as a Gift." In *The Ten Commandments: The Reciprocity of Faithfulness*, edited by William P. Brown, 133-45. Library of Theological Ethics. Louisville, KY: Westminster John Knox.

Sweeney, Marvin A. 2010. "The Nash Papyrus: Preview of Coming Attractions." *BAR* 36, no. 4: 43-48, 77.

Tappy, Ron E. 2000. "The Code of Kinship in the Ten Commandments." *RB* 107: 321-37.

Tomasino, Anthony J. 2000. *Written upon the Heart: The Ten Commandments for Today's Christian*. Eugene, OR: Wipf & Stock.

Verkuyl, Johannes. 1978. *Kapita Selekta*. Etika Kristen II/5. Reprint, Jakarta: BPK Gunung Mulia.

Wallace, Ronald S. 1965. *The Ten Commandments: A Study of Ethical Freedom*. Edinburgh: Oliver & Boyd.

Walton, John H. 2012. "The Decalogue Structure of the Deuteronomic Law." In *Interpreting Deuteronomy: Issues and Approaches*, edited by David G. Firth and Philip S. Johnston, 93-117. Nottingham: Apollos.

Weinfeld, Moshe. 1985a. "The Decalogue: Its Significance, Uniqueness, and Place in Israel's Tradition." In *Religion and Law: Biblical-Judaic and Islamic Perspectives*, edited by Edwin B. Firmage, Bernard G. Weiss, and John W. Welch, 3-47. Winona Lake, IN: Eisenbrauns, 1990. Translated from Hebrew, 1985. (Substantially the same as Weinfeld 1985b.)

———. 1985b. "The Uniqueness of the Decalogue and Its Place in Jewish Tradition." In *The Ten Commandments in History and Tradition*, edited by Ben-Zion Segal and Gershon Levi, 1-44. Publications of the Perry Foundation for Biblical Research. Jerusalem: Magnes, 1990. Translated from Hebrew, 1985. (Substantially the same as Weinfeld 1985a.)

Weiss, Meir. 1985. "The Decalogue in Prophetic Literature." In *The Ten Commandments in History and Tradition*, edited by Ben-Zion Segal and Gershon Levi, 67-81. Publications of the Perry Foundation for Biblical Research. Jerusalem: Magnes, 1990. Translated from Hebrew, 1985.

Wénin, André. 1997. "Le Décalogue: Approche contextuelle, théologie et anthropologie." In *La Loi dans l'un et l'autre Testament*, edited by Camille Focant, 9-43. Lectio Divina 168. Paris: Cerf.

Wright, Christopher J. H. 1979. "The Israelite Household and the Decalogue: The Social Background and Significance of Some Commandments." *TynBul* 30: 101-24.

Youngblood, Ronald. 1994. "Counting the Ten Commandments." *Bible Review* 10, no. 6: 30-35, 50, 52.

1. ONE GOD

Albright, William F. 1946. *From the Stone Age to Christianity: Monotheism and the Historical Process.* 2nd ed. Baltimore: Johns Hopkins. Paperback ed. Doubleday, 1957.

Allen, James P. 2006. "Monotheism in Ancient Egypt." In *Text, Artifact, and Image: Revealing Ancient Israelite Religion*, edited by Gary Beckman and Theodore J. Lewis, 319-25. Brown Judaic Studies 346. Providence, RI: Brown University.

Assmann, J. 2008. *Of God and Gods: Egypt, Israel, and the Rise of Monotheism.* George L. Mosse Series in Modern European Cultural and Intellectual History. Madison: University of Wisconsin Press.

Capetz, Paul E. 2004. "The First Commandment as a Theological and Ethical Principle." In *The Ten Commandments: The Reciprocity of Faithfulness*, edited by William P. Brown, 174-92. Library of Theological Ethics. Louisville, KY: Westminster John Knox.

Coetzee, Carel F. C. 2014. "Calvin's Interpretation of the First Commandment and the Implications for Religious Pluralism and Equality of Religion." *In die Skriflig* 48, no. 1: 1-9. www.indieskriflig.org.za/index.php/skriflig/article/viewFile/1810/2798.

Fretheim, Terence E. 2007. "God, OT View of." In *NIDB*, 2:603-18.

Gnuse, Robert Karl. 1997. *No Other Gods: Emergent Monotheism in Israel*. Sheffield: Sheffield Academic.

Hart, David Bentley. 2005. "God or Nothingness." In *I Am the Lord Your God: Christian Reflections on the Ten Commandments*, edited by Carl E. Braaten and Christopher R. Seitz, 55-76. Grand Rapids: Eerdmans.

Heiser, Michael S. 2008. "Monotheism, Polytheism, Monolatry, or Henotheism? Toward an Assessment of Divine Plurality in the Hebrew Bible." *BBR* 18, no. 1: 1-30.

Higginbotham, Carolyn R. 2006. "Ahkenaten." In *NIDB*, 1:92-94.

Knierim, Rolf P. 1965. "Das erste Gebot." *ZAW* 77: 20-39.

Lang, Bernhard. 1983. *Monotheism and the Prophetic Minority: An Essay in Biblical History and Sociology*. Social World of Biblical Antiquity 1. Sheffield: Almond.

MacDonald, Nathan. 2012. *Deuteronomy and the Meaning of "Monotheism."* 2nd ed. FAT 2.1. Tübingen: Mohr Siebeck.

MacDonald, Nathan, and Ken Brown, eds. 2014. *Monotheism in Late Prophetic and Early Apocalyptic Literature*. FAT 2.72. Tübingen: Mohr Siebeck.

McBride, S. Dean. 2006. "The Essence of Orthodoxy: Deuteronomy 5:6-10 and Exodus 20:2-6." *Interpretation* 60: 133-50.

Millard, Alan R. 1993. "Abraham, Akhenaten, Moses and Monotheism." In *He Swore an Oath: Biblical Themes from Genesis 12-50*, edited by Richard S. Hess, Gordon J. Wenham, and Philip E. Satterthwaite, 119-29. Cambridge: Tyndale House.

Miller, Patrick D. 2004a. *The God You Have: Politics and the First Commandment*. Minneapolis: Fortress.

de Moor, Johannes C. 1997. *The Rise of Yahwism: The Roots of Israelite Monotheism*. Rev. ed. Bibliotheca Ephemeridum Theologicarum Lovaniensium 91. Leuven: Peeters.

Oden, Thomas C. 2005. "No Other Gods." In *I Am the Lord Your God: Christian Reflections on the Ten Commandments*, edited by Carl E. Braaten and Christopher R. Seitz, 41-54. Grand Rapids: Eerdmans.

Patrick, Dale. 1994. "Is the Truth of the First Commandment Known by Reason?" *CBQ* 56: 423-41.

———. 1995. "The First Commandment in the Structure of the Pentateuch." *VT* 45: 107-18.

Petersen, David L. 1988. "Israel and Monotheism: The Unfinished Agenda." In *Canon, Theology, and Old Testament Interpretation: Essays in Honor of Brevard S. Childs*, edited by Gene M. Tucker, David L. Petersen, and Robert R. Wilson, 92-107. Philadelphia: Fortress.

Price, Timothy Shaun. 2008. "A Comparative Analysis of John Calvin and Martin Luther Concerning the First and Second Commandments." *Ashland Theological Journal* 40: 61-73.

Redford, Donald B. 1992. "Akhenaten." In *ABD*, vol. 1: 135-37.

———. 1997. "The Monotheism of Akhenaten." In *Aspects of Monotheism: How God Is One*, edited by Hershel Shanks and Jack Meinhardt, 11-26. Washington, DC: Biblical Archaeology Society.

Schmidt, Werner H. 1969. *Das erste Gebot: Seine Bedeutung für das Alte Testament.* Theologische Existenz heute, N.F. 165. Munich: Kaiser.

Scullion, John J. 1992. "God in the OT." In *ABD*, vol. 2: 1041-48.

Smith, Mark S. 2001. *The Origins of Biblical Monotheism: Israel's Polytheistic Background and the Ugaritic Texts.* Oxford: Oxford University Press.

———. 2002. *The Early History of God: Yahweh and the Other Deities in Ancient Israel.* 2nd ed. Grand Rapids: Eerdmans.

Zimmerli, Walther. 1953. "I Am Yahweh." In *I Am Yahweh*, edited by Walter Brueggemann, 1-28. Atlanta: John Knox, 1982. Translated from German, 1953.

2. IMAGES/IDOLATRY

Ararat, Nisan. 1995. "The Second Commandment: 'Thou Shalt Not Bow Down unto Them, nor Serve Them, for I the Lord Thy God Am a Jealous God.'" *Shofar: An Interdisciplinary Journal of Jewish Studies* 13: 44-57.

Baranov, Vladimir. 2007. "The Second Commandment and 'True Worship' in the Iconoclastic Controversy." In *Congress Volume Ljubljana 2007*, edited by André Lemaire, 541-54. Leiden: Brill.

Barton, John. 1999. "'The Work of Human Hands' (Psalm 115:4): Idolatry in the Old Testament." In *The Ten Commandments: The Reciprocity of Faithfulness*, edited by William P. Brown, 194-203. Library of Theological Ethics. Louisville, KY: Westminster John Knox, 2004. Reprinted from *Ex Auditu* 15 (1999): 63-72.

Barton, Stephen C., ed. 2007. *Idolatry: False Worship in the Bible, Early Judaism and Christianity.* London: T&T Clark.

Beale, G. K. 2008. *We Become What We Worship: A Biblical Theology of Idolatry.* Downers Grove, IL: InterVarsity Press.

Berlejung, Angelika. 1997. "Washing the Mouth: The Consecration of Divine Images in Mesopotamia." In *The Image and the Book: Iconic Cults, Aniconism, and the Rise of Book Religion in Israel and the Ancient Near East*, edited by Karel van der Toorn, 45-72. Contributions to Biblical Exegesis and Theology 21. Leuven: Peeters.

Bernhardt, Karl Heinz. 1956. *Gott und Bild: Ein Beitrag zur Begründung und Deutung des Bilderverbotes im Alten Testament.* Berlin: Evangelische Verlagsanstalt.

Boldrick, Stacy, Leslie Brubaker, and Richard Clay, eds. 2013. *Striking Images, Iconoclasms Past and Present*. Farnham, England: Ashgate.

Carroll, Robert P. 1977. "The Aniconic God and the Cult of Images." *Studia Theologica* 31: 51-64.

Clines, David J. A. 1968. "The Image of God in Man." *TynBul* 19: 53-103.

Curtis, Edward M. 1990. "Images in Mesopotamia and the Bible: A Comparative Study." In *The Bible in the Light of Cuneiform Literature: Scripture in Context III*, edited by William W. Hallo, Bruce William Jones, and Gerard L. Mattingly, 31-56. Ancient Near Eastern Texts and Studies 8. Lewiston, NY: Mellen.

———. 1992. "Idol, Idolatry." In *ABD*, vol. 3: 376-81.

Dick, Michael B., ed. 1999. *Born in Heaven, Made on Earth: The Making of the Cult Image in the Ancient Near East*. Winona Lake, IN: Eisenbrauns.

Dohmen, Christoph. 1985. *Das Bilderverbot: Seine Entstehung und seine Entwicklung im Alten Testament*. Bonner biblische Beiträge 62. Königstein, Germany: Hanstein.

———. 2012. *Studien zu Bilderverbot und Bildtheologie des Alten Testaments*. Stuttgart: Katholisches Bibelwerk.

Duff, Nancy J. 2006. "Locating God in All the Wrong Places: The Second Commandment and American Politics." *Interpretation* 60: 182-93.

Eire, Carlos M. N. 1986. *War Against the Idols: The Reformation of Worship from Erasmus to Calvin*. Cambridge: Cambridge University Press.

Elias, Jamal J. 2013. "The Taliban, Bamiyan, and Revisionist Iconoclasm." In *Striking Images, Iconoclasms Past and Present*, edited by Stacy Boldrick, Leslie Brubaker, and Richard Clay, 145-64. Farnham, England: Ashgate.

Evans, Carl D. 1995. "Cult Images, Royal Policies and the Origins of Aniconism." In *The Pitcher Is Broken*, edited by Steven W. Holloway and Lowell K. Handy, 192-212. JSOTSup 190. Sheffield: Sheffield Academic.

Goudzwaard, Bob. 1981. *Idols of Our Time*. Downers Grove, IL: InterVarsity Press, 1984. Translated from Dutch, 1981.

Gutmann, Joseph. 1961. "The 'Second Commandment' and the Image in Judaism." *HUCA* 32: 161-74.

Hadley, Judith M. 2000. *The Cult of Asherah in Ancient Israel and Judah: Evidence for a Hebrew Goddess*. University of Cambridge Oriental Publications 57. Cambridge: Cambridge University Press.

Halbertal, Moshe, and Avishai Margalit. 1992. *Idolatry*. Cambridge, MA: Harvard University Press. Translated from Hebrew.

Haug, Kari S., and Knut Holter. 2000. "No Graven Image? Reading the Second Commandment in a Thai Context." *Asia Journal of Theology* 14: 20-36.

Hendel, Ronald S. 1988. "The Social Origins of the Aniconic Tradition in Early Israel." *CBQ* 50: 365-82.

———. 1997. "Aniconism and Anthropomorphism in Ancient Israel." In *The Image and the Book: Iconic Cults, Aniconism, and the Rise of Book Religion in Israel and the Ancient Near East*, edited by Karel van der Toorn, 205-28. Contributions to Biblical Exegesis and Theology 21. Leuven: Peeters.

Holter, Knut. 2003. *Deuteronomy 4 and the Second Commandment*. Studies in Biblical Literature 60. New York: Lang.

Hurowitz, Victor. 1994. "Did King Solomon Violate the Second Commandment?" *Bible Review* 10, no. 5: 24-33, 57.

Jacobsen, Thorkild. 1987. "The Graven Image." In *Ancient Israelite Religion: Essays in Honor of Frank Moore Cross*, edited by Patrick D. Miller, Paul D. Hanson, and S. Dean McBride, 15-32. Philadelphia: Fortress.

Johnston, Philip S. 2003. "Figuring Out Figurines." *TynBul* 54, no. 2: 81-104.

Keel, Othmar, and Christoph Uehlinger. 1992. *Gods, Goddesses, and Images of God in Ancient Israel*. Translated by Thomas H. Trapp. Edinburgh: T&T Clark, 1998. Translated from German, 1992.

Kletter, Raz. 1996. *The Judean Pillar-Figurines and the Archaeology of Asherah*. British Archaeological Reports International Series 636. Oxford: Tempus Reparatum.

Konikoff, Carmel. 1973. *The Second Commandment and Its Interpretation in the Art of Ancient Israel*. Geneva: Imprimerie du Journal de Genève.

Lewis, Theodore J. 1998. "Divine Images and Aniconism in Ancient Israel." Review of *No Graven Image?*, by Tryggve N. D. Mettinger. *JAOS* 118 (1995): 36-53.

Lints, Richard. 2015. *Identity and Idolatry: The Image of God and Its Inversion*. New Studies in Biblical Theology 36. Nottingham: Apollos.

Lorton, David. 1999. "The Theology of Cult Statues in Ancient Egypt." In *Born in Heaven, Made on Earth: The Making of the Cult Image in the Ancient Near East*, edited by Michael B. Dick, 123-210. Winona Lake, IN: Eisenbrauns.

Marcus, Joel. 2006. "Idolatry in the New Testament." *Interpretation* 60: 152-64.

Mettinger, Tryggve N. D. 1995. *No Graven Image? Israelite Aniconism in Its Ancient Near Eastern Context*. Stockholm: Almqvist & Wiksell.

———. 1997. "Israelite Aniconism: Developments and Origins." In *The Image and the Book: Iconic Cults, Aniconism, and the Rise of Book Religion in Israel and the Ancient Near East*, edited by Karel van der Toorn, 173-204. Contributions to Biblical Exegesis and Theology 21. Leuven: Peeters.

Michalski, Sergiusz. 1993. *The Reformation and the Visual Arts: The Protestant Image Question in Western and Eastern Europe*. Christianity and Society in the Modern World. London: Routledge.

Moorey, P. R. S. 2003. *Idols of the People: Miniature Images of Clay in the Ancient Near East*. Oxford: Oxford University Press.

North, Christopher R. 1961. "The Essence of Idolatry." In *Von Ugarit nach Qumran: Beiträge zur alttestamentlichen und altorientalischen Forschung, Otto Eissfeldt zum 1,* edited by Johannes Hempel and Leonhard Rost, 151-60. BZAW 77. Berlin: Töpelmann.

Obbink, H. Th. 1929. "Jahwebilder." *ZAW* 47: 264-74.

Patrich, Joseph. 1990. *The Formation of Nabatean Art: Prohibition of a Graven Image Among the Nabateans.* Jerusalem: Magnes.

Phillips, John. 1973. *The Reformation of Images: Destruction of Art in England, 1535–1660.* Berkeley: University of California Press.

Price, Timothy Shaun. 2008. "A Comparative Analysis of John Calvin and Martin Luther Concerning the First and Second Commandments." *Ashland Theological Journal* 40: 61-73.

Reno, R. R. 2006. "Pride and Idolatry." *Interpretation* 60: 166-80.

Satyavani, Puttagunta. 2014. *Seeing the Face of God: Exploring an Old Testament Theme.* Carlisle, England: Langham Monographs.

Schmidt, Brian B. 1995. "The Aniconic Tradition: On Reading Images and Viewing Texts." In *The Triumph of Elohim: From Yahwisms to Judaisms,* edited by Diana V. Edelman, 75-105. Grand Rapids: Eerdmans, 1996. Reprinted from Kampen, Netherlands: Kok Pharos, 1995.

Tatum, W. Barnes. 1986. "The LXX Version of the Second Commandment (Ex.20,3-6 = Deut.5,7-10): A Polemic Against Idols, Not Images." *Journal for the Study of Judaism* 17: 177-95.

Uehlinger, Christoph. 1997. "Anthropomorphic Cult Statuary in Iron Age Palestine and the Search for Yahweh's Cult Images." In *The Image and the Book: Iconic Cults, Aniconism, and the Rise of Book Religion in Israel and the Ancient Near East,* edited by Karel van der Toorn, 97-155. Contributions to Biblical Exegesis and Theology 21. Leuven: Peeters.

Urbach, E. E. 1959. "The Rabbinical Laws of Idolatry in the Second and Third Centuries in the Light of Archaeological and Historical Facts." *IEJ* 9: 149-65, 229-45.

Vandrunen, David. 2004. "Iconoclasm, Incarnation and Eschatology: Toward a Catholic Understanding of the Reformed Doctrine of the 'Second' Commandment." *International Journal of Systematic Theology* 6: 130-47.

Walker, Christopher, and Michael B. Dick. 1999. "The Induction of the Cult Image in Ancient Mesopotamia: The Mesopotamian *mīs pî* Ritual." In *Born in Heaven, Made on Earth: The Making of the Cult Image in the Ancient Near East,* edited by Michael B. Dick, 55-121. Winona Lake, IN: Eisenbrauns.

Walls, Neal H., ed. 2005. *Cult Image and Divine Representation in the Ancient Near East.* ASOR Books 10. Boston: American Schools of Oriental Research.

Winiarski, Catherine E. 2006. "Adultery, Idolatry, and the Subject of Monotheism." *Religion & Literature* 38, no. 3: 41-63.

3. GOD'S NAME

Andrew, M. E. 1963b. "Using God: Exodus xx.7." *ExpTim* 74: 304-7.

Arand, Charles P. 1998. "'And Use Satanic Arts'? Another Look at Luther's Explanation of the Second Commandment." *Concordia Journal* 24: 219-24.

Carrón, Julián. 1993. "The Second Commandment in the New Testament: Your Yes Is Yes, Your No Is No." *Communio* 20: 5-25.

Coffin, F. J. 1900. "The Third Commandment." *JBL* 19: 166-88.

Derby, Josiah. 1993a. "The Third Commandment." *JBQ* 21: 24-27.

Freedman, David Noel. 1960. "The Name of the God of Moses." *JBL* 79: 151-56.

Harman, Allan M. 1988. "The Interpretation of the Third Commandment." *Reformed Theological Review* 47: 1-7.

Huffmon, Herbert B. 1995. "The Fundamental Code Illustrated: The Third Commandment." In *Pomegranates and Golden Bells: Studies in Biblical, Jewish, and Near Eastern Ritual, Law, and Literature in Honor of Jacob Milgrom*, edited by David P. Wright, David N. Freedman, and Avi Hurvitz, 363-71. Winona Lake, IN: Eisenbrauns.

Radner, Ephraim. 2005. "Taking the Lord's Name in Vain." In *I Am the Lord Your God: Christian Reflections on the Ten Commandments*, edited by Carl E. Braaten and Christopher R. Seitz, 77-94. Grand Rapids: Eerdmans.

Rose, Martin. 1992. "Names of God in the OT." In *ABD*, vol. 4: 1001-11.

Sales, Michel. 1993. "Who Can Utter the Name of God? From the Holiness of His Name to the Seriousness of All Words." *Communio* 20: 26-48.

Slesinski, Robert. 1993. "The Name of God in Byzantine Tradition: From Hesychasm to Imyaslavie." *Communio* 20: 49-62.

Staples, W. E. 1939. "The Third Commandment." *JBL* 58: 325-29.

Wilson, John A. 1948. "The Oath in Ancient Egypt." *JNES* 7: 129-56.

4. SABBATH/REST

Andreasen, Niels-Erik. 1972. *The Old Testament Sabbath: A Tradition-Historical Investigation*. SBL Dissertation Series 7. Missoula, MT: Society of Biblical Literature.

———. 1974a. "Festival and Freedom: A Study of an Old Testament Theme." *Interpretation* 28: 281-97.

———. 1974b. "Recent Studies of the Old Testament Sabbath: Some Observations." *ZAW* 86: 453-69.

Bacchiocchi, Samuele. 1977. *From Sabbath to Sunday: A Historical Investigation of the Rise of Sunday Observance in Early Christianity*. Rome: Pontifical Gregorian University.

———. 1980. *Divine Rest for Human Restlessness: A Theological Study of the Good News of the Sabbath for Today.* Rome: private publication.

Barker, Paul A. 2003. "Sabbath, Sabbatical Year, Jubilee." In *DOTPe*, 695-706.

Bass, Dorothy C. 2005. "Christian Formation in and for Sabbath Rest." *Interpretation* 59: 25-37.

Bauckham, Richard. 1982. "The Lord's Day." In *From Sabbath to Lord's Day: A Biblical, Historical, and Theological Investigation,* edited by Donald A. Carson, 221-50. Grand Rapids: Zondervan.

Beckwith, Roger T. 1996. *Calendar and Chronology, Jewish and Christian: Biblical, Intertestamental and Patristic Studies.* Arbeiten zur Geschichte des antiken Judentums und des Urchristentums 33. Leiden: Brill.

Beckwith, Roger T., and Wilfrid Stott. 1978. *This Is the Day: The Biblical Doctrine of the Christian Sunday in Its Jewish and Early Church Setting.* London: Marshall, Morgan & Scott. Reprinted as *The Christian Sunday: A Biblical and Historical Study.* Grand Rapids: Baker, 1980.

Beuken, W. A. M. 1985. "Exodus 16.5, 23: A Rule Regarding the Keeping of the Sabbath?" *JSOT* 32: 3-14.

Bockmuehl, Markus. 2005. "'Keeping It Holy': Old Testament Commandment and New Testament Faith." In *I Am the Lord Your God: Christian Reflections on the Ten Commandments,* edited by Carl E. Braaten and Christopher R. Seitz, 95-124. Grand Rapids: Eerdmans.

Bosman, Hendrik L. 1997. "Sabbath." In *NIDOTTE*, 4:1157-62.

Burer, Michael H. 2012. *Divine Sabbath Work.* Winona Lake, IN: Eisenbrauns.

Carson, Donald A. 1982a. "Jesus and the Sabbath in the Four Gospels." In *From Sabbath to Lord's Day: A Biblical, Historical, and Theological Investigation,* edited by Donald A. Carson, 57-97. Grand Rapids: Zondervan.

———, ed. 1982b. *From Sabbath to Lord's Day: A Biblical, Historical, and Theological Investigation.* Grand Rapids: Zondervan.

Cole, H. R. 2000. "The Sabbath and the Alien." *Andrews University Seminary Studies* 38: 223-29.

Derby, Josiah. 1994. "The Fourth Commandment." *JBQ* 22: 26-31.

Doering, Lutz. 1999. *Schabbat.* Texts and Studies in Ancient Judaism 78. Tübingen: Mohr Siebeck.

Dressler, Harold H. P. 1982. "The Sabbath in the Old Testament." In *From Sabbath to Lord's Day: A Biblical, Historical, and Theological Investigation,* edited by Donald A. Carson, 21-41. Grand Rapids: Zondervan.

Eder, Asher. 1997. "The Sabbath Commandment: Its Two Versions." *JBQ* 25: 188-91.

———. 2006. "The Sabbath: To Remember, to Observe, to Make." *JBQ* 34: 104-9.

Eskenazi, Tamara C., Daniel J. Harrington, and William W. Shea, eds. 1991. *The Sabbath in Jewish and Christian Traditions*. New York: Crossroad.

Frey, Mathilde. 2006. "The Sabbath Commandment in the Book of the Covenant: Ethics on Behalf of the Outcast." *Journal of Asia Adventist Seminary* 9: 3-11.

Geller, Stephen A. 2005. "Manna and Sabbath: A Literary-Theological Reading of Exodus 16." *Interpretation* 59: 5-16.

Gordis, Robert, ed. 1982. "The Sabbath Is Forever—A Symposium." *Judaism* 31: 6-98.

Gosse, Bernard. 2005. "Sabbath, Identity and Universalism Go Together After the Return from Exile." *JSOT* 29: 359-70.

Greene-McCreight, Kathryn. 1995. "Restless Until We Rest in God: The Fourth Commandment as Test Case in Christian 'Plain Sense' Interpretation." In *The Ten Commandments: The Reciprocity of Faithfulness*, edited by William P. Brown, 223-36. Library of Theological Ethics. Louisville, KY: Westminster John Knox, 2004. Reprinted from *Ex Auditu* 11 (1995): 29-41.

Grund, Alexandra. 2011. *Die Entstehung des Sabbats: Seine Bedeutung für Israels Zeitkonzept und Erinnerungskultur*. Tübingen: Mohr Siebeck.

Haag, E. 1993. "שָׁבַת *šābat*; שַׁבָּת *šabbāt*." In *TDOT*, vol. 14: 381-97.

Hallo, William W. 1977. "New Moons and Sabbaths: A Case-Study in the Contrastive Approach." *HUCA* 48: 1-18.

Hasel, Gerhard F. 1992. "Sabbath." In *ABD*, vol. 5: 849-56.

Heschel, Abraham J. 1951a. "A Palace in Time." In *The Ten Commandments: The Reciprocity of Faithfulness*, edited by William P. Brown, 214-22. Library of Theological Ethics. Louisville, KY: Westminster John Knox, 2004. Reprinted from *The Sabbath: Its Meaning for Modern Man*. New York: Farrar, Straus & Young, 1951: 13-24.

———. 1951b. *The Sabbath: Its Meaning for Modern Man*. New York: Farrar, Straus & Young.

Instone-Brewer, David. 2013. "Sabbath—Rest or Recreation?" *Premier Christianity* (March). www.premierchristianity.com/Past-Issues/2013/March-2013/Sabbath-rest -or-recreation.

Jenni, Ernst. 1956. *Die theologische Begründung des Sabbatgebotes im Alten Testament*. Theologische Studien 46. Zurich: Evangelischer.

Jewett, Paul K. 1971. *The Lord's Day: A Theological Guide to the Christian Day of Worship*. Grand Rapids: Eerdmans.

Kahn, Pinchas. 2004. "The Expanding Perspectives of the Sabbath." *JBQ* 32: 239-44.

Klagsbrun, Francine. 2002. *The Fourth Commandment: Remember the Sabbath Day*. New York: Harmony.

Klingbeil, Gerald A. 2010. "The Sabbath Law in the Decalogue(s): Creation and Liberation as a Paradigm for Community." *RB* 117: 491-509.

Lee, Francis Nigel. 1966. *The Covenantal Sabbath*. London: Lord's Day Observance Society.

Lowery, Richard H. 2000. *Sabbath and Jubilee*. Understanding Biblical Themes. St Louis, MO: Chalice.

McKay, Heather A. 1994. *Sabbath and Synagogue: The Question of Sabbath Worship in Ancient Judaism*. Religions in the Graeco-Roman World 122. Leiden: Brill.

North, Robert G. 1955. "The Derivation of Sabbath." *Biblica* 36: 182-201.

Ratzinger, Joseph. 1994. "The Meaning of Sunday." *Communio* 21: 5-26.

Ringe, Sharon H. 2005. "'Holy, as the Lord Your God Commanded You': Sabbath in the New Testament." *Interpretation* 59: 17-24.

Robinson, Gnana. 1980. "The Idea of Rest in the Old Testament and the Search for the Basic Character of Sabbath." *ZAW* 92: 32-42.

———. 1988. *The Origin and Development of the Old Testament Sabbath: A Comprehensive Exegetical Approach*. Beiträge zur biblischen Exegese und Theologie 21. Frankfurt: Lang.

Rordorf, Willy. 1962. *Sunday: The History of the Day of Rest and Worship in the Earliest Centuries of the Christian Church*. London: SCM, 1968. Translated from German, 1962.

Rowland, Christopher. 1982. "A Summary of Sabbath Observance in Judaism at the Beginning of the Christian Era." In *From Sabbath to Lord's Day: A Biblical, Historical, and Theological Investigation*, edited by Donald A. Carson, 43-55. Grand Rapids: Zondervan.

Sales, Michel. 1994. "The Fulfillment of the Sabbath: From the Holiness of the Seventh Day to God's Resting in God." *Communio* 21: 27-48.

Sanders, E. P. 1990. *Jewish Law from Jesus to the Mishnah: Five Studies*. London: SCM.

Shead, Andrew G. 2002. "An Old Testament Theology of the Sabbath Year and Jubilee." *Reformed Theological Review* 61: 19-33.

Sherman, Robert. 2005. "Reclaimed by Sabbath Rest." *Interpretation* 59: 38-50.

Siker, Jeffrey S. 1981. "The Theology of the Sabbath in the Old Testament: A Canonical Approach." *Studia Biblica et Theologica* 11: 5-20.

Sturcke, Henry. 2005. *Encountering the Rest of God: How Jesus Came to Personify the Sabbath*. Zürich: Theologischer Verlag.

Swartley, Willard M. 1983. *Slavery, Sabbath, War, and Women: Case Issues in Biblical Interpretation*. Scottdale, PA: Herald.

Timmer, Daniel C. 2009. *Creation, Tabernacle, and Sabbath: The Sabbath Frame of Exodus 31:12-17; 35:1-3 in Exegetical and Theological Perspective*. Göttingen: Vandenhoeck & Ruprecht.

Tsevat, Matitiahu. 1972. "The Basic Meaning of the Biblical Sabbath." *ZAW* 84: 447-59.

Turner, Max M. B. 1982. "The Sabbath, Sunday, and the Law in Luke/Acts." In *From Sabbath to Lord's Day: A Biblical, Historical, and Theological Investigation*, edited by Donald A. Carson, 99-157. Grand Rapids: Zondervan.

Weiss, Herold. 2003. *A Day of Gladness: The Sabbath Among Jews and Christians in Antiquity*. Columbia: University of South Carolina.

5. HONORING PARENTS/FAMILY

Albertz, Rainer. 1978. "Hintergrund und Bedeutung des Elterngebots im Dekalog." *ZAW* 90: 348-74.

Bailey, Jon Nelson. 2000. "Vowing Away the Fifth Commandment: Matthew 15:3-6// Mark 7:9-13." *Restoration Quarterly* 42: 193-209.

Baker, David L. 2011. "The Fifth Commandment in Context." In *On Stone and Scroll: Essays in Honour of Graham Ivor Davies*, edited by James K. Aitken, Katharine J. Dell, and Brian A. Mastin, 253-67. BZAW 420. Berlin: de Gruyter.

Balch, David L., and Carolyn Osiek, eds. 2003. *Early Christian Families in Context: An Interdisciplinary Dialogue*. Religion, Marriage, and Family. Grand Rapids: Eerdmans.

Barton, Stephen C., ed. 1996. *The Family in Theological Perspective*. Edinburgh: T&T Clark.

Bayliss, Miranda. 1973. "The Cult of Dead Kin in Assyria and Babylonia." *Iraq* 35: 115-25.

Bellefontaine, Elizabeth. 1979. "Deuteronomy 21:18-21: Reviewing the Case of the Rebellious Son." *JSOT* 13: 13-31.

Blenkinsopp, Joseph. 1997. "The Family in First Temple Israel." In *Families in Ancient Israel*, edited by Leo G. Perdue, Joseph Blenkinsopp, John J. Collins, and Carol Meyers, 48-103. Family, Religion, and Culture. Louisville, KY: Westminster John Knox.

Blessing, Kamila. 2010. *Families of the Bible: A New Perspective*. Psychology, Religion, and Spirituality. Santa Barbara, CA: Praeger.

Blidstein, Gerald. 1975. *Honor Thy Father and Mother: Filial Responsibility in Jewish Law and Ethics*. Library of Jewish Law and Ethics. New York: Ktav.

Bloch-Smith, Elizabeth. 1992. *Judahite Burial Practices and Beliefs About the Dead*. JSOTSup 123. Sheffield: Sheffield Academic.

de Boer, P. A. H. 1974. *Fatherhood and Motherhood in Israelite and Judean Piety*. Leiden: Brill.

Brichto, Herbert Chanan. 1973. "Kin, Cult, Land and Afterlife: A Biblical Complex." *HUCA* 44: 1-54.

Callaway, Phillip R. 1984. "Deut 21:18-21: Proverbial Wisdom and Law." *JBL* 103: 341-52.

Cohen, Shaye J. D. 1993. *The Jewish Family in Antiquity*. Brown Judaic Studies 289. Atlanta: Scholars.

Dearman, John Andrew, Stephen C. Barton, Sally B. Purvis, and Larry Kent Graham. 1998. "Symposium on 'The Family.'" *Interpretation* 52: 116-77.

Fishbane, Mona DeKoven. 2009. "'Honor Your Father and Your Mother': Intergenerational Values and Jewish Tradition." In *Spiritual Resources in Family Therapy*, edited by Froma Walsh, 174-93. 2nd ed. New York: Guilford.

Gamberoni, Johann. 1964. "Das Elterngebot im Alten Testament." *BZ* 8: 161-90.

Garland, David E., and Diana R. Garland. 2007. *Flawed Families of the Bible: How God's Grace Works Through Imperfect Relationships*. Grand Rapids: Brazos.

Hagedorn, Anselm C. 2000. "Guarding the Parents' Honor—Deuteronomy 21.18-21." *JSOT* 88: 101-21.

Hallo, William W. 1992. "Royal Ancestor Worship in the Biblical World." In *Sha'arei Talmon: Studies in the Bible, Qumran, and the Ancient Near East Presented to Shemaryahu Talmon*, edited by Michael Fishbane and Emanuel Tov, 381-401. Winona Lake, IN: Eisenbrauns.

Harrisville, Roy A. 1969. "Jesus and the Family." *Interpretation* 23: 425-38.

Healey, John F. 1979. "The Pietas of an Ideal Son in Ugarit." *UF* 11: 353-56.

van Henten, Jan Willem, and Athalya Brenner. 2000. *Families and Family Relations: As Represented in Early Judaisms and Early Christianities: Texts and Fictions*. Studies in Theology and Religion 2. Leiden: Deo.

Hess, Richard S., and M. Daniel Carroll Rodas. 2003. *Family in the Bible: Exploring Customs, Culture, and Context*. Grand Rapids: Baker Academic.

Johnston, Philip S. 2002. *Shades of Sheol: Death and Afterlife in the Old Testament*. Leicester, England: Apollos.

Jungbauer, Harry. 2002. *"Ehre Vater und Mutter": Der Weg des Elterngebots in der biblischen Tradition*. Tübingen: Mohr Siebeck.

Kennedy, Charles A. 1992. "Dead, Cult of the." In *ABD*, vol. 2: 105-8.

Levine, Baruch A., and Jean-Michel de Tarragon. 1984. "Dead Kings and Rephaim: The Patrons of the Ugaritic Dynasty." *JAOS* 104: 649-59.

Lewis, Theodore J. 1989. *Cults of the Dead in Ancient Israel and Ugarit*. Harvard Semitic Monographs 39. Atlanta: Scholars.

———. 1991. "The Ancestral Estate (נַחֲלַת אֱלֹהִים) in 2 Samuel 14:16." *JBL* 110: 597-612.

Loretz, Oswald. 1979. "Das biblische Elterngebot und die Sohnespflichten in der ugaritischen Aqht-Legende." *Biblische Notizen* 8: 14-17.

Millard, Matthias. 2000. "Das Elterngebot im Dekalog: Zum Problem der Gliederung des Dekalogs." In *Mincha: Festgabe für Rolf Rendtorff zum 75. Geburtstag*, edited by Erhard Blum, 193-215. Neukirchen-Vluyn, Germany: Neukirchener.

Moxnes, Halvor, ed. 1997. *Constructing Early Christian Families: Family as Social Reality and Metaphor*. London: Routledge.

Nuyen, A. T. 2004. "The Contemporary Relevance of the Confucian Idea of Filial Piety." *Journal of Chinese Philosophy* 31: 433-50.

Pardee, Dennis. 2002. *Ritual and Cult at Ugarit*. Writings from the Ancient World 10. Leiden: Brill.

Perdue, Leo G., Joseph Blenkinsopp, John J. Collins, and Carol Meyers. 1997. *Families in Ancient Israel*. Louisville, KY: Westminster John Knox.

Pope, Marvin H. 1981. "The Cult of the Dead at Ugarit." In *Ugarit in Retrospect: Fifty Years of Ugarit and Ugaritic*, edited by Gordon D. Young, 159-79. Winona Lake, IN: Eisenbrauns.

Portier-Young, Anathea E. 2007. "Response to 'Honoring Parents' by Byron L. Sherwin." In *The Ten Commandments for Jews, Christians, and Others*, edited by Roger E. van Harn, 100-111. Grand Rapids: Eerdmans.

Rhee, Song Nai. 1965. "Fear God and Honor Your Father and Mother: Two Injunctions in the Book of Proverbs and the Confucian Classics." *Encounter* 26: 207-14.

Ro, Bong Rin, ed. 1985. *Christian Alternatives to Ancestor Practices*. Taichung, Taiwan: Asia Theological Association.

Roth, Martha T. 2006. "Elder Abuse: LH §195." In *If a Man Builds a Joyful House: Assyriological Studies in Honor of Erle Verdun Leichty*, edited by Ann K. Guinan et al., 349-56. Leiden: Brill.

Sanders, James A. 2002. "The Family in the Bible." *BTB* 32: 117-28.

Schmidt, Brian B. 1994. *Israel's Beneficent Dead: Ancestor Cult and Necromancy in Ancient Israelite Religion and Tradition*. Tübingen: Mohr Siebeck. Reprinted, Winona Lake, IN: Eisenbrauns, 1996.

Scott, Marshall S. 1988. "Honor Thy Father and Mother: Scriptural Resources for Victims of Incest and Parental Abuse." *Journal of Pastoral Care* 42: 139-48.

Sherwin, Byron L. 2007. "The Fifth Word: Honoring Parents." In *The Ten Commandments for Jews, Christians, and Others*, edited by Roger E. van Harn, 87-99. Grand Rapids: Eerdmans.

Skaist, Aaron. 1980. "The Ancestor Cult and Succession in Mesopotamia." In *Death in Mesopotamia*, edited by Bendt Alster, 123-28. Mesopotamia 8. Copenhagen: Akademisk.

Spronk, Klaas. 1986. *Beatific Afterlife in Ancient Israel and in the Ancient Near East*. Alter Orient und Altes Testament 219. Kevelaer, Germany: Butzon & Bercker.

Stol, Marten. 1998. "Care of the Elderly in Mesopotamia in the Old Babylonian Period." In *The Care of the Elderly in the Ancient Near East*, edited by Marten Stol and S. P. Vleeming, 59-118. Leiden: Brill.

Stol, Marten, and S. P. Vleeming, eds. 1998. *The Care of the Elderly in the Ancient Near East*. Studies in the History and Culture of the Ancient Near East 14. Leiden: Brill.

van der Toorn, Karel. 1996. *Family Religion in Babylonia, Syria and Israel: Continuity and Change in the Forms of Religious Life*. Studies in the History and Culture of the Ancient Near East 7. Leiden: Brill.

Westbrook, Raymond. 1998. "Legal Aspects of Care of the Elderly in the Ancient Near East: Introduction." In *The Care of the Elderly in the Ancient Near East*, edited by Marten Stol and S. P. Vleeming, 1-22. Leiden: Brill.

Wright, Christopher J. H. 1992. "Family." In *ABD*, vol. 2: 761-69.

Yisraeli, Oded. 2009. "Honoring Father and Mother in Early Kabbalah: From Ethos to Mythos." *JQR* 99: 396-415.

6. HOMICIDE/LIFE

Bailey, Wilma Ann. 2005. *"You Shall Not Kill" or "You Shall Not Murder"? The Assault on a Biblical Text*. Collegeville, MN: Liturgical.

Barmash, Pamela. 2005. *Homicide in the Biblical World*. Cambridge: Cambridge University Press.

Becking, Bob. 2011. "What Forms of Life Are to Be Protected? Exegetical Remarks on Patrick Miller's Interpretation of the Fifth (or) Sixth Commandment." *ZABR* 17: 149-59.

Burnside, Jonathan. 2010b. "Homicide and Vengeance." In *God, Justice, and Society: Aspects of Law and Legality in the Bible*, 253-83. Oxford: Oxford University Press.

Cavanaugh, William T. 2005. "Killing in the Name of God." In *I Am the Lord Your God: Christian Reflections on the Ten Commandments*, edited by Carl E. Braaten and Christopher R. Seitz, 127-47. Grand Rapids: Eerdmans.

Hoch, James, and Sara E. Orel. 1992. "Murder in Ancient Egypt." In *Death and Taxes in the Ancient Near East*, edited by Sara E. Orel, 87-128. Lewiston, NY: Mellen.

Hossfeld, Frank-Lothar. 1992. "רָצַח *rāṣaḥ*." In *TDOT*, vol. 13 (2004): 630-40. Translated from German, 1992.

———. 2003. *"Du sollst nicht Töten!": Das Fünfte Dekaloggebot im Kontext alttestamentlicher Ethik*. Stuttgart: Kohlhammer.

Jacobsen, Thorkild. 1959. "An Ancient Mesopotamian Trial for Homicide." In *Toward the Image of Tammuz and Other Essays on Mesopotamian History and Culture*, edited by William L. Moran, 193-214. Harvard Semitic Series 21. Cambridge, MA: Harvard University Press, 1970. Reprinted from *Studia Biblica et Orientalia III*, 130-50. Rome: Pontifical Biblical Institute.

LaCocque, André, and Paul Ricoeur. 1998. "Exodus 20:13." In *Thinking Biblically: Exegetical and Hermeneutical Studies*, translated by David Pellauer, 69-138. Chicago: University of Chicago Press.

Loewenstamm, Samuel E. 1962. "The Laws of Adultery and Murder in Biblical and Mesopotamian Law." In *Comparative Studies in Biblical and Ancient Oriental Literatures*, 146-53. Alter Orient und Altes Testament 204. Kevelaer: Butzon & Bercker, 1980. Translated from Hebrew, 1962.

McKeating, Henry. 1975. "The Development of the Law on Homicide in Ancient Israel." *VT* 25: 46-68.

Phillips, Anthony. 1977. "Another Look at Murder." *JJS* 28: 105-26.

———. 1983b. "Respect for Life in the Old Testament." *King's Theological Review* 6: 32-35. Reprinted in *Essays on Biblical Law*, 139-47. JSOTSup 344. Sheffield: Sheffield Academic Press, 2002.

Roth, Martha T. 1987. "Homicide in the Neo-Assyrian Period." In *Language, Literature, and History: Philological and Historical Studies Presented to Erica Reiner*, edited by Francesca Rochberg-Halton, 351-65. American Oriental Series 67. New Haven, CT: American Oriental Society.

Simpson, Gary M. 2004. "'Thou Shalt Not Kill'—The First Commandment of the Just War Tradition." In *The Ten Commandments: The Reciprocity of Faithfulness*, edited by William P. Brown, 249-65. Library of Theological Ethics. Louisville, KY: Westminster John Knox.

Sulzberger, Mayer. 1915. *The Ancient Hebrew Law of Homicide*. Philadelphia: Greenstone.

Tinker, Melvin. 2003. "Living in a World Where Life Is Cheap: The Relevance of the Book of Deuteronomy and the Sixth Commandment for the Debate on the Sanctity of Human Life." *Themelios* 29, no. 1: 5-17.

Wannenwetsch, Bernd. 2005. "You Shall Not Kill—What Does It Take? Why We Need the Other Commandments If We Are to Abstain from Killing." In *I Am the Lord Your God: Christian Reflections on the Ten Commandments*, edited by Carl E. Braaten and Christopher R. Seitz, 148-74. Grand Rapids: Eerdmans.

Wiseman, Donald J. 1974. "Murder in Mesopotamia." *Iraq* 36: 249-60.

7. ADULTERY/MARRIAGE

Abasili, Alexander Izuchukwu. 2016. *The Understanding of Adultery in the Hebrew Bible: A Critical Survey*. Bloomington, IN: Xlibris.

Ash, Christopher. 2003. *Marriage: Sex in the Service of God*. Leicester, England: Inter-Varsity Press.

Baker, David L. 2007. "Concubines and Conjugal Rights: ענה in Exodus 21:10 and Deuteronomy 21:14." *ZABR* 13: 87-101.

Bosman, Hendrik L. 1988. "Adultery, Prophetic Tradition, and the Decalogue." In *The Ten Commandments: The Reciprocity of Faithfulness*, edited by William P. Brown, 267-74. Library of Theological Ethics. Louisville, KY: Westminster John Knox, 2004. Reprinted from *Wünschet Jerusalem Frieden*, 21-30. International Organization for the Study of the Old Testament Papers 1986. Frankfurt: Lang, 1988.

Brichto, Herbert Chanan. 1975. "The Case of the *Sōṭā* and a Reconsideration of Biblical 'Law.'" *HUCA* 46: 55-70.

Cornes, Andrew. 1993. *Divorce and Remarriage: Biblical Principles and Pastoral Practice*. London: Hodder & Stoughton.

Edenburg, Cynthia. 2009. "Ideology and Social Context of the Deuteronomic Women's Sex Laws (Deuteronomy 22:13-29)." *JBL* 128: 43-60.

Eyre, Christopher J. 1984. "Crime and Adultery in Ancient Egypt." *Journal of Egyptian Archaeology* 70: 92-105.

Feldhahn, Shaunti, and Tally Whitehead. 2014. *The Good News About Marriage: Debunking Discouraging Myths About Marriage and Divorce*. Colorado Springs, CO: Multnomah.

Finkelstein, Jacob J. 1966. "Sex Offenses in Sumerian Laws." *JAOS* 86: 355-72.

Fishbane, Michael. 1974. "Accusations of Adultery: A Study of Law and Scribal Practice in Numbers 5:11-31." *HUCA* 45: 25-45.

Frymer-Kensky, Tikva. 1984. "The Strange Case of the Suspected Sotah (Numbers v 11-31)." *VT* 34: 11-26.

Goodfriend, Elaine Adler. 1992. "Adultery." In *ABD*, vol. 1: 82-86.

Greengus, Samuel. 1969–1970. "A Textbook Case of Adultery in Ancient Mesopotamia." *HUCA* 40–41: 33-44.

Hamilton, Victor P., and Raymond F. Collins. 1992. "Marriage." In *ABD*, vol. 4: 559-72.

Instone-Brewer, David. 2002. *Divorce & Remarriage in the Bible: The Social and Literary Context*. Grand Rapids: Eerdmans.

———. 2003. *Divorce and Remarriage in the Church: Biblical Solutions for Pastoral Realities*. Milton Keynes, England: Paternoster.

Jenson, Robert W. 2005. "Male and Female He Created Them." In *I Am the Lord Your God: Christian Reflections on the Ten Commandments*, edited by Carl E. Braaten and Christopher R. Seitz, 175-88. Grand Rapids: Eerdmans.

Kornfeld, Walter. 1950. "L'Adultère dans l'Orient antique." *RB* 57: 92-109.

Köstenberger, Andreas J., and David W. Jones. 2010. *God, Marriage, and Family: Rebuilding the Biblical Foundation*. 2nd ed. Wheaton, IL: Crossway.

Loewenstamm, Samuel E. 1962. "The Laws of Adultery and Murder in Biblical and Mesopotamian Law." In *Comparative Studies in Biblical and Ancient Oriental*

Literatures, 146-53. Alter Orient und Altes Testament 204. Kevelaer, Germany: Butzon & Bercker, 1980. Translated from Hebrew, 1962.

Mace, D. R. 1953. *Hebrew Marriage: A Sociological Study*. London: Epworth.

Márquez Rowe, Ignacio. 2000. "The King of Ugarit, His Wife, Her Brothers, and Her Lovers." *UF* 32: 365-72.

Marsman, Hennie J. 2003. *Women in Ugarit and Israel: Their Social and Religious Position in the Context of the Ancient Near East*. Oudtestamentische Studiën 49. Leiden: Brill.

McKeating, Henry. 1979. "Sanctions Against Adultery in Ancient Israelite Society, with Some Reflections on Methodology in the Study of Old Testament Ethics." *JSOT* 11: 57-72.

Milgrom, Jacob. 1985. "On the Suspected Adulteress (Numbers v 11-31)." *VT* 35: 368-69.

Moran, William L. 1959. "The Scandal of the 'Great Sin' at Ugarit." *JNES* 18: 280-81.

Niditch, Susan. 1979. "The Wrong Woman Righted: An Analysis of Genesis 38." *HTR* 72: 143-49.

Phillips, Anthony. 1981. "Another Look at Adultery." *JSOT* 20: 3-25.

Pressler, Carolyn. 1993. *The View of Women Found in the Deuteronomic Family Laws*. BZAW 216. Berlin: de Gruyter.

Rabinowitz, Jacob J. 1959. "The 'Great Sin' in Ancient Egyptian Marriage Contracts." *JNES* 18: 73.

Roth, Martha T. 1988. "'She Will Die by the Iron Dagger': Adultery and Neo-Babylonian Marriage." *JESHO* 31: 186-206.

Wall, Robert W. 1992. "Divorce." In *ABD*, vol. 2: 217-19.

Wells, Bruce. 2015. "Sex Crimes in the Laws of the Hebrew Bible." *Near Eastern Archaeology* 78: 294-300.

Wenham, Gordon J., and William E. Heth. 2002. *Jesus and Divorce*. Rev. ed. Carlisle, England: Paternoster.

Westbrook, Raymond. 1984. "The Enforcement of Morals in Mesopotamian Law." *JAOS* 104: 753-56.

——. 1990. "Adultery in Ancient Near Eastern Law." *RB* 97: 542-80.

van Wolde, Ellen. 2002. "Does 'Innâ Denote Rape? A Semantic Analysis of a Controversial Word." *VT* 52: 528-44.

8. THEFT/PROPERTY

Alcock, Pete. 1997. *Understanding Poverty*. 2nd ed. Basingstoke, England: Macmillan.

Alt, Albrecht. 1949. "Das Verbot des Diebstahls im Dekalog." In *Kleine Schriften zur Geschichte des Volkes Israel*. Vol. 1, 333-40. Munich: Beck, 1953. Reprinted from unpublished paper, 1949.

Anderson, Cheryl B. 2004. "The Eighth Commandment: A Way to King's 'Beloved Community'?" In *The Ten Commandments: The Reciprocity of Faithfulness*, edited by William P. Brown, 276-89. Library of Theological Ethics. Louisville, KY: Westminster John Knox.

Belfield, Chris, Jonathan Cribb, Andrew Hood, and Robert Joyce. 2015. *Living Standards, Poverty and Inequality in the UK: 2015*. London: Institute for Fiscal Studies.

Burnside, Jonathan. 2010c. "Theft and Burglary." In *God, Justice, and Society: Aspects of Law and Legality in the Bible*, 285-316. Oxford: Oxford University Press.

Canuto, Otaviano, and Håvard Halland. 2013. "A Billion-Dollar Opportunity for Developing Countries." *Growth and Crisis Blog*. World Bank Institute. Published October 22, 2013. https://blogs.worldbank.org/growth/billion-dollar-opportunity -developing-countries.

Cater, John James, Lorna A. Collins, and Brent D. Beal. 2015. "Ethics, Faith, and Profit: Exploring the Motives of the U.S. Fair Trade Social Entrepreneurs." *Journal of Business Ethics*: 1-17.

Černý, Jaroslav. 1937. "Restitution of, and Penalty Attaching to, Stolen Property in Ramesside Times." *Journal of Egyptian Archaeology* 23: 186-89.

Gnuse, Robert Karl. 1985. *You Shall Not Steal: Community and Property in the Biblical Tradition*. Maryknoll, NY: Orbis.

Gordon, Cyrus H. 1936. "Nuzi Tablets Relating to Theft." *Orientalia* 5: 305-30.

Gottstein, Moshe H. 1953. "Du sollst nicht stehlen." *Theologische Zeitschrift* 9: 394-95.

Griffiths, Peter. 2011. "Ethical Objections to Fairtrade." *Journal of Business Ethics* 105: 357-73.

Hamp, Vinzenz. 1974. "גָּנַב *gānabh*." In *TDOT*, vol. 3 (1978): 39-53. Translated from German, 1974.

Harary, Charles J. 2003. "Stealing to Save Someone's Life." *Jewish Law*. Accessed February 17, 2005. www.jlaw.com/Articles/ch_stealsavelife.html.

Hickel, Jason. 2013. "Aid in Reverse: How Poor Countries Develop Rich Countries." *Global Policy*. December 12. www.globalpolicyjournal.com/blog/12/12/2013 /donors%E2%80%99-dilemma-aid-reverse-how-poor-countries-develop-rich -countries.

Horst, Friedrich. 1935. "Der Diebstahl im Alten Testament." In *Festschrift Paul Kahle*, 19-28. Leiden: Brill. Reprinted in *Gottes Recht: Gesammelte Studien zum Recht im Alten Testament*, 167-75. Theologische Bücherei 12. Munich: Kaiser, 1961.

Jackson, Bernard S. 1972. *Theft in Early Jewish Law*. Oxford: Clarendon.

———. 1975a. "Principles and Cases: The Theft Laws of Hammurabi." In *Essays in Jewish and Comparative Legal History*, 64-74. Studies in Judaism in Late Antiquity 103. Leiden: Brill.

Kidwell, Jeremy. 2014. "Merchants in the Kingdom?" The Kirby Laing Institute for Christian Ethics. *KLICE Comment*. http://tyndalehouse.createsend1.com/t/View Email/r/91EF42EAF02E701E2540EF23F30FEDED.

Klein, H. 1976. "Verbot des Menschendiebstahls im Dekalog? Prüfung einer These Albrecht Alts." *VT* 26: 161-69.

Landes, David S. 1998. *The Wealth and Poverty of Nations: Why Some Are So Rich and Some So Poor*. London: Little Brown.

Larkin, William J., Jr. 1982. "The Ethics of Inflation: A Biblical Critique of the Causes and Consequences." *Grace Theological Journal* 31: 89-105.

Little, David. 1980. "Exodus 20:15, 'Thou Shalt Not Steal.'" *Interpretation* 34: 399-405.

Piff, Paul K., Michael W. Kraus, Stéphanie Côté, Bonnie Hayden Cheng, Dacher Keltner. 2010. "Having Less, Giving More: The Influence of Social Class on Pro-social Behavior." *Journal of Personality and Social Psychology* 99: 771-84.

————. 2012. "Higher Social Class Predicts Increased Unethical Behavior." *Proceedings of the National Academy of Sciences of the United States of America* 109: 4086-91.

Provost, Claire, and Mark Tran. 2013. "Value of Aid Overstated by Billions of Dollars as Donors Reap Interest on Loans." *The Guardian*. April 30. www.theguardian.com/globaldevelopment/2013/apr/30/aid-overstated-donors-interest-payments.

Sacks, Jonathan. 1999. *Morals and Markets: Seventh Annual Hayek Memorial Lecture*, with commentaries by Norman Barry, Robert Davidson, and Michael Novak. Occasional Paper 108. London: Institute of Economic Affairs.

Salvador, Rommel O., Altaf Merchant, and Elizabeth A. Alexander. 2013. "Faith and Fair Trade: The Moderating Role of Contextual Religious Salience." *Journal of Business Ethics* 121: 353-71.

Schoneveld, J. 1973. "Le sang du cambrioleur: Exode XXII 1,2." In *Symbolae biblicae et Mesopotamicae: Francisco Mario Theodoro de Liagre Böhl Dedicatae*, edited by M. A. Beek, A. A. Kampmann, C. Nijland, and J. Ryckmans, 335-40. Studia Francisci Scholten Memoriae Dicata 4. Leiden: Brill.

Shin, Laura. 2014. "The 85 Richest People in the World Have as Much Wealth as the 3.5 Billion Poorest." *Forbes*. January 23. www.forbes.com/sites/laurashin/2014/01/23/the-85-richest-people-in-the-world-have-as-much-wealth-as-the-3-5-billion-poorest.

Smith, Alastair. 2009. "Fair Trade, Diversification and Structural Change: Towards a Broader Theoretical Framework of Analysis." *Oxford Development Studies* 37, no. 4: 457-78.

Sprinkle, Joe M. 2003. "Theft and Deprivation of Property." In *DOTPe*: 841-45.

Steinrücken, Torsten, and Sebastian Jaenichen. 2007. "The Fair Trade Idea: Towards an Economics of Social Labels." *Journal of Consumer Policy* 30: 201-17.

UN News. 2003. "Development Funds Moving from Poor Countries to Rich Ones, Annan Says." UN News Centre, October 30. www.un.org/apps/news/story.asp?Ne wsID=8722&Cr=financing&Cr1= development.

UNDP. 2011. "Towards Human Resilience: Sustaining MDG Progress in an Age of Economic Uncertainty." United Nations Development Programme. www.undp .org/content/dam/undp/library/Poverty%20Reduction/Towards_SustainingMDG _Web1005.pdf.

Waterman, Anthony. 1982. "Private Property, Inequality, Theft." In *Voice from the Mountain: New Life for the Old Law*, edited by Philip Jefferson, 96-108. Toronto: Anglican Book Centre.

Wehmeier, Gerhard. 1977. "The Prohibition of Theft in the Decalogue." *Indian Journal of Theology* 26: 181-91.

Wright, Christopher J. H. 1990. *God's People in God's Land: Family, Land, and Property in the Old Testament*. Grand Rapids: Eerdmans.

9. TRUTH

Andrew, M. E. 1963a. "Falsehood and Truth: An Amplified Sermon on Exodus 20:16." *Interpretation* 17: 425-38.

Braaten, Carl E. 2005. "Sins of the Tongue." In *I Am the Lord Your God: Christian Reflections on the Ten Commandments*, edited by Carl E. Braaten and Christopher R. Seitz, 206-17. Grand Rapids: Eerdmans.

Brueggemann, Walter. 1997b. "Truth-Telling as Subversive Obedience." In *The Ten Commandments: The Reciprocity of Faithfulness*, edited by William P. Brown, 291-300. Library of Theological Ethics. Louisville, KY: Westminster John Knox, 2004. Reprinted from *Journal for Preachers* 20, no. 2 (1997): 2-9.

Craven, Toni. 1989. "Women Who Lied for the Faith." In *Justice and the Holy: Essays in Honor of Walter Harrelson*, edited by Douglas A. Knight and Peter J. Paris, 35-49. Atlanta: Scholars.

Crüsemann, Frank. 1987. "'Auge um Auge . . .' (Ex 21,24f): Zum sozialgeschichtlichen Sinn des Talionsgesetzes im Bundesbuch." *Evangelische Theologie* 47: 411–26.

Freund, Richard A. 1991. "Lying and Deception in the Biblical and Post-Biblical Judaic Tradition." *Scandinavian Journal of the Old Testament* 5: 45-61.

Frymer-Kensky, Tikva. 1980. "Tit for Tat: The Principle of Equal Retribution in Near Eastern and Biblical Law." *BA* 43: 230-34.

Fuchs, Esther. 1988. "'For I Have the Way of Women': Deception, Gender, and Ideology in Biblical Narrative." *Semeia* 42: 68-83.

Griffiths, Paul J. 2004. *Lying: An Augustinian Theology of Duplicity*. Eugene, OR: Wipf & Stock.

Haase, Richard. 1997. "Talion und spiegelnde Strafe in den keilschriftlichen Rechtscorpora." *ZABR* 3: 195-201.

Hütter, Reinhard. 2005. "The Tongue—Fallen and Restored: Some Reflections on the Three Voices of the Eighth Commandment." In *I Am the Lord Your God: Christian Reflections on the Ten Commandments*, edited by Carl E. Braaten and Christopher R. Seitz, 189-205. Grand Rapids: Eerdmans.

Klopfenstein, Martin A. 1964. *Die Lüge nach dem Alten Testament: Ihr Begriff, ihre Bedeutung und ihre Beurteilung*. Zurich: Gotthelf.

Meilaender, Gilbert. 2006. *The Way That Leads There: Augustinian Reflections on the Christian Life*. Grand Rapids: Eerdmans.

Nel, Philip J. 1994. "The Talion Principle in Old Testament Narratives." *JNSL* 20, no. 1: 21-29.

Otto, Eckart. 1991. "Die Geschichte der Talion im Alten Orient und Israel." In *Ernten, Was Man Sät: Festschrift für Klaus Koch zu seinem 65. Geburstag*, edited by Dwight R. Daniels, Uwe Glessmer, and Martin Rösel, 101-30. Neukirchen-Vluyn, Germany: Neukirchener.

Piattelli, Daniela. 1995. "Zedaqà: Pursuit of Justice and the Instrument of 'Ius Talionis.'" *Israel Law Review* 29: 65-78.

Prouser, Ora Horn. 1994. "The Truth About Women and Lying." *JSOT* 61: 15-28.

Rowe, Jonathan Y. 2014. "Truthful Lies: The Ethics of Lying in the Old Testament." *Ethics in Brief* 19, no. 4. www.klice.co.uk/uploads/Ethics%20in%20Brief/EIB _Rowe_19-4.pdf.

Simian-Yofre, Horacio. 1986. "עוד '*wd*.'" In *TDOT*, vol. 10 (1999): 495-515. Translated from German, 1986.

Strozier, Robert. 1966. "The Euphemism." *Language Learning* 16: 63-70.

Williams, Michael James. 2001. *Deception in Genesis: An Investigation into the Morality of a Unique Biblical Phenomenon*. Studies in Biblical Literature 32. New York: Peter Lang.

10. COVETING

Baker, David L. 2005b. "Last but Not Least: The Tenth Commandment." *HBT* 27: 3-24.

Bartholomew, Craig G., and Thorsten Moritz, eds. 2000. *Christ and Consumerism: A Critical Analysis of the Spirit of the Age*. Carlisle: Paternoster.

Block, Daniel I. 2010. "'You Shall Not Covet Your Neighbor's Wife': A Study in Deuteronomic Domestic Ideology." *Journal of the Evangelical Theological Society* 53: 449-74.

Bothwell, John. 1982. "Coveting Amid Affluence." In *Voice from the Mountain: New Life for the Old Law*, edited by Philip Jefferson, 117-26. Toronto: Anglican Book Centre.

Botica, Aurelian. 2014. "The Tenth Commandment and the Concept of 'Inward Liability.'" In *Windows to the Ancient World of the Hebrew Bible: Essays in Honor of Samuel Greengus*, edited by Bill T. Arnold, Nancy L. Erickson, and John H. Walton, 51-66. Winona Lake, IN: Eisenbrauns.

Buchanan, George W. 1968. "The 'Spiritual' Commandment." *Journal of the American Academy of Religion* 36: 126-27.

Ceresko, Anthony R. 1988. "The Challenge of the Tenth Commandment." In *Psalmists and Sages: Studies in Old Testament Poetry and Religion*, 237-39. Indian Theological Studies Supplements 2. Bangalore, India: St. Peter's Institute, 1994. Reprinted from *Compass: A Jesuit Journal* 6 (1988).

Chaney, Marvin L. 2004. "'Coveting Your Neighbor's House' in Social Context." In *The Ten Commandments: The Reciprocity of Faithfulness*, edited by William P. Brown, 302-17. Library of Theological Ethics. Louisville, KY: Westminster John Knox. Excerpts originally published in *Pacific Theological Review* 15, no. 2 (1982): 3-13.

Coates, J. R. 1934. "'Thou Shalt Not Covet.'" *ZAW* 52: 238-39.

Gordon, Cyrus H. 1963. "A Note on the Tenth Commandment." *Journal of Bible and Religion* 31: 208-9.

Herrmann, Johannes. 1927. "Das zehnte Gebot." In *Beiträge zur Religionsgeschichte und Archäologie Palästinas Ernst Sellin zum 60. Geburtstage*, edited by Anton Jirku, 69-82. Leipzig: Deichertsche.

Jackson, Bernard S. 1971. "Liability for Mere Intention in Early Jewish Law." *HUCA* 42: 197-225.

Lang, Bernhard. 1981. "'Du sollst nicht nach der Frau eines Anderen Verlangen': Eine neue Deutung des 9. und 10. Gebots." *ZAW* 93: 216-24.

Matlock, Michael D. 2007. "Obeying the First Part of the Tenth Commandment: Applications from the Levirate Marriage Law." *JSOT* 31: 295-310.

Mayer, Günter. 1971. "אָוָה *āvāh*." In *TDOT*, vol. 1. (1977), 134-37. Rev. ed. Translated from German, 1971.

Moran, William L. 1967. "The Conclusion of the Decalogue (Ex 20,17 = Dt 5,21)." *CBQ* 29: 543-54.

Premnath, D. N. 1988. "Latifundialization and Isaiah 5.8-10." *JSOT* 40: 49-60.

Reno, R. R. 2005. "God or Mammon." In *I Am the Lord Your God: Christian Reflections on the Ten Commandments*, edited by Carl E. Braaten and Christopher R. Seitz, 218-36. Grand Rapids: Eerdmans.

Rofé, Alexander. 1985. "The Tenth Commandment in the Light of Four Deuteronomic Laws." In *The Ten Commandments in History and Tradition*, edited by Ben-Zion Segal and Gershon Levi, 45-65. Publications of the Perry Foundation for Biblical Research. Jerusalem: Magnes, 1990. Translated from Hebrew, 1985.

Schunck, Klaus-Dietrich. 1984. "Das 9. und 10. Gebot—Jüngstes Glied des Dekalogs?" *ZAW* 96: 104-9.

———. 1992. "Wanting and Desiring." In *ABD*, vol. 6: 866-67.

Svebakken, Hans. 2012. *Philo of Alexandria's Exposition on the Tenth Commandment.*
Studia Philonica Monographs. Atlanta: Society of Biblical Literature.

Vasholz, Robert I. 1987. "You Shall Not Covet Your Neighbor's Wife." *Westminster
Theological Journal* 49: 397-403.

Wallis, G. 1977. "חָמַד *chāmadh.*" In *TDOT*, vol. 4 (1980): 452-61. Translated from
German, 1977.

OTHER WORKS

Albright, William F. 1976. "Moses in Historical and Theological Perspective." In *Mag-
nalia Dei, the Mighty Acts of God: Essays on the Bible and Archaeology in Memory
of G. Ernest Wright*, edited by Frank Moore Cross, Werner E. Lemke, and Patrick
D. Miller, 120-31. Garden City, NY: Doubleday.

Alt, Albrecht. 1934. "The Origins of Israelite Law." In *Essays on Old Testament History
and Religion*, 79-132. Oxford: Blackwell, 1966. Translated from German, 1934.

Anderson, A. A. 1972. *The Book of Psalms.* Vol. 1. New Century Bible. London: Oli-
phants.

Arnold, Bill T. 1999. "Religion in Ancient Israel." In *The Face of Old Testament
Studies: A Survey of Contemporary Approaches*, edited by David W. Baker and Bill
T. Arnold, 391-420. Grand Rapids: Baker.

Badenas, Robert. 1985. *Christ the End of the Law: Romans 10.4 in Pauline Perspective.*
JSNTSup 10. Sheffield: JSOT Press.

Baker, David L. 2009. *Tight Fists or Open Hands? Wealth and Poverty in Old Testament Law.* Grand Rapids: Eerdmans.

———. 2010. *Two Testaments, One Bible: The Theological Relationship Between the Old
and New Testaments.* 3rd ed. Nottingham: Apollos.

Baltzer, Klaus. 1964. *The Covenant Formulary: In Old Testament, Jewish, and Early
Christian Writings.* Oxford: Blackwell, 1971. Translated from German, 2nd ed.,
1964.

Barclay, William. 1975. *The Gospel of Matthew.* Vol. 1, *Chapters 1 to 10.* Rev. ed. Daily
Study Bible. Edinburgh: Saint Andrew.

Barth, Karl. 1951. *Church Dogmatics.* Vol. 3.4. Edinburgh: T&T Clark, 1961. Translated from German, 1951.

Beale, G. K. 1999. *The Book of Revelation: A Commentary on the Greek Text.* New
International Greek Testament Commentary. Grand Rapids: Eerdmans.

Beckman, Gary. 1999. *Hittite Diplomatic Texts.* 2nd ed. Writings from the Ancient
World 7. Atlanta: Scholars.

Beegle, Dewey M. 1992. "Moses: Old Testament." In *ABD*, vol. 4: 909-18.

Beyerlin, Walter. 1961. *Origins and History of the Oldest Sinaitic Traditions*. Oxford: Blackwell, 1965. Translated from German, 1961.

——, ed. 1975. *Near Eastern Religious Texts Relating to the Old Testament*. OTL. London: SCM, 1978. Translated from German, 1975.

Biddle, Mark E. 2003. *Deuteronomy*. Smyth & Helwys Bible Commentary. Macon, GA: Smyth & Helwys.

Block, Daniel I. 2012. *Deuteronomy*. NIV Application Commentary. Grand Rapids: Zondervan.

Bowman, John, ed. 1977. *Samaritan Documents: Relating to Their History, Religion and Life*. Pittsburgh Original Texts and Translation Series 2. Pittsburgh, PA: Pickwick.

Bright, John. 1981. *A History of Israel*. 3rd ed. Philadelphia: Westminster.

Bruce, F. F. 1962. *Commentary on the Book of the Acts: The English Text with Introduction, Exposition and Notes*. 3rd ed. London: Marshall, Morgan & Scott.

Brueggemann, Walter. 1994. "The Book of Exodus." In *The New Interpreter's Bible*. Vol. 1, edited by Leander E. Keck et al., 675-981. Nashville, TN: Abingdon.

——. 1997a. *Theology of the Old Testament: Testimony, Dispute, Advocacy*. Minneapolis: Fortress.

Buber, Martin. 1946. *Moses*. East & West Library. Oxford: Phaidon.

Budde, Karl. 1899. *Religion of Israel to the Exile*. American Lectures on the History of Religions 1898–1899. New York: Knickerbocker. Translated from German manuscript.

Bullard, Roger A., and Howard A. Hatton. 2001. *A Handbook on Tobit and Judith*. UBS Handbook Series. New York: United Bible Societies.

Burney, C. F. 1908. "A Theory of the Developement of Israelite Religion in Early Times." *JTS* 9: 321-52.

Burnside, Jonathan. 2010a. *God, Justice, and Society: Aspects of Law and Legality in the Bible*. Oxford: Oxford University Press.

Calvin, John. 1536–1559. *Institutes of the Christian Religion*. Library of Christian Classics 20–21. Philadelphia: Westminster, 1960. Translated from Latin/French eds., 1536–1559.

Carpenter, Eugene E. 2009. "Deuteronomy." In *ZIBBC*, vol. 1, edited by John H. Walton, 418-547. Grand Rapids: Zondervan.

Cassuto, Umberto. 1951. *A Commentary on the Book of Exodus*. Jerusalem: Magnes, 1967. Translated from Hebrew, 1951.

Catagnoni, Amalia. 2003. "Anatolia and the Levant: Ebla." In *HANEL*, vol. 1: 227-39.

Childs, Brevard S. 1974. *Exodus: A Commentary*. OTL. London: SCM.

Christensen, Duane L. 2001. *Deuteronomy 1:1–21:9*. Rev. ed. WBC 6a. Nashville, TN: Nelson.

Civil, Miguel. 2011. "The Law Collection of Ur-Namma." In *Cuneiform Royal Inscriptions and Related Texts in the Schøyen Collection*, edited by A. R. George, 221-86. Cornell University Studies in Assyriology and Sumerology 17. Bethesda, MD: CDL.

Coats, George W. 1988. *Moses: Heroic Man, Man of God*. JSOTSup 57. Sheffield: JSOT Press.

Cole, R. Alan. 1973. *Exodus: An Introduction and Commentary*. TOTC. London: Tyndale.

Craigie, Peter C. 1976. *The Book of Deuteronomy*. NICOT. Grand Rapids: Eerdmans.

———. 1983. *Psalms 1–50*. WBC 19. Waco, TX: Word.

Dandama[y]ev, Muhammad A. 1984. *Slavery in Babylonia: From Nabopolassar to Alexander the Great (626–331 BC)*. DeKalb: Northern Illinois University Press. Revised and translated from Russian, 1974.

Daube, David. 1947. *Studies in Biblical Law*. Cambridge: Cambridge University Press.

Davies, Benedict G. 1999. *Who's Who at Deir El-Medina: A Prosopographic Study of the Royal Workmen's Community*. Leiden: Nederlands Instituut voor het Nabije Oosten.

Davies, Graham I. 2004. "Was There an Exodus?" In *In Search of Pre-Exilic Israel: Proceedings of the Oxford Old Testament Seminar*, edited by John Day, 23-40. JSOTSup 406. London: T&T Clark.

Dever, William G. 1987. "The Contribution of Archaeology to the Study of Canaanite and Early Israelite Religion." In *Ancient Israelite Religion: Essays in Honor of Frank Moore Cross*, edited by Patrick D. Miller, Paul D. Hanson, and S. Dean McBride, 209-47. Philadelphia: Fortress.

Dozeman, Thomas B. 2009. *Commentary on Exodus*. Eerdmans Critical Commentary. Grand Rapids: Eerdmans.

Driver, G. R., and John C. Miles, eds. 1935. *The Assyrian Laws*. Ancient Codes and Laws of the Near East. Oxford: Clarendon.

———, eds. 1952. *The Babylonian Laws*. Vol. 1, *Legal Commentary*. Ancient Codes and Laws of the Near East. Oxford: Clarendon. Reprinted with minor corrections in 1960.

Driver, S. R. 1902. *A Critical and Exegetical Commentary on Deuteronomy*. 3rd ed. ICC. Edinburgh: T&T Clark. Reprinted 1996.

Dunn, James D. G., ed. 1996. *Paul and the Mosaic Law: The Third Durham-Tübingen Research Symposium on Earliest Christianity and Judaism (Durham, September, 1994)*. Wissenschaftliche Untersuchungen zum Neuen Testament 89. Tübingen: Mohr.

Durham, John I. 1987. *Exodus*. WBC 3. Waco, TX: Word.

Ebeling, Erich. 1916. "Die '7 Todsünden' bei den Babylonieren." *Orientalische Literatur-Zeitung* 19: 296-98.

———, ed. 1919. *Keilschrifttexte aus Assur Religiösen Inhalts.* Vol. 1. Ausgrabungen der Deutschen Orient-Gesellschaft in Assur E: Inschriften, 2, 28. Leipzig: Hinrichs.

Eckermann, Johann Peter, and Johann Wolfgang von Goethe. 1823–1832. *Conversations with Goethe.* Everyman's Library 851. London: Dent, 1971. Translated from German, 1823–1832.

Eichrodt, Walther. 1933. *Theology of the Old Testament.* Vol. 1. OTL. London: SCM, 1961. Translated from German, 1933.

Ewald, Heinrich. 1876. *The History of Israel*, vol. 2. Edited by Russell Martineau. 3rd ed. London: Longmans, Green, & Co.

Finkelstein, Jacob J. 1981. *The Ox That Gored.* Transactions of the American Philosophical Society 71.2. Philadelphia: American Philosophical Society.

Foster, Benjamin R. 2005. *Before the Muses: An Anthology of Akkadian Literature.* 3rd ed. Bethesda, MY: CDL.

Frame, John M. 2008. *The Doctrine of the Christian Life.* Phillipsburg, NJ: P&R.

Fretheim, Terence E. 1991. *Exodus.* Interpretation. Louisville, KY: John Knox.

———. 2003. "Law in the Service of Life: A Dynamic Understanding of Law in Deuteronomy." In *A God So Near: Essays on Old Testament Theology in Honor of Patrick D. Miller*, edited by Brent A. Strawn and Nancy R. Bowen, 183-200. Winona Lake, IN: Eisenbrauns.

Friedmann, Daniel. 2002. *To Kill and Take Possession: Law, Morality, and Society in Biblical Stories.* Peabody, MA: Hendrickson. Revised and translated from Hebrew, 2000.

Gerstenberger, Erhard S. 1965a. "Covenant and Commandment." *JBL* 84: 38-51.

———. 1965b. *Wesen und Herkunft des "Apodiktischen Rechts."* WMANT 20. Neukirchen-Vluyn, Germany: Neukirchener.

Goldingay, John. 2003. *Old Testament Theology.* Vol. 1, *Israel's Gospel.* Downers Grove, IL: InterVarsity Press.

Goppelt, Leonhard. 1975. *Theology of the New Testament.* Vol. 1, *The Ministry of Jesus in Its Theological Significance*, translated by John Alsup. Grand Rapids: Eerdmans, 1981. Translated from German, 1975.

Gordon, Cyrus H. 1949. "Azitawadd's Phoenician Inscription." *JNES* 8: 108-15.

Green, Bradley G. 2014. *Covenant and Commandment: Works, Obedience and Faithfulness in the Christian Life.* New Studies in Biblical Theology 33. Downers Grove, IL: IVP Academic.

Greenberg, Moshe. 1960. "Some Postulates of Biblical Criminal Law." In *Yehezkel Kaufmann Jubilee Volume: Studies in Bible and Jewish Religion*, edited by Menahem Haran, 5-28. Jerusalem: Magnes.

———. 1986. "More Reflections on Biblical Criminal Law." In *Studies in Bible, 1986*, edited by Sara Japhet, 1-17. Scripta Hierosolymitana 31. Jerusalem: Magnes.

Greengus, Samuel. 2011. *Laws in the Bible and in Early Rabbinic Collections: The Legal Legacy of the Ancient Near East*. Eugene, OR: Cascade.

Gressmann, Hugo. 1913. *Mose und seine Zeit: Ein Kommentar zu den Mose-Sagen*. FRLANT 1. Göttingen: Vandenhoeck & Ruprecht.

Haase, Richard. 2003. "Anatolia and the Levant: The Hittite Kingdom." In *HANEL*, vol. 1: 619-56.

Hallo, William W. 1991. *The Book of the People*. Brown Judaic Studies 225. Atlanta: Scholars.

Hamilton, Victor P. 1990. *The Book of Genesis: Chapters 1-17*. NICOT. Grand Rapids: Eerdmans.

Hartley, John E. 1992. *Leviticus*. WBC 4. Dallas, TX: Word.

Hoffner, Harry A. 1997. *The Laws of the Hittites: A Critical Edition*. Studies in Near Eastern Archaeology and Civilisation 23. Leiden: Brill.

Houtman, Cornelis. 1996. *Exodus*. Vol. 3, *Chapters 20-40*. Historical Commentary on the Old Testament. Leuven: Peeters, 2000. Translated from Dutch, 1996.

Jackson, Bernard S. 1975b. "Reflections on Biblical Criminal Law." In *Essays in Jewish and Comparative Legal History*, 25-63. Studies in Judaism in Late Antiquity 103. Leiden: Brill. Reprinted with minor revisions from *Journal of Jewish Studies* 24, no. 1 (1973): 8-38.

———. 2002. "Models in Legal History: The Case of Biblical Law." *Journal of Law and Religion* 18: 1-30.

Janzen, Waldemar. 1994. *Old Testament Ethics: A Paradigmatic Approach*. Louisville, KY: Westminster John Knox.

Jasnow, Richard. 2003. "Egypt: New Kingdom." In *HANEL*, vol. 1: 289-359.

Jenson, Philip. 2010. *How to Interpret Old Testament Law*. Grove Biblical Series 58. Cambridge: Grove.

Jeremias, Joachim. 1971. *New Testament Theology*. Vol. 1, *The Proclamation of Jesus*. NTL. London: SCM.

John Paul II. 1993. "Veritatis Splendor." Encyclical letter. August 6. http://w2.vatican .va/content/john-paul-ii/en/encyclicals/documents/hf_jp-ii_enc_06081993_veritatis -splendor.html.

Johnstone, William. 2014. *Exodus 20-40*. Smyth & Helwys Bible Commentary. Macon, GA: Smyth and Helwys.

Kaufman, Stephen A. 1979. "The Structure of the Deuteronomic Law." *Maarav* 1: 105-58.

Kaufmann, Yehezkel. 1961. *The Religion of Israel: From Its Beginnings to the Babylonian Exile*. London: Allen & Unwin.

King, Philip J., and Lawrence E. Stager. 2001. *Life in Biblical Israel.* Library of Ancient Israel. Louisville, KY: Westminster John Knox.

Kline, Meredith G. 1963. *Treaty of the Great King: The Covenant Structure of Deuteronomy.* Grand Rapids: Eerdmans.

Knudtzon, J. A., ed. 1915. *Die el-Amarna-Tafeln, mit Einleitung und Erläuterungen.* Vorderasiatische Bibliothek. Aalen, Germany: Otto Zeller.

Kuenen, A. 1885. *An Historico-Critical Inquiry into the Origin and Composition of the Hexateuch.* London: Macmillan, 1886. Translated from Dutch, 1885.

Lafont, Bertrand, and Raymond Westbrook. 2003. "Mesopotamia: Neo-Sumerian Period (Ur III)." In *HANEL*, vol. 1: 183-226.

Lambert, W. G. 1974. "Dingir.šà.dib.ba Incantations." *JNES* 33: 267-70, 272-322.

Lauterbach, Jacob Z. 1935. *Mekilta de-Rabbi Ishmael.* Vol. 3. JPS Library of Jewish Classics. Philadelphia: Jewish Publication Society.

Levine, Etan. 2000. *Heaven and Earth, Law and Love: Studies in Biblical Thought.* BZAW 303. Berlin: de Gruyter.

Lewis, C. S. 1952. *Mere Christianity.* Reprinted by New York: HarperCollins, 2009.

Lindenberger, James M. 2003. *Ancient Aramaic and Hebrew Letters.* Edited by Kent Harold Richards. 2nd ed. Writings from the Ancient World 14. Atlanta: SBL.

Lohfink, Norbert L. 1977. *Great Themes from the Old Testament.* Edinburgh: T&T Clark, 1982. Translated from German, 1977.

Lundbom, Jack R. 2013. *Deuteronomy: A Commentary.* Grand Rapids: Eerdmans.

Luther, Martin. 1520. *A Treatise on Good Works.* Grand Rapids: Christian Classics Ethereal Library.

———. 1529. *The Large Catechism.* Grand Rapids: Christian Classics Ethereal Library.

Marcus, Ralph, and Ignace J. Gelb. 1949. "The Phoenician Stele Inscription from Cilicia." *JNES* 8: 116-20.

McCarthy, Dennis J. 1978. *Treaty and Covenant: A Study in Form in the Ancient Oriental Documents and in the Old Testament.* Updated ed. Analecta biblica 21a. Rome: Pontifical Biblical Institute.

McConville, J. Gordon. 2002a. *Deuteronomy.* Apollos Old Testament Commentary 5. Leicester, England: Apollos.

———. 2002b. "Singular Address in the Deuteronomic Law and the Politics of Legal Administration." *JSOT* 97: 19-36.

Mendenhall, George E. 1954a. "Ancient Oriental and Biblical Law." *BA* 17: 26-46.

———. 1954b. "Covenant Forms in Israelite Tradition." *BA* 17: 50-76.

Meshorer, Ya'akov. 1982. *Ancient Jewish Coinage.* Vol. 1, *Persian Period Through Hasmonaeans.* New York: Amphora.

Milgrom, Jacob. 2000. *Leviticus 17–22: A New Translation with Introduction and Commentary.* Anchor Bible 3a. New York: Doubleday.

Millard, Alan R. 2014. "The Hebrew Divine Name in Cuneiform and Hebrew Texts." In *Bible et Proche-Orient: Mélanges André Lemaire III*, edited by Josette Elayi and Jean-Marie Durand, 113-25. Paris: Gabalda.

Miller, Patrick D. 2004d. *The Way of the Lord: Essays in Old Testament Theology*. FAT 39. Tübingen: Mohr Siebeck.

Miskotte, Kornelis H. 1963. *When the Gods Are Silent*. London: Collins, 1967. Translated from Dutch, 1956, with revisions for German edition, 1963.

Moltmann, Jürgen. 1985. *God in Creation: An Ecological Doctrine of Creation*. Gifford lectures, 1984–1985. London: SCM.

Moore, Carey A. 1996. *Tobit: A New Translation with Introduction and Commentary*. Anchor Bible 40a. New York: Doubleday.

Morenz, Siegfried. 1960. *Egyptian Religion*. Methuen's Handbooks of Archeology. London: Methuen, 1973. Translated from German, 1960.

Motyer, J. Alec. 2005. *The Message of Exodus: The Days of Our Pilgrimage*. Bible Speaks Today. Leicester, England: Inter-Varsity Press.

Mowinckel, Sigmund. 1921–1924. *Psalm Studies*. Vol. 1. SBL History of Biblical Studies 2. Atlanta: SBL, 2014. Translated from German, 1921–24.

———. 1962. *The Psalms in Israel's Worship*. Vol. 1. Oxford: Blackwell.

Oakes, Lorna, and Lucia Gahlin. 2002. *Ancient Egypt: An Illustrated Reference to the Myths, Religions, Pyramids and Temples of the Land of the Pharaohs*. London: Hermes House.

Oelsner, Joachim, Bruce Wells, and Cornelia Wunsch. 2003. "Mesopotamia: Neo-Babylonian Period." In *HANEL*, vol. 2: 911-74.

Olson, Dennis T. 1994. *Deuteronomy and the Death of Moses: A Theological Reading*. Overtures to Biblical Theology. Minneapolis: Fortress.

Oswalt, John N. 1998. *The Book of Isaiah: Chapters 40–66*. NICOT. Grand Rapids: Eerdmans.

Paul, Shalom M. 1970. *Studies in the Book of the Covenant in the Light of Cuneiform and Biblical Law*. VTSup 18. Leiden: Brill.

Phillips, Anthony. 1984a. "A Fresh Look at the Sinai Pericope: Part 1." *VT* 34: 39-52.

———. 1984b. "A Fresh Look at the Sinai Pericope: Part 2." *VT* 34: 282-94.

Propp, William H. C. 2006. *Exodus 19–40: A New Translation with Introduction and Commentary*. Anchor Bible 2a. New York: Doubleday.

Rabast, Karlheinz. 1949. *Das apodiktische Recht im Deuteronomium und im Heiligkeitsgesetz*. Berlin: Heimatdienst.

von Rad, Gerhard. 1957. *Old Testament Theology*. Vol. 1, *The Theology of Israel's Historical Traditions*. Edinburgh: Oliver & Boyd, 1962. Translated from German, 1957.

———. 1964. *Deuteronomy: A Commentary.* OTL. London: SCM, 1966. Translated from German, 1964.

———. 1972. *Genesis: A Commentary.* 3rd rev. ed. OTL. London: SCM, 1972. Translated from German, 1972.

Reiner, Erica. 1958. *Šurpu: A Collection of Sumerian and Akkadian Incantations.* Archiv für Orientforschung Beiheft 11. Graz, Austria: Im Selbstverlage des Herausgebers.

Rodd, Cyril S. 2001. *Glimpses of a Strange Land: Studies in Old Testament Ethics.* Old Testament Studies. Edinburgh: T&T Clark.

Rosner, Brian S. 2013. *Paul and the Law: Keeping the Commandments of God.* New Studies in Biblical Theology 31. Nottingham: Apollos.

Roth, Martha T. 1997. *Law Collections from Mesopotamia and Asia Minor.* 2nd ed., with a contribution by Harry A. Hoffner. Writings from the Ancient World 6. Atlanta: Scholars.

Sanders, E. P. 1983. *Paul, the Law, and the Jewish People.* Minneapolis: Fortress.

Sarna, Nahum M. 1991. *Exodus.* JPS Torah Commentary. Philadelphia: Jewish Publication Society.

Sellin, Ernst. 1924. *Geschichte des Israelitisch-Jüdischen Volkes.* Vol. 1. Leipzig: von Quelle & Meyer.

Seux, Marie-Joseph. 1976. *Hymnes et prières aux dieux de Babylonie et d'Assyrie.* Littératures anciennes du Proche-Orient. Paris: Cerf.

Shupak, Nili. 1993. *Where Can Wisdom Be Found? The Sage's Language in the Bible and in Ancient Egyptian Literature.* OBO 130. Göttingen: Vandenhoeck & Ruprecht.

Slanski, Kathryn E. 2003. "Mesopotamia: Middle Babylonian Period." In *HANEL*, vol. 1: 485-520.

Sprinkle, Joe M. 1994. *"The Book of the Covenant": A Literary Approach.* JSOTSup 174. Sheffield: JSOT Press.

Stott, John R. W. 1990. *The Message of Acts: To the Ends of the Earth.* Bible Speaks Today. Leicester, England: Inter-Varsity Press.

Strack, Hermann L., and Paul Billerbeck. 1922. *Kommentar zum Neuen Testament aus Talmud und Midrasch.* Vol. 1. Munich: Beck.

Thiselton, Anthony C. 2000. *The First Epistle to the Corinthians: A Commentary on the Greek Text.* New International Greek Testament Commentary. Grand Rapids: Eerdmans.

Tigay, Jeffrey H. 1986. *You Shall Have No Other Gods: Israelite Religion in the Light of Hebrew Inscriptions.* Harvard Semitic Studies 31. Atlanta: Scholars.

———. 1996. *Deuteronomy.* JPS Torah Commentary. Philadelphia: Jewish Publication Society.

van der Toorn, Karel. 1985. *Sin and Sanction in Israel and Mesopotamia: A Comparative Study*. Studia Semitica Neerlandica 22. Assen, Netherlands: van Gorcum.

Trueblood, Elton. 1961. *Foundations for Reconstruction*. Rev. ed. New York: Harper & Row.

de Vaux, Roland. 1961. *Ancient Israel: Its Life and Institutions*. London: Darton, Longman & Todd.

———. 1971. *The Early History of Israel: To the Exodus and Covenant of Sinai*. London: Darton, Longman & Todd, 1978. Translated from French, 1971.

Veenhof, Klaas R. 2003. "Mesopotamia: Old Assyrian Period." In *HANEL*, vol. 1: 431-83.

Volz, Paul. 1932. *Mose und sein Werk*. 2nd ed. Tübingen: Mohr.

Walton, John H. 2006. *Ancient Near Eastern Thought and the Old Testament: Introducing the Conceptual World of the Hebrew Bible*. Grand Rapids: Baker.

Watts, John D. W. 2005. *Isaiah 34–66*. Rev. ed. WBC 25. Nashville, TN: Nelson.

Weinfeld, Moshe. 1991. *Deuteronomy 1–11*. Anchor Bible 5. New York: Doubleday.

Wellhausen, Julius. 1883. *Prolegomena to the History of Israel*. Edinburgh: Black, 1885. Translated from German, 1883.

———. 1889. *Die Composition des Hexateuchs und der historischen Bücher des Alten Testaments*. Reprint with addenda. Berlin: Reimer.

Wells, Bruce. 2009. "Exodus." In *ZIBBC*, vol. 1, edited by John H. Walton, 160-283. Grand Rapids: Zondervan.

Wenham, Gordon J. 1978. "Law and the Legal System in the Old Testament." In *Law, Morality and the Bible*, edited by Bruce N. Kaye and Gordon J. Wenham, 24-52. Leicester, England: Inter-Varsity Press.

———. 1979. *The Book of Leviticus*. NICOT. Grand Rapids: Eerdmans.

———. 1987. *Genesis 1–15*. WBC 1. Waco, TX: Word.

———. 2000. *Story as Torah: Reading the Old Testament Ethically*. Old Testament Studies. Edinburgh: T&T Clark.

Westbrook, Raymond. 1988. *Studies in Biblical and Cuneiform Law*. Cahiers de la Revue biblique 26. Paris: Gabalda.

———. 1991. "The Dowry." In *Property and the Family in Biblical Law*, 142-64. JSOTSup 113. Sheffield: Sheffield Academic.

———. 2003a. "The Character of Ancient Near Eastern Law." In *HANEL*, vol. 1: 1-90.

———. 2003b. "Mesopotamia: Old Babylonian Period." In *HANEL*, vol. 1: 361-430.

Westerholm, Stephen. 1988. *Israel's Law and the Church's Faith: Paul and His Recent Interpreters*. Grand Rapids: Eerdmans.

Westermann, Claus. 1974. *Genesis 1–11*. Continental Commentary. London: SPCK, 1984. Translated from German, 1974.

———. 1978. *Elements of Old Testament Theology*. Atlanta: John Knox, 1982. Translated from German, 1978.

Williamson, Paul R. 2008. "Promises with Strings Attached: Covenant and Law in Exodus 19–24." In *Exploring Exodus: Literary, Theological and Contemporary Approaches*, edited by Brian S. Rosner and Paul R. Williamson, 89-122. Nottingham: Apollos.

Willis, Timothy M. 2001. *The Elders of the City: A Study of the Elders-Laws in Deuteronomy*. Atlanta: SBL.

Wilson, Ian. 1995. *Out of the Midst of the Fire: Divine Presence in Deuteronomy*. SBL Dissertation Series 151. Atlanta: Scholars.

Wright, Christopher J. H. 2004. *Old Testament Ethics for the People of God*. Leicester, England: Inter-Varsity Press.

Zimmerli, Walther. 1975. *Old Testament Theology in Outline*. Edinburgh: T&T Clark, 1978. Translated from German, 1975.

AUTHOR INDEX

SUBJECT INDEX

SCRIPTURE INDEX